SPANISH
PHRASEBOOK

Izaskun Arretxe
Allison Jones

Spanish phrasebook
  1st edition

Published by
  Lonely Planet Publications
  Head Office: PO Box 617, Hawthorn, Vic 3122, Australia
  Branches: 155 Filbert Street, Suite 251, Oakland CA 94607, USA
                     10 Barley Mow Passage, Chiswick. London W4 4PH, UK
                     71 bis rue de Cardinal Lemoine, 75005 Paris, France

Printed by
Colorcraft Ltd, Hong Kong

Cover Illustration
  En el Bar by Penelope Richardson

Published
  August 1997

National Library of Australia Cataloguing in Publication Data

Arretxe, Izaskun
  Spanish phrasebook
  1st ed.
  Includes index.
  ISBN 0 86442 475 2.

  1. Spanish language – Conversation and phrase books – English. I.
  Jones, Allison, 1968- II. Title. (Series: Lonely Planet language survival
  kit)

  468.3421

  © Lonely Planet Publications Pty Ltd, 1997
  Cover Illustration © Lonely Planet

All rights reserved. No part of this publication may be reproduced, stored
in a retrieval system or transmitted in any form by any means, electronic,
mechanical, photocopying, recording or otherwise, except brief extracts
for the purpose of review, without the written permission of the publisher
and copyright owner.

CONTENTS

3

About the Authors

Allison Jones has travelled and studied extensively in Spain and speaks Spanish and Catalan. She currently works in the Australian book publishing industry.

Izaskun Arretxe was born in the Basque Country but has spent most of her life in Barcelona. She has just returned there after four years in Melbourne, where she taught Spanish and Catalan at La Trobe University.

Allison and Izaskun wrote the Spanish and Catalan sections of the book, with assistance from Carlos Uxo in Madrid and Carlotta Guerrero in Barcelona.

Robert Neal Baxter works as a freelance translator and interpreter in Santiago de Compostela. He wrote the Galician section with assistance from David Rei Vázquez.

Mikel Edorta Morris Pagoeta is an American Basque living in Gipuzkoa. He is a writer and translator who has just completed a Basque-English, English-Basque dictionary.

From the Authors

Thanks to Nick Bolger for his ideas, to Paul Matthews, who tried out many of the phrases in Spain, and to Stewart King for checking the Catalan section and being such a fabulous host in Barcelona. Thanks to the other people who helped us on the book.

From the Publisher

This book was produced in a tremendous team effort by Sally Steward, who edited the book and instigated several long Bacchanalian nights that threw so many ideas our way; Lou Callan who planned, proofread and put our ideas together; Penelope Richardson who painted, drew and designed everything with such flair; Pete D'Onghia who slaved away on the dictionary, and Sergio Mariscal for finishing work to deadline even after we'd plied him with sangria. Thanks also to Richard Plunkett for providing excellent crosswords.

Un beso to Isabel Moutinho who wrote the Spanish chapter of the Lonely Planet *Western Europe* phrasebook, from which this book developed.

INTRODUCTION

Spanish, or Castilian, as it is often and more precisely called, is the most widely spoken of the Romance languages — the group of languages derived from Latin which includes French, Italian and Portuguese. Outside Spain, it is the language of all of South America, except Brazil and the Guianas; of Mexico, Central America, and most of the West Indies; to some extent, of the Philippines and Guam, as well as of some areas of the African coast and within the USA. In Spain itself, three Romance languages are spoken: Castilian (the main one) in the north, centre and south; Catalan in the east; and Galician in the north-west. Basque, a non-Latin language, is spoken in parts of the north. Each language is considered an official national language of Spain, although Castilian, or Spanish, covers by far the largest territory. Castilian itself has many dialects, which mainly involve differences in pronunciation.

Spanish is the neo-Latin language derived from the Vulgar Latin which Roman soldiers and merchants brought to the Iberian Peninsula during the period of the Roman conquest (third to first century BC). By 19 BC Spain had become totally Roman, and Latin became the language of the Peninsula in the four centuries of Romanisation which followed. It almost completely obliterated the languages of the Celtic and Iberian indigenous tribes – only Basque has survived in its original form.

In 711 AD an African Berber army invaded the Peninsula. Soon many more Arabs came from the African Maghreb (North-West Africa), and it was not until the ninth century that the reconquest of Spain began, led by the Christians who had taken refuge in the mountains of the north. As the reconquest advanced southwards, the Latin spoken by those Christians was progressively brought back to central and, eventually, southern Spain. Although the Arabs were not completely driven from the south for centuries yet, and although many people spoke Arabic as well as Vulgar Latin during that period, the influence of the Arabic language on Spanish is limited to vocabulary innovations. Examples of Arabic-Spanish words are **alfombra** ('rug'), **arroz** ('rice'), **tambor** ('drum') and **alcalde** ('mayor').

With Columbus' discovery of the New World in 1492 began an era of Spanish expansion in America, which is reflected in the language. **Patata**, **tomate**, **cacao** and **chocolate** are a few examples of words taken from the indigenous American languages. But the essentials of the language – its core vocabulary, grammar and word structure – have always remained neo-Latin.

Spanish literature begins in the 12th century with the famous epic poem *Cantar de mio Cid*. Cervantes' 17th century *Don Quijote* is universally known. Nowadays Spain has an equally thriving literature, some of which is available in English translation. Novelists such as Ana María Matute, Carmen Martín Gaite, Juan Goytisolo, Miguel Delibes and the 1989 Nobel Prize winner, Camilo José Cela, have had some of their works translated into English and other languages, and they will give visitors a valuable insight into contemporary Spanish society.

Castilian-speakers today are intensely proud of their language and generally expect visitors to know at least a little. English is less widely spoken in Spain than in many other European countries, especially outside the major cities. Here you will find not only the words and phrases you need to get by and find your way but also the basic tools for conversing with Spaniards and making friends.

ARTHUR OR MARTHA?

Spanish has two noun forms, known as masculine and feminine. In this book we have placed the feminine form first, the masculine second. While there is no difference between the two forms in terms of priority, language books have consistently placed the masculine first. We wanted to counteract that preference. Ideally we'd have mixed orders, but as this would be confusing to readers new to the language we have stuck with the feminine first throughout.

ABBREVIATIONS USED IN THIS BOOK

col   colloquial usage
f   feminine
inf   informal
pol   polite
m   masculine
sg   singular
pl   plural
v   verb

HOW TO USE THE PHRASEBOOK
You *Can* Speak Another Language

It's true – anyone can speak another language. Don't worry if you haven't studied languages before, or that you studied a language at school for years and can't remember any of it. It doesn't even matter if you failed English grammar. After all, that's never affected your ability to speak English! And this is the key to picking up a language in another country. You don't need to sit down and memorise endless grammatical details and you don't need to memorise long lists of vocabulary. You just need to start speaking. Once you start, you'll be amazed how many prompts you'll get to help you build on those first words. You'll hear people speaking, pick up sounds from TV, catch a word or two that you think you know from the local radio, see something on a billboard – all these things help to build your understanding.

Plunge In

There's just one thing you need to start speaking another language – courage. Your biggest hurdle is overcoming the fear of saying aloud what may seem to you to be just a bunch of sounds. There are a number of ways to do this.

Firstly, think of some Spanish words or phrases you are familiar with. Such as **hasta la vista** and **que sera, sera** (remember that one!?). These are phrases you are already able to say fluently – and you'll even get a response. From these basic beginnings, provided you can get past the 'courage to speak' barrier, you can start making sentences. You probably know cuando means 'when' (cuando is Spanish, quando is Italian and Portuguese – they all sound much the same). So, let's imagine you think the bus will arrive tomorrow. You could ask ¿cuando sera? – 'when will that be?' Don't worry that you're not getting a whole sentence right first time. People will understand if you stick to the key words of the sentence. And you'll find that once you're in the country it won't take long to remember the complete sentence.

The best way to start overcoming your fear is to memorise a few key words. These are the words you know you'll be saying again and again, like 'hello', 'thankyou' and 'how much?'. Here's an important hint though: right from the beginning, learn at least one phrase that will be useful but not essential. Such as 'good morning' or 'good afternoon', 'see you later' or even a conversational piece like 'lovely day, isn't it?' or 'it's cold today' (people everywhere love to talk about the weather). Having this extra phrase (just start with one, if you like, and learn to say it really well) will enable you to move away from the basics, and when you get a reply and a smile, it'll also boost your confidence. You'll find that people you speak to will like it too, as they'll understand that at least you've tried to learn more of the language than just the usual essential words.

Ways to Remember

There are several ways to learn a language. Most people find they learn from a variety of these, although people usually have a preferred way to remember. Some like to see the written word and remember the sound from what they see. Some like to just hear it spoken in context (if this is you, try talking to yourself in Spanish, but do it in the car or somewhere private, to give yourself confidence, and so others don't wonder about your sanity!). Others, especially the more mathematically inclined, like to analyse the grammar of a language, and piece together words according to the rules of grammar. The very visually inclined like to associate the written word and even sounds with some visual stimulus, such as from illustrations, TV and general things they see in the street. As you learn, you'll discover what works best for you – be aware of what made you really remember a particular word, and if it sticks in your mind, keep using that method.

Kicking Off

Chances are you'll want to learn some of the language before you go. So you won't be hearing it around you. The first thing to do is to memorise those essential phrases and words. Check out the basics (page 43) ... and don't forget that extra phrase (see Plunge In!). Try the sections on making conversation or greeting people for a phrase you'd like to use. Write some of these words down on a separate piece of paper and stick them up around the place. On the fridge, by the bed, on your computer, as a bookmark – somewhere where you'll see them often. Try putting some words in context – the 'How much is it?' note, for instance, could go in your wallet.

Building the Picture

We include a chapter on grammar in our books for two main reasons.

Firstly, some people have an aptitude for grammar and find understanding it a key tool to their learning. If you're such a person, then the grammar chapter in a phrasebook will help you build a picture of the language, as it works through all the basics.

The second reason for the grammar chapter is that it gives answers to questions you might raise as you hear or memorise some key phrases. You may find a particular word is always used when there is a question – check out the grammar heading on questions and it should explain why. This way you don't have to read the grammar chapter from start to finish, nor do you need to memorise a grammatical point. It will simply present itself to you in the course of your learning. Key grammatical points are repeated through the book.

Any Questions?

Try to learn the main question words (see page 41). As you read through different situations, you'll see these words used in the example sentences, and this will help you remember them. So if you want to hire a bicycle, turn to the Bicycles section in Getting Around (use the Contents or Index pages to find it quickly). You've already tried to memorise the word for 'where' and you'll see the word for 'bicycle'. When you come across the sentence 'Where can I hire a bicycle?', you'll recognise the key words and this will help you remember the whole phrase. If there's no category for your need, try the dictionary (the question words are repeated there too, with examples), and memorise the phrases 'Please write that down' and 'How do you say ...?' (page 47).

I've Got a Flat Tyre

Doesn't seem like the phrase you're going to need? Well, in fact it could be very useful. As are all the phrases in this book, provided you have the courage to mix and match them. We have given specific examples within each section. But the key words remain the same even when the situation changes. So while you may not be planning on any cycling during your trip, the first part of the phrase 'I've got ...' could refer to anything else, and there are plenty of words in the dictionary that, we hope, will fit your needs. So whether it's 'a ticket', 'a visa' or 'a condom', you'll be able to put the words together to convey your meaning.

Finally

Don't be concerned if you feel you can't memorise words. On the inside front and back covers are the most essential words and phrases you'll need. You could also try tagging a few pages for other key phrases, or use the notes pages to write your own reminders.

PRONUNCIATION

Pronunciation of Spanish is not difficult. There is a clear and consistent relationship between pronunciation and spelling, and English speakers will find that many Spanish sounds are similar to their English counterparts. If you stick to the following rules you should have very few problems being understood.

VOWELS

Unlike English, each of the vowels in Spanish has a uniform pronunciation which does not vary. For example, the Spanish **a** has one pronunciation rather than the numerous pronunciations we find in English, such as the 'a's in 'cake', 'art' and 'all'. Vowels are pronounced clearly, even in unstressed positions or at the end of a word.

a   as the 'u' in 'nut', or a shorter sound than the 'a' in 'art'
e   as the 'e' in 'met'
i   similar to the 'i' sound in 'marine' but not so drawn out or strong; between that sound and the 'i' in 'flip'
o   similar to the 'o' in 'hot'
u   as the 'oo' in 'fool'

PRONUNCIATION HINTS

Some of the key sounds to remember are:

c, which is hard, like 'k' before **a, o, u** and consonants, but as the 'th' in 'thumb' (that lisping sound!) just about everywhere else.

ñ, which is pretty easy to remember as the 'ny' sound

d is much softer than in English, almost a 'th' as in 'the'

and finally ... remember that the vowels are short, not rounded as in British English, and not slanted as in American English.

CONSONANTS

Some Spanish consonants are the same as their English counterparts. Pronunciation of other consonants varies according to which vowel follows, and also according to what part of Spain you are in. The Spanish alphabet also contains three consonants which are not found in the English alphabet: ch, ll and ñ.

b   generally a much softer 'b' than the English one: somewhere between an English 'b' and 'v' – try saying this with your lips slightly closed, (the English 'b' is pronounced with closed lips) and your top teeth on your bottom lip (the English 'v' is pronounced this way, though with open lips). When initial, or preceded by a nasal sound, the sound is as the 'b' in 'book'.

c   a hard 'c' as in 'cat' when followed by 'a', 'o', 'u' or a consonant; as the 'th' in 'thin' before 'e' or 'i' (resulting in a lisping sound)

ch   as the 'ch' in 'choose'

d   in an initial position, as the 'd' in 'dog'; elsewhere as the 'th' in 'then'

g   in an initial position, as the 'g' in 'gate' before 'a', 'o' and 'u'; everywhere else, the Spanish 'g' is much softer than the English one. Before 'e' or 'i' it is a harsh, breathy sound, similar to the 'h' in 'hit'.

h   silent, never pronounced

j   a harsh, guttural sound similar to the 'ch' in the Scottish *loch* or German *ich*

ll   between the 'ly' sound in 'million' and the 'y' in 'yes'

ñ   this is a nasal sound like the 'ny' sound in 'onion' or 'canyon'

q   as the 'k' in kick; as in English the 'q' is always followed by a silent 'u'. It is only combined with 'e' as in 'que' and 'i' as in 'qui'.

r   a rolled 'r' sound; a longer and stronger sound when it is a double 'rr' or when a word begins with 'r'

s   as the 's' in 'send'

PRONUNCIATION

v   the same sound as the Spanish 'b'
x   as the 'x' in 'taxi', when between two vowels; as the 's' in
    'say' when the 'x' precedes a consonant
z   as the 'th' in 'thin'

ACCENTS & DIALECTS

There are many dialectic variations in Castilian Spanish, mainly
affecting the spoken language. In areas like Catalonia, Galicia
and the Basque country, spoken Spanish has been heavily influ-
enced by the other languages spoken there (you can see how
some of these influences have affected Castilian by reading their
respective sections in this book).

The other major dialectic variation occurs in the Canary Is-
lands and the south of Spain, in Andalucia, Extremadura and
Murcia. These regions have their own unique dialects, based on
Castilian but sharing several common variations from it:

- not distinguishing between s, c and z (a usage known as el
  seseo), all of which are pronounced as 's'
    servesa (beer) instead of cerveza

- substituting the ll sound with a 'y' sound (a usage known as
  el yeísmo)
    caye (street) instead of calle

- not distinguishing between r and l
    arto (tall) instead of alto

- emphasising the h- at the beginning of a word so that it
  more closely resembles a
    jarta (fed up) instead of harta

- not pronouncing the final -s
    la tre (three o'clock) instead of las tres

PRONUNCIATION

OCTOPUS IN THE GARAGE

speak of the devil!	hablando del Papa de Roma, por la puerta asoma
	- speaking of the Pope of Rome, here he is coming through the door!
you can't make a silk purse out of a sow's ear	aunque la mona se vista de seda, mona se queda
	- a nun can wear silk, but she's still a nun
she/he is a good person	es un trozo de pan
	- she/he's a piece of bread
to feel out of place	encontrarse como un pulpo en un garaje
	- to be like an octopus in a garage

echar margaritas a los cerdos
- *to feed daisies to the pigs*
    (said when you do something for someone but feel that they don't deserve it)

Éramos pocos y parió la abuela
- *there were a few of us and then granny gave birth*
    (said when you already have a lot of problems, and then all of a sudden you have another one)

Es más largo que un día sin pan
- *longer than a day without bread*
    (said when something is particularly tedious and dragging on and on)

Donde comen doe comen tres
- *where two can eat, three can*
    (said to someone who is feeling shy about joining in a meal after an impromptu invite)

GRAMMAR

This chapter is designed to give you an idea of how Spanish phrases are put together, providing you with the basic rules to help you to construct your own sentences.

WORD ORDER
Generally, the word order of sentences is similar to English word order (subject-verb-object).

Ana is drinking beer.   **Ana bebe cerveza.**

ARTICLES
In English and Spanish there are two articles: the definite article ('the' in English) and the indefinite article ('a'). Spanish, however, has feminine and masculine forms as well as singular and plural forms for each.

Feminine
the house	la casa	the houses	las casas
a house	una casa	some houses	unas casas

Masculine
the book	el libro	the books	los libros
a book	un libro	some books	unos libros

DID YOU KNOW ...

There are some ways to tell if a word should have a feminine or masculine form, even if it doesn't end in the usual -a or -a For instance, words derived from ancient Greek are often feminine, such as those ending in **-dad** (la eternidad) and in **-cion** (la nación).

NOUNS

In Spanish, nouns always have a feminine or masculine form. Fortunately, there are some rules governing this though, as with all rules, there are always exceptions.

Feminine

- Nouns descriptive of females:

the woman	la mujer
the girl	la chica
the teacher	la profesora

- Generally, nouns ending in -a:

the house	la casa
the mountain	la montaña
the food	la comida

- Nouns ending in -ción, -sión and -dad:

the song	la canción
the university	la universidad
the address	la dirección
the occasion	la ocasión

Masculine

- Nouns descriptive of men:

the man	el hombre
the boy	el chico
the teacher	el profesor

- Generally, nouns ending in -o and -or:

the book	el libro
the glass	el vaso
the engine	el motor

- Days of the week, months, rivers, mountains, sea and oceans:

| Monday | el lunes |
| the Mediterranean | el Mediterráneo |

GRAMMAR

PLURALS

In general, you can simply add an -s to nouns to form the plural:

| bed | cama |
| beds | camas |

If the noun ends in a consonant, the plural is made by adding es:

| flower | flor |
| flowers | flores |

DIMINUTIVES

The use of diminutive suffixes is common in Spanish. These are additions to nouns and adjectives to express smallness or affection; for example, when expressing the smallness and cuteness of a puppy. The most common of these suffixes are -ita/o, -cita/o and, to a lesser extent, -illa/o and -cilla/o.

café	coffee	cafecito
amor	love	amorcito
animal	animal	animalito
perro	dog	perrito

Note: When looking up a word in the dictionary, be aware of such things as diminutives, which are not listed. If the word you've heard ends in -ita/o; -cita/o; -illa/o or -cilla/o, try looking for the base word. For instance, to find perrito, try perro.

GRAMMAR

DID YOU KNOW ... A common colloquial saying you hear in Spain is **la España cañí**. There is no direct translation but it means 'The real Spain' – probably the type of thing you, as the traveller, are keen to come across.

GRAMMAR

MISTAKES TO WATCH FOR – ENGLISH SPEAKERS

It's useful to know what the most common mistakes are for English and Spanish speakers as each attempts to speak and understand the other language. By checking this list from time to time, you can remind yourself of possible mistakes to avoid.

- Unlike English, Spanish nouns can be either masculine or feminine. English-speakers often have difficulty remembering the gender of a particular word.

So ... say el coche ✓	not	la coche ✗
la gente ✓	not	el gente ✗

- Although there are basic rules governing the use of genders (see page 32), the inevitable exceptions can be a real source of confusion. Check the dictionary for the correct article.

So ... say la mano ✓	not	el mano ✗
el mapa ✓	not	la mapa ✗

- In English, adjectives are placed *before* the noun (eg the big dog), so it's easy to forget that Spanish generally places them *after* the noun.

el perro grande ✓	not	el grande perro ✗
la casa blanca ✓	not	la blanca casa ✗

- The existence of two verbs in Spanish for the English 'to be' is a real headache for English-speakers, who frequently confuse them. Follow the basic rules outlined in the Grammar section, page 32.

Ella es joven ✓	not	Ella está joven ✗
Isabel está contenta ✓	not	Isabel es contenta ✗

- In Spanish, to say you like something, you say 'something is pleasing to you', using the verb **gustar** ('to please/taste') and the pronouns **me, te, le, os, nos, les** to indicate who it is pleasing to (see page 23 & 37).

Me gusta Bilbao. ✔	*not*	Me gusto Bilbao. ✘
Nos gustan las patatas. ✔	*not*	Nos gustamos las patatas. ✘

  - The subjunctive is frequently used in Spanish, unlike English, and is therefore often ignored or misused. You won't be misunderstood if you don't use the subjunctive, but it does help to get it right. See page 29 for more details.

Quiero que vengas conmigo al cine. ✔	*not*	Quiero que vienes conmigo al cine. ✘

  - In English there is only one verb for 'to know' whilst Spanish has **saber** ('to have knowledge of, be aware of, be able to do something') and **conocer** ('to be acquainted with people and places'). See page 30 for more details.

¿Conoces a mi hermano? ✔ *not*		¿Sabes a mi hermano? ✘
¿Saben leer? ✔	*not*	¿Conocen leer? ✘

- Prepositions 'in, on, at, to, by' etc are used quite differently in English and Spanish and it is quite common for English-speakers to use the wrong one. For complete details, you'll have to get hold of a comprehensive grammar book, though listening to what native speakers say is generally the best way to pick these usages up.

mañana voy a ir de viaje a Granada ✔	*not*	mañana voy a ir de viaje en Granada ✘

PRONOUNS

Subject Pronouns

The English singular 'you' has two forms in Spanish - tú, which is generally used in familiar and informal situations and usted, which is a more formal term. Tú is by far the most commonly used today and you should generally avoid the use of usted unless you find yourself in a highly formal situation or wish to show your respect to someone much older than yourself. As a more general rule, you should respond in the same form that you are addressed in.

In this chapter all forms are included. Throughout the rest of the book we've stuck mainly to the informal tú, with the exception of certain categories where the formal usted is more appropriate (eg At Customs, Booking Accommodation, Dealing with the Police).

GRAMMAR

I	**yo**	we	**nosotras/os**
you	**tú** (sg, inf)	you	**vosotras/os** (pl, inf)
you	**usted** (sg, polite)	you	**ustedes** (pl, polite)
she/it	**ella**	they	**ellas/ellos**
he/it	**él**		

You'll find that the subject pronoun is usually omitted in Spanish, because the subject is understood from the verb conjugation and the corresponding ending.

I'm travelling to Europe.	Viajo a Europa.
We speak some Spanish.	Hablamos un poco castellano.

If there is a chance of ambiguity the subject pronoun should be included.

Object Pronouns

Direct object pronouns are used in Spanish to refer to people as 'him', 'them', etc.

me	me	us	nos
you	te (sg, inf)	you	os (pl, inf)
her, it, you	la (polite)	them, you	las/los (polite)
him, it, you	lo (polite)		

I don't know him.   No lo conozco.
Can you see me?   ¿Me ves?

Indirect objects are used to describe 'to him', 'to them', etc.

to me	me	to us	nos
to you	te (sg, inf)	to you	os (pl, inf)
to her, him	le	to them,	les
to you	le (polite)	to you	les (pl, polite)

I'm talking to her.   Le hablo.
I'm writing them a letter.   Les escribo una carta.

GRAMMAR

WAITER!

The word ¡Permiso! is useful for getting past people. To catch someone's attention, try ¡Disculpe! or ¡Perdón!

MISTAKES TO WATCH FOR – SPANISH SPEAKERS

- Spanish speakers tend to find the pronunciation of some English words particularly difficult. For example, words beginning with 's' are often pronounced with an initial 'e'.

  'estarting *instead of* starting'

- Distinguishing between a 'b' and 'v' also presents a problem and they are often both pronounced as a 'b'.

  'best *instead of* vest'

- Because Spanish speakers rarely use 'he/she' before a verb, they commonly confuse the two in English, as well as the pronouns 'him/her'.

  'Do you know my brother Txabi? She is coming tonight.'

- Just like English speakers, Spaniards often confuse the order of the adjective and noun.

  'a tomato red'

- In Spanish the partitive ('a half', 'a bit', etc) generally goes after the noun instead of before and thus is often misused in English.

  'one hour and a half' *instead of* 'one and a half hours'

- The Spanish verb **hacer** can be translated as both 'to do' and 'to make', which is why Spanish speakers commonly confuse the two in English.

  'Make me a favor: shut up!'

- Another difference in the use of prepositions in Spanish and English is highlighted by this common error.

  'What for are you using this phrasebook?' *instead of* 'What are you using this phrasebook for?'

GRAMMAR

- Spanish uses **hay**, **hubo** and **había**, all singular words, to express 'there is; there are' 'there was; there were' (see page 31). Because of this, Spanish speakers will often say 'there is/was' when 'there was/were' is needed.

    'There was onions in the basket.'

- Spanish speakers may use two forms of the past tense together in questions and negative statements. This is because such sentences in Spanish don't use an auxiliary verb (eg 'Did you say?' would be 'You said?': ¿Dijiste?)

    'I didn't washed my hair yesterday.'
    'Did you slept alone last night?'

- Many English verbs change their meaning according to the preposition that is used with them, a good example being 'to look', which has many different meanings when used with 'around, after, at, away, back on, down on, for, forward to, into, out, over, through' and 'up to'.

    'I'm looking at the window.' *instead of*
    'I'm looking through the window.'

- A common mistake which Spanish speakers make in English is to use the third person singular of the verb ('he, she, it ...') incorrectly, using the form of the first or second person ('I, you, we ...') or the third person plural ('they ...').

    'She eat paella.'
    'My mother have a beautiful bike.'

- 'People' is always used as a plural word whilst its Spanish counterpart, **gente** is singular.

    'People is very strange in Granada.' *instead of*
    'People are very strange in Granada.'

VERBS

There are three different categories of verb in Spanish - those ending in -ar, -er and -ir. Tenses are formed by adding various endings to the verb stem, and these endings vary according to whether the verb is an -ar, -er or -ir verb. There are quite a few exceptions to the rules when forming these endings. However the following standard forms are useful to know:

	-ar	-er	-ir
Infinitive	comprar	comer	vivir
	(to buy)	(to eat)	(to live)
Stem	compr-	com-	viv-

Present Tense

	-ar	-er	-ir
I	compro	como	vivo
you (inf)	compras	comes	vives
she/he/it/you (polite)	compra	come	vive
we	compramos	comemos	vivimos
you (pl, inf)	compráis	coméis	vivís
they/you (pl, polite)	compran	comen	viven

Future Tense

This is the easiest tense to form as the endings are the same regardless of whether the verb ends with -ar, -er or -ir. You simply add the endings to the infinitive of the verb:

	-ar	-er	-ir
I	compraré	comeré	viviré
you (inf)	comprarás	comerás	vivirás
she/he/it/you (polite)	comprará	comerá	vivirá
we	compraremos	comeremos	viviremos
you (pl inf)	compraréis	comeréis	viviréis
they/you (pl, polite)	comprarán	comerán	vivirán

GRAMMAR

Going to ...

As in English, a more common way of creating the future tense, particularly when you are discussing the immediate future, is to use the verb ir ('to go') in the present tense, followed by the preposition a ('to/at') and the verb infinitive.

I go/am going to ...	voy
you go/are going to ... (inf)	vas
he/she/it/you go/are going to ... (polite)	va
we go/are going to ...	vamos
you go/are going to ... (pl, inf)	vais
they/you go/are going to ... (pl, polite)	van

I am going to eat later.   Voy a comer más tarde.
It's going to rain this   Va a llover esta tarde.
afternoon.

Past Tense

There are three ways of referring to the past:

1) The preterite, or simple past tense, is used to express completed past actions, which usually only happened once.

	-ar	-er	-ir
I	compré	comí	viví
you (inf)	compraste	comiste	viviste
he/she/it/you (polite)	compró	comió	vivió
we	compramos	comimos	vivimos
you (pl, inf)	comprasteis	comisteis	vivisteis
they/you (pl, polite)	compraron	comieron	vivieron

I bought a shirt yesterday.   Compré una camisa ayer.
It rained last Wednesday.   Llovió el miércoles pasado.

GRAMMAR

2) The imperfect is used for past actions which went on for some time, happened repeatedly, or were going on when a completed action (simple past) took place. So, in the sentence 'I was reading when John knocked at the door', 'I was reading' is the imperfect as it was going on during the time that 'John knocked'. The imperfect is expressed in English as 'I was buying, 'I bought' (on several occasions) or 'I used to buy'.

	-ar	-er	-ir
I	compraba	comía	vivía
you (inf)	comprabas	comías	vivías
he/she/it/you (polite)	compraba	comía	vivía
we	comprábamos	comíamos	vivíamos
you (pl, inf)	comprabais	comíais	vivíais
they/you (pl, polite)	compraban	comían	vivían

GRAMMAR

We were living together in Scotland.	Vivíamos juntos en Escocia.
They ate all day.	Comían todo el día.
You (pl, inf) bought vegetables every week.	Comprabais verduras todas las semanas.

3) The present perfect is used for a completed past action which implies a strong connection with the present. It is formed with the verb haber ('to have') plus the past participle.

An example of the present perfect in English is 'I have bought' – the verb 'have' plus the past participle of 'to buy'. Generally, to create the past participle for -ar verbs you add -ado to the stem; for -er and -ir verbs the past participle is the stem plus -ido. For exceptions, refer to the vocabulary.

comprar 'to buy'	becomes	comprado 'bought'
comer 'to eat'	becomes	comido 'ate'
vivir 'to live'	becomes	vivido 'lived'

The Subjunctive Tense

The subjunctive is frequently used in Spanish, unlike English, and is therefore often ignored or misused. You won't be misunderstood if you don't use the subjunctive but it is worth trying to learn the basics. The subjunctive form is used in Spanish to denote irreality, doubt or desire.

	-ar	-er	-ir
I	compre	coma	viva
you (inf)	compres	comas	vivas
she/he/it/you (polite)	compre	coma	viva
we	compremos	comamos	vivamos
you (pl, inf)	compreis	comais	vivais
they/you (pl, polite)	compren	coman	vivan

I don't want that to happen.	No quiero que suceda esto.
I hope he comes.	Espero que venga.
I doubt we'll eat early tonight.	Dudo que cenemos pronto esta noche.

The Gerund

The gerund is that verb which, in English, is portrayed by the addition of '-ing' to the verb stem. In Spanish, the equivalent is -ando for the -ar verbs, and -endo for both the -er and -ir verbs, and they are used with the verb

We're watching TV.	Estamos mirando la tele.
I'm waiting for my friend.	Estoy esperando mi amiga.
It's raining.	Está lloviendo.

However, in Spanish it is often common to simply use the present tense for the same meaning. Thus 'It's raining' can also be **llueve** 'We're going' is usually just **Vamos**; 'I'm going', **Voy**

TO KNOW

In Spanish there are two words for 'to know', saber (to have knowledge of, be aware of, be able to) and conocer (to be acquainted with people or places).

Do you know my brother?	¿Conoces a mi hermano?
Do you know Italy?	¿Conoces Italia?
Can you read?	¿Sabes leer?
Have you heard the latest about Amanda?	¿Sabes lo último de Amanda?

KEY VERBS

to be	ser; estar
to bring	traer
to come	venir
to come; arrive	llegar
to cost	costar; valer
to depart (leave)	partir; salir de
to do	hacer
to go	ir; partir
to have	tener; haber
to know (someone)	conocer
to know (something)	saber
to like	gustarle; apreciar
to live (life)	vivir
to live (somewhere)	vivir; ocupar
to make	hacer; fabricar
to meet	encontrar
to need	necesitar
to prefer	preferir
to return	volver; regresar
to say	decir
to stay (remain)	quedarse
to stay (somewhere)	alojarse; hospedarse
to take	llevar
to understand	entender; comprender
to want	querer; desear

GRAMMAR

TO HAVE

The verb 'to have' has two forms in Spanish, haber and tener

Haber

As we have seen, haber is used as an auxiliary verb to form the present perfect tense.

Haber	
I have	he
you have (inf)	has
she/he/it has, you have (polite)	ha
we have	hemos
you have (pl, inf)	habéis
they/you have (pl, polite)	han

We have bought tickets.	Hemos comprado billetes.
I have eaten too much.	He comido demasiado.
I have lived in France.	He vivido en Francia.

To find out the past participles of other verbs, see the following page or refer to the listings in the dictionary.

Hay

One word you'll often hear is the impersonal form of haber: hay. This is used to mean 'there is/are', and in questions meaning 'are/is there?' or 'do you have…/have you…?'

Do you have any rooms?	¿Hay habitaciones?
Do you have fresh bread?	¿Hay pan de hoy?
We don't have any/ There isn't any.	No hay.

GRAMMAR

Tener

This form of 'to have' can be used to express both possession and compulsion (having to do something - see page 37).

Tener	
I have	**tengo**
you have (inf)	**tienes**
she/he/it/has, you have (polite)	**tiene**
we have	**tenemos**
you have (pl, inf)	**tenéis**
they/you have (pl, polite)	**tienen**

A small number of phrases consisting of 'to be + adjective' in English, are expressed in Spanish by 'to have' (**tener**) + noun (see also **estar**, page 33).

to be hungry	**tener hambre** (lit: to have hunger)
to be thirsty	**tener sed** (lit: to have thirst)
to be afraid	**tener miedo** (lit: to have fear)
to be right (correct)	**tener razón** (lit: to have reason)

TO BE

The verb 'to be' has two forms in Spanish, **ser** and **estar**. To know exactly when to use which verb takes practice but here are some basic rules to help you.

Ser

Ser	
I am	**soy**
you are (inf)	**eres**
she/he/it is, you are (polite)	**es**
we are	**somos**
you are (pl, inf)	**sois**
they/you are (pl, polite)	**son**

The verb ser is used in situations that have a degree of permanence about them:

- characteristics of persons or things

  Maria is pretty.   María es guapa.

  The book is yellow.   El libro es amarillo.

- occupations and nationality

  I am a student.   Soy estudiante.

  They are Australian.   Son australianas/os.

- telling the time and location of events

  It's one o'clock.   Es la una.

  It's 3.30.   Son las tres y media.

  The party is at my house. La fiesta es en mi casa.

Estar

Estar	
I am	estoy
you are (inf)	estás
she/he/it is, you are (polite)	está
we are	estamos
you are (pl, inf)	estáis
they/you are (pl, polite)	están

The verb estar connotes temporary characteristics, or those which are the result of an action:

  The food is cold.   La comida está fría.

  The coffee is too sweet. El café está demasiado dulce.

- it is used with the location of persons or things

  I am in Cádiz.   Estoy en Cádiz.

  The city is far away.   La ciudad está lejos.

- it is used to indicate mood

  They (f) are happy.   Están contentas.

  She/He is sad.   Está triste.

GRAMMAR

KEY VERBS
Regular Verbs

The following three verb forms are regular forms. Most other verbs follow the same conjugations. The three forms are those ending in -ar, -er and -ir.

comprar (to buy)   *past participle:* (haber) comprado

	present	simple past	imperfect past	future
I	compro	compré	compraba	compraré
you (inf)	compras	compraste	comprabas	comprarás
he/she/it/you	compra	compró	compraba	comprará
we	compramos	compramos	comprábamos	compraremos
you (pl, inf)	compráis	comprasteis	comprabais	compraréis
they/you	compran	compraron	compraban	comprarán

comer (to eat)   *past participle:* (haber) comido

	present	simple past	imperfect past	future
I	como	comí	comía	comeré
you (inf)	comes	comiste	comías	comerás
he/she/it/you	come	comió	comía	comerá
we	comemos	comimos	comíamos	comeremos
you (pl, inf)	coméis	comisteis	comíais	comeréis
they/you	comen	comieron	comían	comerán

vivir (to live)   *past participle:* (haber) vivido

	present	simple past	imperfect past	future
I	vivo	viví	vivía	viviré
you (inf)	vives	viviste	vivías	vivirás
he/she/it/you	vive	vivió	vivía	vivirá
we	vivimos	vivimos	vivíamos	viviremos
you (pl, inf)	vivís	vivisteis	vivíais	viviréis
they/you	viven	vivieron	vivían	vivirán

Useful Irregular Verbs

estar (to be)   *past participle:* (haber) estado

	present	simple past	imperfect past	future
I	estoy	estuve	estuviera	estaré
you (inf)	estás	estuviste	estuvieras	estarás
he/she/it/you	está	estuvo	estuviera	estará
we	estamos	estuvimos	estuviéramos	estaremos
you (pl, inf)	estáis	estuvisteis	estuvierais	estaréis
they/you	están	estuvieron	estuvieran	estarán

GRAMMAR

ir (to go)

past participle: (haber) **ido**

	present	simple past	imperfect past	future
I	voy	fui	iba	iré
you (inf)	vas	fuiste	ibas	irás
he/she/it/you	va	fue	iba	irá
we	vamos	fuimos	íbamos	iremos
you (pl, inf)	vais	fuisteis	ibais	iréis
they/you	van	fueron	iban	irán

haber (to have)

past participle: (haber) **habido**

	present	simple past	imperfect past	future
I	hube	había	habré	
you (inf)	has	hubiste	habías	habrás
he/she/it/you	ha	hubo	había	habrá
we	hemos	hubimos	habíamos	habremos
you (pl, inf)	habéis	hubisteis	habíais	habréis
they/you	han	hubieron	habían	habrán

poder (to be able)

past participle: (haber) **podido**

	present	simple past	imperfect past	future
I	puedo	pude	podía	podré
you (inf)	puedes	pudiste	podías	podrás
he/she/it/you	puede	pudo	podía	podrá
we	podemos	pudimos	podíamos	podremos
you (pl, inf)	podeis	pudisteis	podíais	podréis
they/you	pueden	pudieron	podían	podrán

ser (to be)

past participle: (haber) **sido**

	present	simple past	imperfect past	future
I	soy	fui	era	seré
you (inf)	eres	fuiste	eras	serás
he/she/it/you	es	fue	era	será
we	somos	fuimos	éramos	seremos
you (pl, inf)	sois	fuisteis	erais	seréis
they/you	son	fueron	eran	serán

tener (to have)

past participle: (haber) **tenido**

	present	simple past	imperfect past	future
I	tengo	tuve	tenía	tendré
you (inf)	tienes	tuviste	tenías	tendrás
he/she/it/you	tiene	tuvo	tenía	tendrá
we	tenemos	tuvimos	teníamos	tendremos
you (pl, inf)	tenéis	tuvisteis	teníais	tendréis
they/you	tienen	tuvieron	tenían	tendrán

GRAMMAR

traer (to bring)   *past participle:* (haber) traído

	present	simple past	imperfect past	future
I	traigo	traje	traía	traeré
you (inf)	traes	trajiste	traías	traerás
he/she/it/you	trae	trajo	traía	traerá
we	traemos	trajimos	traíamos	traeremos
you (pl, inf)	traéis	trajísteis	traíais	traeréis
they/you	traen	trajeron	traían	traerán

dar (to give)   *past participle:* (haber) dado

	present	simple past	imperfect past	future
I	doy	di	daba	daré
you (inf)	das	diste	dabas	darás
he/she/it/you	da	dio	daba	dará
we	damos	dimos	dábamos	daremos
you (pl, inf)	dais	disteis	dabais	daréis
they/you	dan	dieron	daban	darán

saber (to know)   *past participle:* (haber) sabido

	present	simple past	imperfect past	future
I	sé	supe	sabía	sabré
you (inf)	sabes	supiste	sabías	sabrás
he/she/it/you	sabe	supo	sabía	sabrá
we	sabemos	supimos	sabíamos	sabremos
you (pl, inf)	sabéis	supisteis	sabíais	sabréis
they/you	saben	supieron	sabían	sabrán

hacer (to make/do)   *past participle:* (haber) hecho

	present	simple past	imperfect past	future
I	hago	hice	hacía	hará
you (inf)	haces	hiciste	hacías	harás
he/she/it/you	hace	hizo	hacía	hará
we	hacemos	hicimos	hacíamos	haremos
you (pl, inf)	hacéis	hicisteis	hacíais	hareis
they/you	hacen	hicieron	hacían	harán

querer (to want)   *past participle:* (haber) querido

	present	simple past	imperfect past	future
I	quiero	quise	quería	querré
you (inf)	quieres	quisiste	querías	querrás
he/she/it/you	quiere	quiso	quería	querrá
we	queremos	quisimos	queríamos	querremos
you (pl, inf)	queréis	quisisteis	queríais	querréis
they/you	quieren	quisieron	querían	querrán

GRAMMAR

MODALS
Must/Have To/Need To

In order to express having to do something, you can use the verb tener followed by que and then the infinitive of the verb.

I have to change some money.	Tengo que cambiar dinero.

Can/To Be Able

There are several ways to express 'can/to be able'. The verb can be used, while you may also hear es posible [que], 'it is possible [that]'.

Can (may) I take a photo?	¿Puedo sacar una foto?
Can you show it to me on the map?	¿Me lo puede mostrar en el mapa?
Can you do it?	¿Puedes hacerlo?; ¿Es posible hacerlo?

To Like

In Spanish, in order to say you like something, you say 'something pleases you'. You use the verb gustar ('to please/taste') with the indirect object pronouns (see page 23).

I like beer.	Me gusta la cerveza.
	('beer pleases me')
We like it.	Nos gusta.
	('it pleases us')
They like ice cream.	Les gusta el helado.
	('the icecream pleases them')
I like action films.	Me gustan las películas de acción.
	('action films please me')
I like you (inf).	Me gustas.
	('you please me')
You like me (inf).	Te gusto.
	('I please you')

GRAMMAR

ADJECTIVES

Adjectives in Spanish agree in gender and number with the nouns they relate to, so they have different endings depending upon whether the noun is masculine, feminine, singular or plural. Unlike English, they almost always come after the noun.

a pretty house	una casa bonita
some pretty houses	unas casas bonitas
a white hat	un sombrero blanco
some white hats	unos sombreros blancos

Adjectives of quantity such as 'much', 'a lot of', 'little/few', 'too much'; cardinal and ordinal numbers, and possessive adjectives always precede the noun.

a lot of tourists	muchos turistas
first class	primera clase
my car	mi coche

Comparatives

more ... than	richer than	más rico que
más ... que		(lit: more rich than)
less ... than	less rich than	menos rico que
menos ... que	easier than	más fácil que
as ... as	less easy than	menos fácil que
tan ... como	as easy as	tan fácil como
	as beautiful as	tan bonito como
	better	mejor
	worse	peor

Superlatives

the most ...	the richest	el más rico
el más ...	the least rich	el menos rico
the least ...	the easiest	el más fácil
el menos ...	the least easy	el menos fácil
	the best	el mejor
	the worst	el peor

FALSE FRIENDS

to say ...	use ...	don't use ...	which means ...
to attend	asistir	atender	to help
to board (the ship)	embarcarse	bordar	to embroider
(bus) conductor	cobrador/a	conductor/a	driver
to be constipated	estar estreñida/o	estar constipada/o	to have a cold
date	la fecha	el dato	information/data
embarrassed	avergonzada/o	embarazada	pregnant
exit	la salida	el éxito	success
injury	la herida	la injuria	insult
large	grande	larga/o	long
library	la biblioteca	la librería	bookshop
parents	los padres	los parientes	relatives
to quit	dejar	quitar	to take away
to realize	darse cuenta de	realizar	to carry out
rent	el alquiler	la renta	income
sensible	juiciosa/o	sensible	sensitive
suburb	el barrio	el suburbio	slum district
sympathetic	comprensiva/o	simpática/o	friendly

GRAMMAR

POSSESSION

Possession may be indicated in several ways. The most common way is by using possessive adjectives which agree in number and gender with the noun they describe. They are always placed before the noun.

Possessive Adjectives		
	m/f singular	m/f plural
my	mi	mis
your (inf)	tu	tus
his/her/its/your (polite)	su	sus
our	nuestra/o	nuestras/os
your (pl, inf)	vuestra/o	vuestras/os
their/your (pl, polite)	su	sus

my country	mi país
your (inf) hands	tus manos

Another way to indicate possession is by using possessive pronouns, which also agree in number and gender with the noun and are placed after it.

Possessive Pronouns		
	m/f singular	m/f plural
mine	mía/o	mías/os
yours (inf)	tuya/o	tuyas/os
hers/his/yours (polite)	suya/o	suyas/os
ours	nuestra/o	nuestras/os
yours (pl inf)	vuestra/o	vuestras/os
theirs/yours (pl, polite)	suya/o	suyas/os

The house is mine.	La casa es mía.
These passports are ours.	Estos pasaportes son nuestros.

QUESTIONS

As in English, all questions in Spanish require a rise in intonation at the end of the sentence. In written Spanish a question is introduced by an inverted question mark – this is a clear indication to change your intonation.

> You're (pl) leaving early tomorrow?   ¿Os vais mañana temprano?

Question Words		
Where?	¿Dónde?	Where is the bank? ¿Dónde está el banco?
Why?	¿Por qué?	Why is the museum closed? ¿Por qué está cerrado el museo?
When?	¿Cuándo?	When does the carnival begin? ¿Cuándo empieza el carnaval?
What?	¿Qué?	What is he saying? ¿Qué está diciendo?
How?	¿Cómo?	How do I get to there? ¿Cómo puedo llegar/ir allá?
Who? (sg)	¿Quién?	Who is it? ¿Quién es?
Who? (pl)	¿Quiénes?	Who are they? ¿Quiénes son?
Which?/ What? (sg)	¿Cuál?	Which is the best beach? ¿Cuál es la mejor playa?
Which/ What? (pl)	¿Cuáles?	Which restaurants are the cheapest? ¿Cuáles restaurantes son los más baratos?

NEGATIVES

To form the negative in a sentence, place no before the verb:

We don't want to go to the museum today.	No queremos ir al museo hoy.
I don't know what the time is.	No sé qué hora es.

Contrary to English, you can use double negatives in Spanish:

I don't have anything.	No tengo nada. (lit: I don't have nothing)

MEETING PEOPLE

YOU SHOULD KNOW

If you don't remember any other Spanish words, these will be the ones that always stay in your mind – the essential greetings and politenesses that exist in any language.

Hello.	¡Hola!
Goodbye.	¡Adiós!
Yes/No.	Sí/No.
Excuse me.	Perdón.
Please.	Por favor.
Thank you.	Gracias.
Many thanks.	Muchas gracias.

May I? Do you mind?	¿Puedo?; ¿Me permite?
Sorry. (excuse me, forgive me)	Lo siento; Discúlpeme; Perdón; Perdóneme.
That's fine. You're welcome.	De nada.

GREETINGS

Good morning.	Buenos días.
Good afternoon. (until about 8pm)	Buenas tardes.
Good evening/night.	Buenas noches.
See you later.	Hasta luego.
See you tomorrow.	Hasta mañana.
How are you ?	¿Qué tal?
Well, thanks.	Bien, gracias.
Not too bad.	Tirando.
Not so good.	Pues, no muy bien.

FORMS OF ADDRESS

Mrs	Señora; Doña (rare)
Mr	Señor; Don (rare)
Miss	Señorita

Note that it has become less and less common for women to be addressed as señorita. It's more common now to use señora for all women, regardless of age or marital status.

companion
friend

¡OYE TIO!

Here are some common ways of addressing your friends, or referring to people (a bit like 'you guys' in English)

tía(s); tío(s)
tronca(s); tronco(s)
colega(s)

And in the south ...

pixa(s)/xoxo(s)

FIRST ENCOUNTERS

What's your name?	¿Cómo te llamas? (inf)
	¿Cómo se llama usted? (polite)
My name's …	Me llamo …
I'm a friend of (Maria).	Soy amiga/o de (María).
I'd like to introduce you to …	Quisiera presentarte a …
His/her name is …	Se llama …
(I'm) pleased to meet you.	Mucho gusto; Encantada/o.
I'm here ...	Estoy aquí ...
on holiday	de vacaciones
business	en viaje de negocios
studying	estudiando
Where are you staying?	¿Dónde te alojas?
How long have you been here?	¿Cuánto tiempo llevasaquí?
I've been here (three days).	Llevo aquí (tres días).

MEETING PEOPLE

How long are you here for?	¿Cuánto tiempo te vas a quedar?
We're here for (two weeks).	Nos quedaremos (dos semanas).
This is my first visit to (Spain).	Es la primera vez que visito (España).
I like (Spain) very much.	Me encanta (España).
Are you on your own?	¿Has venido sola/o?
I'm with my partner.	He venido con mi compañera/o.
How did you get here?	¿Cómo has venido?
It was nice talking to you.	Me ha encantado charlar contigo.
I have to get going now.	Ahora tengo que irme.
I had a great day/evening.	Me lo he pasado en grande.
Hope to see you again soon.	Espero verte pronto.
We must do this again sometime.	¡Esto tenemos que repetirlo!
Next time it's on me.	La próxima la pago yo.
I'll give you a call.	Ya te llamaré.
See you soon.	Hasta pronto.

NATIONALITIES

Spain is very much a regional country – it is said that Spaniards are loyal firstly to their home town, then to their region and only finally to Spain. A great conversation-starter in Spain is to ask someone where they come from. Unfortunately we can't list all countries here, however you'll find that many country names in Spanish are similar to English. Remember though that even if a word looks like the English equivalent, it will have Spanish pronunciation. For instance, Japan: *hah-pon*). Listed here are some that differ more considerbly.

Where are you from?	¿De dónde eres?
Are you from around here?	¿Eres de por aquí?

I'm from …
   England
   Germany
   Holland
   New Zealand
   Scotland
   South America

   the USA
   Wales

Soy de …
   Inglaterra
   Alemania
   los Paises Bajos
   Nueva Zelanda
   Escocia
   América del Sur;
     Sudamérica
   los Estados Unidos
   País de Gales

Have you ever been to my
   country?
What is your home town/
   region like?

¿Has estado alguna vez en mi
   país?
¿Cómo es tu ciudad/región?

I come from …/live in …
   the city
   the countryside
   the mountains
   the seaside
   the suburbs of …
   a village

Vengo de …;Vivo en …
   la ciudad
   el campo
   las montañas
   la costa
   las afueras de …
   un pueblo

CULTURAL DIFFERENCES

How do you do this in (your) country?	¿Cómo se hace esto en (vuestro/tu) país?
Is this a local or national custom?	¿Esto es una costumbre local o nacional?
I don't want to offend you.	No quiero ofenderte (inf)/ ofenderos (pol)
I'm sorry, it's not the custom in my country.	Lo siento, pero esto no es costumbre en mi país.
I'm not accustomed to this.	No estoy acostumbrada/o a esto.
I don't mind watching, but I'd prefer not to participate.	No me importa verlo, pero prefiero no participar.

LANGUAGE DIFFICULTIES

Do you speak English?	¿Hablas inglés?
Does anyone speak English?	¿Hay alguien que hable inglés?
I speak a little Spanish.	Hablo un poco de castellano; español.
I'm learning.	Estoy aprendiendo.
Excuse my Spanish!	¡Perdona mi castellano!
I (don't) understand.	(No) Entiendo.
Do you understand?	¿Me entiendes?
Could you speak more slowly please?	Más despacio, por favor.
Could you repeat that?	¿Puedes repetir?
Could you write that down please?	¿Puedes escribirlo, por favor?
How do you say...?	¿Cómo se dice ...?
What is this called in Spanish?	¿Cómo se dice esto en castellano?
What does ... mean?	¿Qué significa ...?
How do you pronounce this word?	¿Cómo se pronuncia esta palabra?
Pardon?; What?	¿Cómo?

MEETING PEOPLE

In my country we …	En mi país …
My culture/religion doesn't allow me to …	Mi cultura/religión no me permite …
practise this	estas prácticas
eat this	esta comida
drink this	esta bebida

For more beliefs and opinions see Interests (page 93) and Social Issues (page 111).

AGE

How old are you?	¿Cuántos años tienes?
I am … years old.	Tengo … años.
Oh! You don't look it!	¡Vaya! ¡Pues no lo pareces!

OCCUPATIONS

Where do you work?	¿De qué trabajas?
What do you do?	¿A qué te dedicas?

I'm (a/an …)	Soy …
artist	artista
business person	comerciante
doctor	doctora/doctor, médica/o
engineer	ingeniera/o
factory worker	obrera/o
farmer	agricultora/agricultor, granjera/o
homemaker	ama/o de casa
journalist	periodista
lawyer	abogada/o
manual worker	obrera/o, trabajadora/trabajador
mechanic	mecánica/o
musician	música/o
nurse	enfermera/o
office worker	oficinista, empleada/o
scientist	científica/o

MEETING PEOPLE

secretary	secretaria/o
self-employed	trabajadora/trabajador autónoma/o
student	estudiante
teacher	profesora/profesor
waiter	camarera/o
writer	escritora/escritor

I'm …	Estoy …
retired	jubilada/o
unemployed	en el paro

Do you enjoy your work?	¿Te gusta tu trabajo?
How long have you been in your job?	¿Desde cuándo trabajas allí?
What are you studying?	¿Qué estudias?

I'm studying …	Estudio …
art	arte
business	economía
education	educación
engineering	ingeniería
humanities	letras
languages	idiomas
law	derecho
medicine	medicina
science	ciencias
social sciences	ciencias sociales
Spanish	español

RELIGION

What is your religion?	¿Cuál es tu religión?
I'm …	Soy …
Buddhist	budista
Catholic	católica/o
Christian	cristiana/o
Hindu	hindú
Jewish	judía/o
Muslim	musulmana/musulmán

MEETING PEOPLE

I'm Catholic, but not practising.	Soy católica/o no practicante.
I think I believe in God, or something like God.	Me parece que creo en Dios, o en algo similar.
I believe in destiny/fate.	Creo en el destino.
I'm not religious.	No soy religiosa/o.
I'm agnostic.	Soy agnóstica/o.
I'm an atheist.	Soy atea/o.

FEELINGS

I'm sorry (condolence).	Lo siento mucho.
I'm grateful.	Le agradezco mucho.

I'm …	Tengo …
Are you …?	¿Tienes …?
afraid	miedo
cold	frío
hot	calor
hungry	hambre
in a hurry	prisa
keen to …	ganas de …
right	razón
sleepy	sueño
thirsty	sed

I'm …	Estoy …
Are you …?	¿Estás …?
angry	enojada/o
happy	feliz
sad	triste
tired	cansada/o
well	bien
worried	preocupada/o

THEY MAY SAY …

You may hear people saying that they are **nerviosa/o**. This doesn't always translate directly as 'nervous' but more often as what we may call 'nervy'.

The word **ansiosa/o** means 'worried' or 'anxious' but it is used so commonly that it often doesn't carry the weight of the equivalent word in English.

GETTING AROUND

FINDING YOUR WAY

Excuse me, can you help me please?	¿Perdone, puede ayudarme por favor?
I'm looking for …	Busco …
How do I get to …?	¿Cómo se va a …?
Where is …?	¿Dónde está …?
the bus station	la estación de autobús/autocares
the bus stop	la parada de autobús
the city centre	el centro de la ciudad
the port	el puerto
the subway station	la parada de metro
the taxi stand	la parada de taxis
the train station	la estación de tren
the ticket office	la taquilla
Is it far from/near here?	¿Está lejos/cerca de aquí?
Where are we now?	¿Dónde estamos ahora?
What's the best way to get there?	¿Cómo se puede ir?
Can I walk there?	¿Se puede ir andando?
Can you show me (on the map)?	¿Lo puede mostrar/indicar (en el mapa)?
Is there another way to get there?	¿Hay otra forma de ir allí/allá?

DIRECTIONS

Turn left …	Doble a la izquierda …
Turn right …	Doble a la derecha …

Cross the road …
    at the next corner
    at the traffic lights
    at the roundabout

Cruce la calle …
    en la próxima esquina
    en el semáforo
    en la rotonda

Go straight ahead.
It's two streets down.

Siga; Vaya todo derecho; recto.
Está a dos calles de aquí.

after	después de
behind	detrás de
between	entre
far	lejos
in front of	enfrente de; delante de
near	cerca
next to	al lado de
opposite	frente a
avenue	avenida
square	plaza
street	calle; paseo
east	este
north	norte
south	sur
west	oeste

THEY MAY SAY …	
De acuerdo.	Okay.
Claro.	Sure.
Vámonos.	Let's go.
¡Ojo!	Careful!
Espera.	Wait.
Espera un segundo.	Just a minute.
¿Estás lista/o?	Are you ready?
Estoy lista/o.	I'm ready.

ADDRESSES

A written Spanish address looks something like this:

Roger Martín
C/ Oro Negro 3
4° 1ª
08026 Barcelona

Deciphered, this means Oro Negro Street (calle), number 3, fourth floor (piso), first door (puerta).

BUYING TICKETS

Excuse me, where is the ticket office?	¿Perdón, dónde está la taquilla?
Where can I buy a ticket?	¿Dónde puedo comprar el billete?
Do you have a timetable please?	¿Tiene un horario?
I want to go to (Toledo).	Quiero ir a (Toledo).
How much is the fare to (Trujillo)?	¿Cuánto vale el billete a (Trujillo)?
What is the cheapest fare to (Nerja)?	¿Cuál es el billete más barato para (Nerja)?
How long does the trip take?	¿Cuánto se tarda?
Is it a direct trip?	¿Es un viaje directo?
Do I need to book?	¿Tengo que reservar?
I'd like to book a seat to (Pamplona).	Quisiera reservar una plaza para (Pamplona).

I'd like …	Quisiera …
a one-way ticket	un billete sencillo
a return ticket	un billete de ida y vuelta
two tickets	dos billetes

a/an … fare	Una tarifa …
adult	de adulto
child's	infantil
student	de estudiante
pensioner	de pensionista

I'd like a window seat, please.	Quisiera un asiento de ventanilla, por favor.
(No) smoking, please.	Quisiera un asiento de (no) fumadores.

I require a … meal.	Deseo una comida …
kosher	kosher
vegetarian	vegetariana

GETTING AROUND

I'd like to … my reservation.	Quisiera … mi reserva.
cancel	cancelar
change	cambiar
confirm	confirmar

| 1st class | primera clase |
| 2nd class | segunda clase |

It's full.	Está completo.
Is it completely full?	¿Está completamente lleno?
Can I go on the standby list?	¿Puede ponerme en la lista de espera?

When booking tickets (especially at bus and train stations) go to the venta inmediata (immediate sale) window if you are travelling on the same day. When buying tickets in advance, go to the venta anticipada (advance sale) window.

Useful Words & Phrases

What time does the … leave/arrive?	¿A qué hora sale/llega el …?
plane	avión
boat	barco
bus (city)	autobús
bus (intercity)/coach	autocar
train	tren
tram	tranvía

AT CUSTOMS

I have nothing to declare.	No tengo nada que declarar.
This is all my luggage.	Este es todo mi equipaje.
May I go through?	¿Puedo pasar?
Do I have to declare this?	¿Tengo que declarar esto?
I would like to declare (five bottles of rum).	Quisiera declarar (cinco botellas de ron).
May I call my embassy/consulate?	¿Puedo llamar a la embajada/al consulado de mi país?

SIGNS	
ADUANA	CUSTOMS
ARTÍCULOS LIBRES DE IMPUESTOS	DUTY-FREE GOODS
INMIGRACIÓN	IMMIGRATION CONTROL
CONTROL DE PASAPORTE	PASSPORT CONTROL

GETTING AROUND

AIR

Is there a flight to …?	¿Hay un vuelo para …?
When is the next flight to …?	¿Cuándo sale el próximo vuelo para …?
How long does the flight take?	¿Cuánto tiempo dura el vuelo?
Is it a nonstop flight?	¿Es un vuelo directo?
What is the flight number?	¿Cuál es el número del vuelo?
What time do I have to check in?	¿A qué hora tengo que facturar mi equipaje?
Is there a bus to the airport?	¿Hay algún autobús para el aeropuerto?
Is there a departure tax here?	¿Hay que pagar impuestos en éste aeropuerto?
I'd like to check-in my luggage.	Quisiera facturar mi equipaje.
What's the charge for each excess kilo?	¿Cuánto vale cada quilo de más?
My luggage hasn't arrived.	Mis maletas se han perdido.

airport tax	tasa del aeropuerto
arrivals	llegadas
baggage claim	recogida de equipajes
boarding pass	tarjeta de embarque
check-in	facturación de equipajes
departures	salidas
domestic	vuelos domésticos
exchange	cambio
flight	vuelo
gate	puerta
international	internacional
passport	pasaporte
plane	avión
transit lounge	tránsito

GETTING AROUND

BUS & COACH

Where is the bus/tram stop?	¿Dónde está la parada de autobús/tranvía?
How often do buses pass by?	¿Cuántas veces pasa el autobús?
Which bus goes to …?	¿Qué autobús va a …?
Do you stop at …?	¿Tiene parada en …?
(Two) tickets, please.	(Dos) billetes, por favor.
Could you let me know when we get to …?	¿Puede avisarme cuando lleguemos a …?
Can you smoke in this bus?	¿Se puede fumar en este autobús?
I want to get off!	¡Quiero bajarme!

What time is the … coach/bus?	¿A qué hora es el … autocar/autobús?
first	primer
next	próximo
last	último

Does this bus go to …?	¿Este autobus va a …?
the beach	la playa
the city centre	el centro de la ciudad
the station	la estación

local/city bus	autobús
long-distance bus/coach	autocar

TRAIN

Where is the nearest train station?	¿Dónde está la estación de tren más cercana?
Is it a … train?	¿Es un tren …?
direct	directo
express	expreso
local	regional

long distance	de largo recorrido
	rápido (daytime)
	estrella (night)
non-direct	semidirecto

Is this the right platform for ...?	¿El tren para ... sale de este andén?
The train leaves from platform ...	El tren sale del andén número ...
Do I have to change trains?	¿Tengo que cambiar de tren?
Passengers must change trains/platforms.	Los pasajeros deben cambiar de tren/andén.
Is that seat taken?	¿Está ocupado este asiento?
Do you mind if I smoke/put the window down?	¿Le importa si fumo/si bajo la ventanilla?
Excuse me. (when making your way to the door)	Perdón.
I'm sorry, I can't find my ticket/train/platform.	Lo siento, pero no encuentro mi billete/tren/andén.

dining car	vagón restaurante
local	de cercanías
long distance	de largo recorrido
platform number	número de andén
sleeping car	coche cama
ticket collector	revisora/revisor
train	tren

RENFE is the name of the Spanish national railway. It offers a range of train services, the quickest and most efficient of which you will see referred to as Talgo, Expreso and Rápido.

Día azúl (Blue day) and Día blanco (White day) are days when cheap rail fares are offered, with the días azules marginally cheaper than the días blancos. Avoid the Día rojo (Red day), when fares are especially expensive.

METRO

Which line takes me to …?	¿Qué línea cojo para …?
What is the next station?	¿Cuál es la próxima estación?
Where do I change for …?	¿Dónde hago el transbordo para …?

SIGNS	
POR AQUÍ A …	THIS WAY TO …
SALIDA	WAY OUT

change (coins)	cambio
destination	destino
line	línea
ticket machine	venta automática de billetes

Petty crime is common on the Madrid and Barcelona underground systems. When travelling on a train, keep your money in a safe place and try not to stand near the doors. These phrases may help you:

Leave me alone!	¡Déjame en paz!
Stop, thief!	¡Socorro, al ladrón!

TAXI

Are you free?	¿Está libre?
Please take me …	Por favor, lléveme …
to this address	a esta dirección
to the airport	al aeropuerto
to the city centre	al centro de la ciudad
to the railway station	a la estación de tren
How much is it to go to …?	¿Cuánto cuesta/vale ir a …?
Does that include luggage?	¿El precio incluye el equipaje?

GETTING AROUND

Can you take five people?	¿Puede llevar a cinco personas?
Do you have change of 5000 pesetas?	¿Tiene cambio de 5000 pesetas?
Please slow down.	Por favor vaya más despacio.
Please hurry.	Por favor, dese prisa.
The next corner, please.	La próxima esquina, por favor.
Continue!	¡Siga!
The next street to the left/right.	La próxima calle a la izquierda/derecha.
Here is fine, thank you.	Aquí está bien, gracias.
Stop here!	¡Pare aquí!
Please wait here.	Por favor, espere aquí.
How much do I owe you?	¿Cuánto le debo?

CAR

SIGNS

CEDA EL PASO	GIVE WAY
DESVÍO	DETOUR
DIRECCIÓN PROHIBIDA	NO ENTRY
FRENE	SLOW DOWN
NO ADELANTAR	DO NOT OVERTAKE
OBRAS	ROADWORKS
PEATONES	PEDESTRIANS
PELIGRO	DANGER
PRECAUCIÓN	CAUTION
PROHIBIDO ESTACIONAR	NO PARKING
SALIDA	EXIT
SENTIDO ÚNICO	ONE WAY
STOP/PARE	STOP
VADO PERMANENTE	24-HOUR ACCESS

Where can I rent a car?	¿Dónde puedo alquilar un coche?
How much is it daily/weekly?	¿Cuánto cuesta por día/por semana?
Does that include insurance/ mileage?	¿Incluye el seguro/ el kilometraje?
Where's the next petrol station?	¿Hay alguna gasolinera por aquí?
Please fill the tank.	Por favor, lléneme el depósito.
I want ... litres of petrol (gas).	Quiero ... litros de gasolina.
I want (2000 pesetas) worth of petrol.	Quiero (2000 pesetas) de gasolina.
Please check the oil, water and air.	Por favor, revise el nivel del aceite, del agua y el aire.
How long can I park here?	¿Cuánto tiempo puedo aparcar aquí?
Does this road lead to ...?	¿Se va a ... por esta carretera?

air	aire
battery	batería; acumulador
brakes	frenos
clutch	embrague
driver's licence	carnet; permiso de conducir
engine	motor
garage	taller
indicator	intermitente
leaded/regular	gasolina normal/con plomo
lights	luces
main road	carretera
map	mapa
mobile breath testing unit	control de alcoholemia
motorway (with tolls)	autopista
oil	aceite
puncture	pinchazo

radiator	radiador
ring-road	carretera de circunvalación/ cinturón
road map	mapa de carreteras
seatbelt	cinturón de seguridad
self-service	autoservicio
speed limit	límite de velocidad
super	súper
toll free motorway	autovía
tyres	neumáticos
unleaded	sin plomo
windscreen	parabrisas

Car Problems

I need a mechanic.	Necesito un mecánico.
What make is it?	¿De qué marca es?
I've had a breakdown at …	He tenido una avería en …
The battery is flat.	La batería está descargada.
The radiator is leaking.	El radiador tiene una fuga.
I have a flat tyre.	Tengo un pinchazo.
It's overheating.	Está recalentándose.
It's not working.	No funciona.
I've lost my car keys.	He perdido las llaves de mi coche.
I've run out of petrol.	Me he quedado sin gasolina.

DID YOU KNOW … There is no specific word for *toes*, instead, they are known as **los dedos de pie** (the fingers of the foot).

BICYCLE

Do you like cycling?	¿Te gusta montar en bicicleta?
Do you cycle?	¿Sabes montar en bicicleta?
Can you recommend a good place for a bike ride?	¿Me puede recomendar algún sitio bonito para pasear en bicicleta?
Is it within cycling distance?	¿Está a distancia de bicicleta?
Is it safe to cycle around here?	¿Es seguro andar en bicicleta aquí?
Where can I find second-hand bicycles for sale?	¿Dónde venden bicicletas de segunda mano?
Where can I hire a bicycle?	¿Dónde se alquilan bicicletas?
How much is it to hire a bicycle for …	¿Cuánto vale alquilar una bicicleta durante …?
an hour	una hora
the morning/afternoon	toda la mañana/tarde
the day	todo el día
Can you lend me a padlock?	¿Me puede prestar un candado?
Can you raise/lower the seat?	¿Me puede subir/bajar el sillín?
Is it compulsory to wear a helmet?	¿Es obligatorio llevar casco?
Where can I leave the bicycle?	¿Dónde puedo aparcar la bicicleta?
Can I leave the bike here?	¿Puedo aparcar la bici aquí?
Where are bike repairs done?	¿Dónde arreglan bicicletas?
I've got a flat tyre.	Se me ha pinchado una rueda.
I came off my bike.	Me he caído de la bici.

bike	bici; bicicleta
brakes	frenos
to cycle	andar en bicicleta
gear stick	cambio de marchas

handlebars	manillar
helmet	casco
to hire	alquilar
inner tube	cámara
lights	luces
mountain bike	mountain bike; bicicleta de montaña
padlock	candado
pump	bomba
puncture	pinchazo
racing bike	bicicleta de carreras
saddle	sillín
tandem	tándem
wheel	rueda

CROSSWORD – GETTING AROUND

Across:
1. Useful when waterskiing
2. Achtung!
3. Not even close
4. Should come with wings

Down:
1. Where to strut your swimwear
2. 'She's got a ... to ride'
3. In the neighbourhood

Answers: page 366

GETTING AROUND

ACCOMMODATION

I'm looking for a …
   cheap hotel
   good hotel
   nearby hotel
   clean hotel

Busco un …
   hotel barato
   buen hotel
   hotel cercano
   hotel limpio

What is the address?
Could you write the address, please?

¿Cuál es la dirección?
¿Puede escribir la dirección, por favor?

For details on camping, see page 153.

SIGNS

CAMPING	CAMPING GROUND
ALBERGUE JUVENIL	YOUTH HOSTEL
REFUGIO DE MONTAÑA	MOUNTAIN LODGE
PENSION (P)/	GUESTHOUSE
CASA DE HUESPEDES (CH)	
HOSTAL (Hs)/	BUDGET HOTEL
HOSTAL-RESIDENCIA (HsR)	
HOTEL (H)	HOTEL

BOOKING AHEAD

I'd like to book a room please.

Quisiera reservar una habitación.

Do you have any rooms available?
For (three) nights.
How much is it per night/ per person?

¿Tiene habitaciones libres?

Para (tres) noches.
¿Cuánto cuesta por noche/ por persona?

65

I will be arriving at (two o'clock).	Llegaré a (las dos).
My name is …	Me llamo …
Is there hot water all day?	¿Hay agua caliente todo el día?
Does it include breakfast?	¿Incluye el desayuno?

CHECKING IN

I've made a reservation.	He hecho una reserva.

I'd like …
    a single room
    a double room
    to share a dorm

Quisiera …
    una habitación individual
    una habitación doble
    compartir un dormitorio

I want a room with a …
    bathroom
    double bed
    shower
    twin beds
    view of the sea/mountain
    window

Quiero una habitación con …
    baño
    cama de matrimonio
    ducha
    dos camas
    vistas al mar/a la montaña
    ventana

It must be …
    quiet
    light

Tiene que ser …
    silenciosa
    luminosa

Can I see it?	¿Puedo verla?
Can I see the bathroom?	¿Puedo ver el baño?
Are there any others?	¿Hay otras?
Are there any cheaper rooms?	¿Hay habitaciones más baratas?
Is there a reduction for students/children?	¿Hay algún precio especial para estudiantes/niños?
Do you charge for the baby?	¿Los bebes también pagan?

Do I have to hire the bedlinen or is it included?	¿Tengo derecho a ropa de cama o tengo que alquilarla?
It's fine, I'll take it.	Vale, la alquilo.
Can I pay by credit card?	¿Puedo pagar con tarjeta de crédito?
Do you require a deposit?	¿Hay que pagar un depósito?

I'm going to stay for ...	Me voy a quedar ...
one day	un día
two days	dos días
one week	una semana

I'm not sure how long I'm staying.	No sé cuánto tiempo me voy a quedar.

THEY MAY SAY ...

Lo siento, no tenemos nada libre.	Sorry, we're full.
¿Cuánto tiempo se queda?	How long will you be staying?
¿Cuántas noches?	How many nights?
¿Tiene carnet de identidad?/ ¿Tiene pasaporte?	Do you have identification?
Su tarjeta de socio, por favor.	Your membership card, please.

---

date	fecha
date of birth	fecha de nacimiento
name	nombre
surname	apellido
signature	firma

ACCOMMODATION

REQUESTS & QUERIES

Do you have a safe?
    ¿Tiene una caja fuerte?
Where is the bathroom?
    ¿Dónde está el baño?

Can I use the kitchen?
Can I use the telephone?
Is there a lift?
I've locked myself out of my
    room.

¿Puedo usar la cocina?
¿Puedo usar el teléfono?
¿Hay ascensor?
Cerré la puerta y se me
    olvidaron las llaves dentro.

Do you change money here?	¿Se cambia dinero en este hotel?
Should I leave my key at reception?	¿Tengo que dejar la llave en la recepción?
Is there a message board?	¿Tienen tablón de anuncios?
Can I leave a message?	¿Puedo dejar un mensaje?
Is there a message for me?	¿Hay algún mensaje para mí?
Can I get my letters sent here?	¿Puedo recibir cartas dirigidas a mí?
The key for room (311) please.	La llave para la habitación (311), por favor.
Please wake me up at (seven) o'clock.	Por favor, despiérteme a las (siete).
The room needs to be cleaned.	Hay que limpiar la habitación.
Please change the sheets.	Por favor, cambie las sábanas.
Can you give me an extra blanket, please? I'm cold.	¿Puede darme otra manta, por favor? Tengo frío.
Is there somewhere to wash clothes?	¿Hay algún lugar donde pueda lavar la ropa?

COMPLAINTS

I can't open/close the window.	No puedo abrir/cerrar la ventana.
I don't like this room.	No me gusta esta habitación.
The toilet won't flush.	La cadena del retrete no funciona.
Can I change to another dormitory?	¿Puede cambiarme a otro dormitorio?
It's ...	Es ...
too small	demasiado pequeña
noisy	ruidosa
too dark	demasiado oscura
expensive	cara
cold	fría

ACCOMMODATION

CHECKING OUT

When do I/we have to check out?	¿A qué hora hay que dejar la habitación?
I am/We are leaving now.	Me voy/Nos vamos ahora.
I would like to pay the bill.	Quiero pagar la cuenta.
Can I leave my backpack at reception until tonight?	¿Puedo dejar mi mochila en la recepción hasta esta noche?
Please call a taxi for me.	¿Puede llamar a un taxi, por favor?

RENTING

I'm here about your ad for a room to rent.	He venido por la habitación que anuncian para alquilar.
Do you have any flats to rent?	¿Tiene pisos en alquiler?
I'm looking for a flat to rent for (three) months.	Estoy buscando un piso para alquilar durante (tres) meses.

I'm looking for something close to the … Busco algo cerca …

city centre	del centro de la ciudad
beach	de la playa
railway station	de la estación

Is there anything cheaper?	¿Hay algo más barato?
Could I see it?	¿Puedo verla/o?
How much is it per week/month?	¿Cuánto vale por semana/mes?
Do you require a deposit?	¿Tengo que dejar un depósito?
I'd like to rent the room for one month.	Me gustaría alquilar la habitación durante un mes.

AROUND TOWN

LOOKING FOR ...

I'm looking for ...	Busco ...
the art gallery	el museo; la galería d'arte
a bank	un banco
a cinema	un cine
the city centre	el centro de la ciudad
the consulate	el consulado
the ... embassy	la embajada ...
my hotel	mi hotel
the main square	la plaza mayor
the market	el mercado
the museum	el museo
the police	la policía
the post office	correos
a public telephone	un teléfono público
a public toilet	servicios; aseos públicos
the telephone centre	el locutorio
the tourist information office	la oficina de turismo

What time does it open?	¿A qué hora abren?
What time does it close?	¿A qué hora cierran?

AT THE BANK

Can I use my credit card to withdraw some money?	¿Puedo usar mi tarjeta de crédito para sacar dinero?
Can I exchange money here?	¿Se cambia dinero aquí?
I want to exchange some money/travellers' cheques.	Quiero cambiar dinero/ cheques de viaje.
What is the exchange rate?	¿Cuál es el tipo de cambio?
How many pesetas per (dollar)?	¿A cuánto está el (dólar)?
Please write it down.	¿Puede escribirlo, por favor?

What is your commission?	¿Cuál es su comisión?
Can I have smaller notes?	¿Me lo puede dar en billetes más pequeños?
The automatic teller has swallowed my credit card.	El cajero automático se ha tragado mi tarjeta de crédito.
Can I have money transferred here from my bank?	¿Pueden transferirme dinero de mi banco a éste?
How long will it take to arrive?	¿Cuánto tiempo tardará en llegar?

Has my money arrived yet?	¿Ya ha llegado mi dinero?
Can I transfer money overseas?	¿Puedo enviar dinero al extranjero?
Where do I sign?	¿Dónde firmo?

ATM (Automatic Teller Machine)	el cajero automático
bank notes	los billetes (de banco)
cashier	la caja
coins	las monedas
credit card	la tarjeta de crédito
exchange	el cambio
identification	la identificación
loose change	las monedas sueltas
signature	la firma

AT THE POST OFFICE

I'd like to send …	Quisiera enviar …
a letter	una carta
a postcard	una postal
a parcel	un paquete
a telegram	un telegrama

I'd like some stamps.	Quisiera unos sellos.
How much is the postage?	¿Cuánto vale el franqueo?
How much does it cost to send this to (London)?	¿Cuánto cuesta enviar esto a (Londres)?
Where is the poste restante section?	¿Dónde está la lista de correos?
Is there any mail for me?	¿Hay alguna carta para mí?

aerogram	una aerograma
air mail	por vía aérea
envelope	un sobre
express mail	el correo urgente

express mail	el correo urgente
mail box	el buzón
parcel	un paquete
pen	el bolígrafo
postcode	el código postal
registered mail	el correo certificado
surface mail	por vía terrestre; marítima

AROUND TOWN

SIGNS

ABIERTO/CERRADO	OPEN/CLOSED
ADUANA	CUSTOMS
CALIENTE/FRÍO	HOT/COLD
ENTRADA	ENTRANCE
ENTRADA GRATIS	FREE ADMISSION
FACTURACIÓN DE EQUIPAJE; CHECK-IN	CHECK-IN COUNTER
INFORMACIÓN	INFORMATION
NO TOCAR	DO NOT TOUCH
NO (USAR EL) FLASH	DO NOT USE FLASH
PROHIBIDO	PROHIBITED
PROHIBIDO COMER	NO EATING
PROHIBIDO EL PASO	NO ENTRY
PROHIBIDO FUMAR	NO SMOKING
PROHIBIDO PISAR LA HIERBA	KEEP OFF THE GRASS
PROHIBIDO TOMAR FOTOS	NO PHOTOGRAPHY
RESERVADO	RESERVED
SALIDA	EXIT
SALIDA DE EMERGENCIA	EMERGENCY EXIT
SERVICIOS; ASEOS	TOILETS
TELÉFONO	TELEPHONE

TELECOMMUNICATIONS

In Spain you can use any public telephone to call locally or internationally, or call from el locutorio, where you pay afterwards. All calls are charged by the minute.

I want to make a call.	Quiero hacer una llamada.
I want to ring (Australia).	Quiero llamar a (Australia).
I want to speak for (three) minutes.	Quiero hablar (tres) minutos.
How much does a three-minute call cost?	¿Cuánto cuesta/vale una llamada de tres minutos?
How much does each extra minute cost?	¿Cuánto cuesta cada minuto adicional?
The number is …	El número es …
What's the area code for …?	¿Cuál es el prefijo de …?
I want to make a reverse-charges phone call.	Quiero hacer una llamada a cobro revertido.
It's engaged.	Está comunicando.
I've been cut off.	Me han cortado (la comunicación).
How can I get Internet access?	¿Cómo puedo acceder a Internet?
Is there a local Internet café?	¿Hay algún servicio local de Internet?
I need to check my email.	Tengo que revisar mi correo electrónico.
Is there a cheap rate for …?	¿Hay alguna tarifa más barata …?
evenings	para las llamadas nocturnas
weekends	durante los fines de semana
answering machine	el contestador automático
dial tone	el tono
home page	home page; la pagina
Internet	Internet

operator	la operadora;el operador
phone book	la guía telefónica
phone box	la cabina telefónica
phonecard	la tarjeta de teléfono
telephone	el teléfono
telephone office	la centralita telefónica
urgent	urgente

Making a Call

Hello! (making a call)	¡Hola!
Hello! (answering a call)	¿Diga?
Can I speak to (Angel)?	¿Está (Angel)?
Who's calling?	¿De parte de quién?
It's (Susana).	De (Susana).
Just a minute, I'll put (him) on.	Un momento, ahora se pone.
I'm sorry (she)'s not here.	Lo siento, pero ahora no está.
What time will (he) be back?	¿A qué hora volverá?
Can I take a message?	¿Quieres dejar un mensaje?
Yes, please tell (her) I called.	Sí, por favor, dile que he llamado.
No, thanks, I'll call back later.	No gracias, ya llamaré más tarde.

SIGHTSEEING

Do you have a guidebook/ local map?	¿Tiene una guía/un mapa de la ciudad?
What are the main attractions?	¿Cuáles son las atracciones principales?
What is that?	¿Qué es eso?
How old is it?	¿Es antiguo? ¿De cuándo es?
Can I take photographs?	¿Puedo tomar fotos?
What time does it open/close?	¿A qué hora abren/cierran?
Is there an admission charge?	¿Hay que pagar?
Is there a discount for …?	¿Hay descuentos para …?
children	niños
students	estudiantes
pensioners	pensionistas

ON THE STREETS

What is this?	¿Qué es esto?
What is happening?	¿Qué pasa?
What happened?	¿Qué ha pasado?
What is s/he doing?	¿Qué está haciendo?
What do you charge?	¿Cuánto cobra?
How much is it?	¿Cuánto vale?
Can I have one please?	Quisiera una/o, por favor.

festival	festival
newspaper kiosk	quiosco
recycling bin	contenedor de reciclaje
street	calle
street demonstration	manifestación
suburb	barrio
tobacco kiosk	quiosco de tabaco

People You See

artist	artista
beggar	mendiga/o
busker	artista callejera/o
clown	payasa/o
flower seller	vendedora/vendedor de flores
fortune teller	adivina/o
lottery ticket seller	vendedora/vendedor de lotería
magician	maga/o
performing artist	artista callejero
portrait sketcher	retratista; caricaturista
street-seller	vendedora/vendedor callejera/o

Things They Sell

crafts	artesanía
earrings	pendientes
paintings	cuadros
posters	posters
scarves	pañuelos y bufandas
T-shirts	camisetas

GUIDED TOURS

Do you organise group tours?	¿Organizan excursiones en grupo?
What type of people participate?	¿Qué tipo de gente participa?
Will I have free time?	¿Voy a tener tiempo libre?
Is it necessary to join in all the group activities?	¿Es obligatorio hacer todas las actividades con el grupo?
How long will we stop for?	¿Cuánto tiempo vamos a parar?
What time do I have to be back?	¿A qué hora tengo que volver?
The guide has paid/will pay.	La/El guía ha pagado/va a pagar.
I'm with them.	Voy con ellos.
I've lost my group.	He perdido a mi grupo.
Have you seen a group of (Australians)?	¿Ha visto a un grupo de (australianos)?

GOING OUT

Socialising is a national pastime in Spain, especially at night when Spaniards of all ages hit the streets in search of friends, food, music and a good time. Especially at weekends, the evening doesn't get started until after 11pm and can go on all night.

Where to Go

What's there to do in the evenings?	¿Qué se puede hacer por las noches?
Where can I find out what's on?	¿Dónde puedo averiguar qué hay esta noche?
What's on tonight?	¿Qué hay esta noche?
Which paper are the concerts listed in?	¿En qué periódico se anuncian los conciertos?
In the entertainment guide.	En la guía del ocio.

I feel like going to ...
a bar/café
the cinema
a concert
a disco
the opera
a restaurant
the theatre

Tengo ganas de ir ...
a un bar/café
al cine
a un concierto
a una discoteca
a la ópera
a un restaurante
al teatro

I feel like ...
a stroll
dancing
going for tapas

Tengo ganas de ...
pasear
bailar
ir de tapas

Invites

What are you doing this evening/this weekend?

¿Qué haces esta noche/este fin de semana?

Would you like to go out somewhere? — ¿Quieres salir conmigo?

Do you know a good restaurant (that is cheap)? — ¿Conoces algún restaurante (que no sea muy caro)?

Would you like to go for a drink/meal? — ¿Quieres que vayamos a tomar algo/a cenar?

My shout (I'll buy). — Te invito.

Do you want to come to the (Barricada) concert with me? — ¿Quieres venir conmigo al concierto de (Barricada)?

We're having a party. — Vamos a hacer una fiesta.
  Come along. — ¿Quieres venir?

Responding to Invites

Sure! — ¡Por supuesto!

Yes, I'd love to. — Me encantaría.

That's very kind of you. (NB this may sound stilted in English, but it's common in Spanish, especially when the situation is formal.) — Es muy amable por tu parte.

Yes, let's. Where shall we go? — Venga, vamos. ¿Pero, dónde?

No, I'm afraid I can't. What about tomorrow? — Lo siento pero no puedo. ¿Qué tal mañana?

Nightclubs & Bars

Are there any discos? — ¿Hay alguna discoteca?

How much is it to get in? — ¿Cuánto cuesta la entrada?

How do you get to this disco? — ¿Cómo se llega a esta discoteca?

Shall we dance? — ¿Vamos a bailar?

I'm sorry, I'm a terrible dancer. — Lo siento, pero bailo fatal.

Come on! — ¡Venga, vamos!

What type of music do you prefer? — ¿Qué tipo de música prefieres?

I really like (reggae).	Me encanta (el reggae).
Where can we dance some (salsa)?	¿Dónde se puede bailar (salsa)?
Do you want to go to a karaoke bar?	¿Quieres ir a un karaoke?
How much is the cover charge?	¿Cuánto vale entrar?
Do you have to pay to enter the ballroom?	¿Vale pasta entrar a la sala de fiestas?
No, it's free.	No, es gratis.
Yes, it's 750 pesetas.	Sí, vale 750 pesetas.

THEY MAY SAY ...

Spanish has many words related to going out. **El ocio** is a concept that can't easily be translated, but basically it means 'going out and enjoying oneself'. All of these verbs mean 'to go out and have a good time':

ir de copas
ir de farra
ir de marcha
ir de juerga
ir de fiesta

This place is great!
¡Este lugar me encanta!
I'm having a great time!
¡Me lo estoy pasando bomba!
I don't like the music here,
La música no me gusta.
Shall we go somewhere else?
¿Vamos a otro sitio?

ARRANGING TO MEET

What time shall we meet?
¿A qué hora quedamos?
Where shall we meet?
¿Dónde quedamos?
Let's meet at (eight o'clock) in the (Plaza Mayor).
Quedamos a las (ocho) en la (Plaza Mayor).
OK. I'll see you then.
De acuerdo. Nos vemos.
Agreed/OK!
¡Hecho!

GOING OUT

I'll come over at (six).	Vendré a las (seis).
I'll pick you up at (nine).	Te recogeré a las (nueve).
I'll try to make it.	Intentaré venir.
If I'm not there by (nine), don't wait for me.	Si no estoy a las (nueve), no me esperéis.
I'll be along later, where will you be?	Llegaré más tarde. ¿Dónde vais a estar?
See you later/tomorrow.	Hasta luego/mañana.
Sorry I'm late.	Siento llegar tarde.
Never mind.	No importa/No pasa nada.

DATING & ROMANCE
The Date

Would you like to do something …?	¿Quieres hacer algo …?
tomorrow	mañana
tonight	esta noche
at the weekend	este fin de semana
Yes, I'd love to.	Me encantaría.
Thanks, but I'd rather not.	Gracias, pero no me apetece.
I'm afraid I'm busy.	Me parece que estoy ocupada/o.

CLASSIC PICK-UP LINES

Would you like a drink?	¿Te apetece una copa?
Do you have a light?	¿Tienes fuego, por favor?
Do you mind if I sit here?	¿Te importa si me siento aquí?
Shall we get some fresh air?	¿Vamos a tomar el aire?
Do you have a girlfriend/ boyfriend?	¿Tienes novia/o?
Can I take you home?	¿Puedo llevarte a casa?

CLASSIC REJECTIONS

No thank you.	No, gracias.
I'd rather not.	Mejor que no.
I'm here with my girlfriend/ boyfriend.	Estoy aquí con mi novia/ novio.
I'm sorry, I've got better things to do ...	Lo siento, pero tengo otras cosas más importantes que hacer.
Stop hassling me.	Por favor, deje de molestarme.
Leave me alone!	¡Déjeme en paz!
Excuse me, I have to go now.	Lo siento, pero tengo que irme.
Get lost!	¡Hasta nunca!

Where would you like to go?	¿Dónde quieres ir?
Will you take me home?	¿Me acompañas a casa?
Do you want to come inside for a while?	¿Quieres subir a tomar algo?
Can I see you again?	¿Quieres que nos veamos de nuevo?
Can I call you?	¿Puedo llamarte?
I'll call you tomorrow.	Te llamaré mañana.
Goodnight.	Buenas noches.

GOING OUT

Useful Words

boyfriend	el novio
to chat up	ligar
girlfriend	la novia
date	una cita
to date	citarse
to go out with	salir con
to pick up	ligar
relationship	una relación
single	soltera/o

INTIMATE BODY

I really like your ...	Me encanta(n) tu(s) ...
body	cuerpo
breasts	pechos
bum; ass	culo
eyes	ojos
hair	pelo
hands	manos
lips	labios
mouth	boca
skin	piel

Making Love

I want you.	Te deseo.
Do you like this?	¿Esto te gusta?
Kiss me.	Bésame.
I (don't) like that.	Esto (no) me gusta.
Please stop!	¡Por favor, para!
Please don't stop!	¡Sigue!
I think we should stop now.	Creo que deberíamos parar.
Kiss me!	¡Dame un beso!
Take this off.	Sácate esto.
Touch me here.	Tócame aquí.
I want to make love to you.	Quiero hacerte el amor.
Let's go to bed!	¡Vámonos a la cama!
Do you have a condom?	¿Tienes un condón?
Let's use a condom.	Quiero que usemos un condón.

INTIMATE SPANISH

cuddle	abrazo	lover	amante
erection	erección	to masturbate	masturbarse
to fuck	follar; joder; echar un polvo	orgasm	orgasmo
		oral sex	sexo oral
kiss	beso	safe sex	sexo seguro

Afterwards

That was great.	Ha sido fantástico.
Would you like a cigarette?	¿Quieres un cigarro?
Can I stay over?	¿Puedo quedarme a pasar la noche?
You can't sleep here tonight.	No puedes quedarte aquí esta noche.
When can I see you again?	¿Podemos vernos alguna otra vez?
I'll call you.	Ya te llamaré.

Love

I love you.	Te quiero; Te amo.
I'm in love with you.	Estoy enamorada/o de ti.
I'm really happy with you.	Soy muy feliz contigo.
Do you love me?	¿Me quieres?; ¿Me amas?
Do you want to go out with me?	¿Quieres salir conmigo?
I'd love to have a relationship with you.	Me gustaría que tuviéramos una relación.
Let's move in together.	¿Por qué no nos vamos a vivir juntos?
Will you marry me?	¿Quieres casarte conmigo?

Leaving & Breaking Up

I have to leave tomorrow.	Tengo que irme mañana.
I'll miss you.	Te voy a echar de menos.
I'll come and visit you.	Vendré a visitarte.
I really want us to keep in touch.	Me gustaría que nos mantuviéramos en contacto.
I don't think it's working out.	Creo que no está funcionando.
I want to end the relationship.	Quiero que lo dejemos.
I want to remain friends.	Me gustaría que quedáramos como amigos.

GOING OUT

CROSSWORD – GOING OUT

GOING OUT

Across:

2. Shows you're not illiterate
4. Ask this, and it's sink or swim
5. Hunger cure
6. Shake them but don't let them wander

Down:

1. Not attached, possibly desperate
3. There's no night like ...
4. Anything from the tango to the stockman's stomp

Answers: page 366

QUESTIONS

Are you married?	¿Estás casada/o?
Do you have a girlfriend/ boyfriend?	¿Tienes novia/o?
How many children do you have?	¿Cuántos hijos tienes?
How many brothers/sisters do you have?	¿Cuántas/os hermanas/os tienes?
How old are they?	¿Cuántos años tienen?
Do you live with your family?	¿Vives con tu familia?
Do you get along with your family?	¿Te llevas bien con tu familia?

REPLIES

I'm …	
single	Soy soltera/o.
married	Estoy casada/o.
separated	Estoy separada/o.
divorced	Estoy divorciada/o.
a widow/widower	Soy viuda/o.
I have a partner.	Tengo pareja.
We live together but we're not married.	Vivimos juntos pero no estamos casados.
I don't have any children.	No tengo hijos.
I have a daughter/a son.	Tengo una hija/un hijo.
I live with my family.	Vivo con mi familia.

DID YOU KNOW … | Todo el mundo means everyone. However, all the world is el mundo entero

FAMILY MEMBERS

baby	el bebé
boy	el chico
brother	el hermano
children	los hijos
christian name	el nombre de pila
dad	el papá
daughter	la hija
family	la familia
father	el padre; papá
father-in-law	el suegro
girl	la chica
grandfather	el abuelo
grandmother	la abuela
husband	el esposo, marido
mother	la madre, mamá
mother-in-law	la suegra
mum	la mamá
nickname	el apodo
sister	la hermana
son	el hijo
wife	la esposa; mujer

TALKING WITH PARENTS

When is the baby due?	¿Para cuándo esperas el bebé?
What are you going to call the baby?	¿Cómo se va a llamar?
Is this your first child?	¿Es tu primer bebé?
How many children do you have?	¿Cuántos hijos tienes?
How old are your children?	¿Cuántos años tienen tus hijas/os?
I can't believe it! You look too young.	¡No me lo puedo creer! Y pareces tan joven.
Does s/he attend school?	¿Va a la escuela?
Is it a private or state school?	¿Va a una escuela privada o pública?

FAMILY

Who looks after the children?	¿Quién cuida de las hijas (f)/ los hijos? (m)
Do you have grandchildren?	¿Tienes nietos?
What's the baby's name?	¿Cómo se llama el bebé?
Is it a boy or a girl?	¿Es niña o niño?
Is s/he well-behaved?	¿Se porta bien?
Does s/he let you sleep at night?	¿Te deja dormir por las noches?
S/he's very big for her/his age!	¡Está muy grande para su edad!
What a beautiful child!	¡Es un niño/a precioso/a!
S/he looks like you.	Se parece a ti.
S/he has your eyes.	Tiene tus ojos.
Who does s/he look like, Mum or Dad?	¿A quién ha salido, al padre o a la madre?

TALKING WITH CHILDREN

What's your name?	¿Cómo te llamas?
How old are you?	¿Cuántos años tienes?
When's your birthday?	¿Cuándo es tu cumpleaños?
Have you got brothers and sisters?	¿Tienes hermanos y hermanas?
Do you have a pet at home?	¿Tienes alguna mascota?
Do you go to school or kinder?	¿Vas a la escuela o a la guardería?
Is your teacher nice?	¿Es simpática/o tu maestra/o?
Do you like school?	¿Te gusta ir a la escuela?
Do you play sport?	¿Practicas algún deporte?
What sport do you play?	¿Que deporte practicas?
What do you do after school?	¿Qué haces después de la escuela?
Do you learn English?	¿Aprendes inglés?
We speak a different language in my country so I don't understand you very well.	En mi país hablamos otra lengua diferente y no te entiendo bien.
I come from very far away.	Vengo de muy lejos.
Do you want to play a game?	¿Quieres jugar conmigo?
What shall we play?	¿A qué jugamos?
Have you lost your parents?	¿Has perdido a tus padres?

FAMILY

PETS

Despite a reputation for being cruel to animals, stemming from the tradition of bullfighting, Spaniards are great pet-owners and even have a special saints' day, 'día de San Antonio', exclusively for pets. Taking place each year on 17 January, pets and even farm animals are taken into the churches to be blessed. The idea comes from the discussion as to whether an animal has a soul, and the blessing is given in case they do.

Do you like animals?	¿Te gustan los animales?
What a cute (puppy)!	¡Qué cachorrillo más lindo!
What's s/he called?	¿Cómo se llama?
Is it female or male?	¿Es hembra o macho?
How old is s/he?	¿Cuánto tiempo tiene?
What breed is s/he?	¿De qué raza es?
Does s/he bite?	¿Muerde?
Do you have any pets?	¿Tienes alguna mascota?

I have a ...   Tengo ...
  bird   un pájaro
  canary   un canario
  cat   una/un gata/o
  dog   una/un perra/o
  fish   un pez
  guinea pig   un conejillo de indias
  hamster   un hámster
  kitten   una/un gatita/o
  mouse   un ratón
  puppy   un cachorro
  rabbit   un conejo
  tortoise   una tortuga

Common Spanish pet names include Rin-Tin-Tin, Rufo and Rosco

COMMON INTERESTS

What do you do in your spare time?	¿Qué te gusta hacer en tu tiempo libre?

Do you like …?	¿Te gusta …?
I (don't) like	(No) me gusta …
basketball	el baloncesto
dancing	bailar
films	el cine
food	la comida
football	el fútbol
hiking	el excursionismo
music	la música
photography	la fotografía
reading	leer
shopping	ir de compras
skiing	esquiar
swimming	nadar
talking	hablar
travelling	viajar

STAYING IN TOUCH

Tomorrow is my last day here.	Mañana es mi último día aquí.
Let's swap addresses.	¿Por qué no nos damos las direcciones?

Do you have a pen and paper?	¿Tienes papel y lápiz?
What's your address?	¿Cuál es tu dirección?
Here's my address.	Ésta es mi dirección.
If you ever visit (Scotland) you must come and visit us.	Si alguna vez vas a (Escocia) tienes que venir a vistarnos.
If you come to (Birmingham) you've got a place to stay.	Si vas a (Birmingham) tienes casa.
Do you have an email address?	¿Tienes dirección de correo electrónico?

Do you have access to a fax machine?	¿Tienes acceso a fax?
I'll send you copies of the photos.	Te enviaré copias de las fotos.
Don't forget to write!	¡No te olvides de escribirme!
It's been great meeting you. Keep in touch!	Me ha encantado conocerte. ¡Nos mantendremos en contacto!

Writing

If you want to impress your new friends by writing to them in Spanish when you get back home, here are some useful words and phrases:

Dear ...	Querida/o ...
I'm sorry it's taken me so long to write.	Siento haber tardado tanto en escribir.
It was great to meet you.	Me encantó conocerte/os. (pl)
Thank you so much for your hospitality.	Muchísimas gracias por tu (sg)/ vuestra (pl) hospitalidad.
I miss you (sg).	Te echo mucho de menos.
I miss you (pl).	Os echo mucho de menos.
I had a fantastic time in Spain.	Me lo pasé genial en España.
My favourite place was ...	Mi lugar preferido fue ...
I hope to visit Spain again soon.	Espero visitar otra vez España pronto.
Say 'hi' to (Isabel) and (Miquel) for me!	Saluda a (Isabel) y a (Miquel) de mi parte.
I'd love to see you again.	Tengo ganas de verte/os otra vez.
Write soon!	¡Escríbeme pronto!
With love/regards,	Un beso/besos/un abrazo

Spaniards tend to be quite informal when ending a letter. It is usual to finish with un abrazo (a hug) or un beso (a kiss), even when writing to casual friends. To work out Spanish addresses, see page 52.

To work out Spanish addresses, see page 52.

INTERESTS

ART
Seeing Art

When is the gallery open?

¿A qué hora abren el museo; la galería?

What kind of art are you interested in?

¿Qué tipo de arte te interesa?

I'm interested in …
animation

Me interesa(n) (pl) …
los dibujos animados; el cómic

cyber art
design
graphic art
painting
performance art
Renaissance art
Romanesque art
sculpture

el arte cibernético
el diseño
el arte gráfico
la pintura
la interpretación
el arte renacentista
el arte románico
la escultura

The previous list is short, as many other words associated with art styles are similar enough to English for you to just try saying the English word. For instance, baroque is **barroco**.

What is in the collection?	¿Qué hay en la colección?
There is a good collection of …	Hay una buena colección de …

altarpiece	el retablo
building	el edificio
church	la iglesia
cloakroom	la guardarropía
curator	una conservadora/un conservador
epoch	la época
etching	el aguafuerte
gardens	los jardines
permanent collection	una exposición permanente
photographer	la/el fotógrafa/o
a print	un grabado
salon	la sala
sculptor	una escultora/un escultor
slide	una diapositiva
souvenir shop	la tienda de recuerdos
statue	una estatua

Opinions

I like the works of …	Me gustan las obras de …
What do you think of …?	¿Qué te parece …?

It's …	Es …
awful	horrible
beautiful	bonito
dramatic	dramático
interesting	interesante
marvellous	maravilloso
unusual	extraño
incomprehensible	incomprensible

It's not as good as …	No es tan bueno como …
It's reminiscent of …	Me recuerda a …

Doing Art

artwork	un obra de arte
bookshop	la librería
canvas	el lienzo
exhibit	exponer
exhibition	una exposición
installation	una instalación
opening	una inauguración
painter	una pintora/un pintor
studio	el estudio
style	el estilo
technique	la técnica

MUSIC
Spanish Music

Tuna
Musical groups, traditionally students, who go
from bar to bar singing
folksongs for money.

Flamenco
This famous Spanish
music and dance is ever-
popular and has many
varieties.

Zarzuela
Spanish operetta.

TRILLS

It's important to
emphasise the rr in
Spanish as it can
mean the difference
between one meaning
and another.

perro = dog
pero = but

Regional Music
Each area of Spain has its own musical and dance styles, some
very old like la sardana, la jota, la muñeira, las sevillanas, and
aurrezku.

INTERESTS

Do you like …?	Te gusta …?
listening to music	escuchar música
to dance	bailar

Do you …?	
play an instrument	¿Tocas algún instrumento?
sing	¿Cantas?

What music do you like?	¿Qué tipo de música te gusta?
Which bands do you like?	¿Qué grupos te gustan?
I like (the) …	Me gustan (los) …
Have you heard the latest record by …?	¿Has escuchado lo último de …?
Which station plays salsa?	¿En qué emisora ponen salsa?

¡GUAY – COOL!

El concierto de la semana que viene será …	The concert next week will be …
Es una película …	It's a … film.
El tiempo ayer fue …	The weather yesterday was …
La excursión de ayer results…	Yesterday's trip was …
La fiesta mañana va a ser muy …	The party tomorrow will be really …
Es/Está …	It's …
una caña	amazing
chachi	great
cojonuda/o	brilliant
un coñazo	crap
loca/o	crazy
guay	cool
heavy	full on
una mierda	shit
de puta madre	fantastic
de pena/de puta pena	terrible

INTERESTS

Which is a good station for (jazz)?	¿Qué emisora es buena para escuchar (jazz)?
What frequency is it on?	¿En qué frecuencia está?
This station, is it FM or AM?	¿Esta emisora, está en la FM o la AM?
Where can you hear traditional music around here?	¿Dónde se puede escuchar música folklórica en esta ciudad?
Where can you see good flamenco in this town?	¿Hay lugares donde se bailan el flamenco auténtico en esta ciudad?
Shall we sit or stand?	¿Sentados o de pie?
Where shall we sit?	¿Dónde nos sentamos?
Shall we go closer to the stage?	¿Vamos más cerca del escenario?
What a fantastic concert!	¡Qué concierto más guay!
It's terrible!	¡Suena fatal!
This singer is brilliant.	Esta/e cantante es genial.

See also On Tour, page 202.

Useful Words

ballroom	la sala de fiestas
band	el grupo
bar with music	el bar musical; pub
concert	el concierto
concert hall	la sala de conciertos
drums	la batería
famous	conocida/o; famosa/o
gig	el bolo
guitar	la guitarra
karaoke bar	karaoke
keyboard	los teclados
musician	una/un música/o
opera	la ópera
opera house	la ópera
orchestra	la orquesta

INTERESTS

performance	la actuación
rock group	el grupo de rock
saxaphone	el saxofón
song	la canción
show	el espectáculo
singer	la/el cantante
singer-songwriter	la cantautora/el cantautor
stage	el escenario
tickets	las entradas
ticket office	la taquilla
tune	la melodía
venue	el local
voice	la voz

CINEMA & THEATRE

Cinema-going is very popular in Spain and the major cities can offer a wide range of Spanish and foreign films. Most foreign-language films are still dubbed (**doblada**) into Spanish, a legacy of Franco's strict censorship. To find ones that aren't, look out for screenings which are **subtitulada** or in **versión original** (**V.O.S.**).

Check the local paper or information guide carefully for details of cinema screening times. There are often specially priced sessions and most cinemas have a weekly **día del espectador** (viewer's day) when tickets are well below the usual cost. Be prepared to queue!

TICKETS PLEASE

You'll come across a couple of different words for tickets:

If you're buying tickets for a show, you'll need to ask for **las entradas**.

Tickets for trains, buses, etc are called **billetes**

INTERESTS

I feel like going to a/an …	Tengo ganas de ir …
ballet	al ballet
comedy	a una comedia
film	al cine
play	al teatro

What's on at the cinema tonight?
¿Qué película dan en el cine esta noche?

Where can I find a cinema guide?
¿Dónde puedo encontrar la cartelera del cine?

Are there any tickets for …?
¿Hay entradas para …?

Sorry, we are sold out.
Lo siento pero se han agotado las localidades.

Is it in English?
¿Es en inglés?

Does it have English subtitles?
¿Tiene subtítulos en inglés?

Is there a short before the film?
¿Hay algún corto antes de la película?

Are those seats taken?
¿Están libres estos asientos?

Have you seen …?
¿Has visto …?

Have you seen the latest film by (Almodóvar)?
¿Has visto la última película de (Almodóvar)?

Who is in it?
¿Quién actúa?

It stars …
Actúa …

Who's it by?
¿Quién la dirige?

It's directed by …
La dirige …

It's been really well reviewed.
La crítica la deja muy bien.

I (don't) like …	(No) me gusta/n …
action movies	las películas de acción
amateur film	el cine amateur
animated films	las películas de dibujos animados
art films	el arte y ensayo
black comedy	la comedia negra
classical theatre	el teatro clásico
comedy	la comedia

INTERESTS

documentary	los documentales
drama	el drama
film noir	el cine negro
horror movies	el cine de terror
period dramas	el cine de época
realism	el cine realista
sci-fi movies	el cine de ciencia ficción
short films	los cortos
thrillers	el cine de suspenso
war films	el cine bélico

Opinions

Did you like the …?	¿Te ha gustado la/el …?
film	película
performance	actuación
play	obra

I liked it very much.	Me ha gustado mucho.
I didn't like it very much.	No me ha gustado demasiado.

I thought it was …	Creo que ha sido …
excellent	fantástica/o
OK	regular

I had a few problems with the language.	He tenido dificultades para entender la lengua.

BAD SPANISH – CURSES

Whether on the big screen or on the street,
you're bound to hear some of the following:

¡Hostia puta!	Fucking hell!
¡Hostia!	Damn!
¡Joder!	Fuck!
¡Coño!	Fuck!
¡Mierda!	Shit!
¡Me cago en dios!	Christ!
¡Me cago en sos!	Gosh!

INTERESTS

LITERATURE

Who is your favourite author?	¿Quién es tu autora/autor favorita/o?
I read (Carmen Martín Gaite).	Leo mucho a (Carmen Martín Gaite).
I've read everything by (Almudena Grandes).	Me lo he leído todo de (Almudena Grandes).
I prefer the works of (Vázquez Montalbán).	Prefiero las obras de (Vázquez Montalbán).
What kind of books do you read?	¿Qué tipo de libros lees?

I (don't) like …	(No) me gusta(n) …
anthologies	las antologías
biography	las biografías
comics	los cómics
contemporary literature	la literatura contemporánea
crime/detective novels	la novela negra
erotic literature	la literatura erótica
fantasy literature	la literatura fantástica
fiction	la ficción
non-fiction	el ensayo
novels	las novelas
poetry	la poesía
romance	la literatura romántica
science-fiction	la ciencia ficción
short stories	los cuentos
the classics	la literatura clásica
travel writing	los libros de viajes

Have you read (One Hundred Years of Solitude)?	¿Has leído (Cien años de soledad)?
What did you think of …?	¿Qué te pareció …?
Can you recommend a book for me?	¿Me puedes recomendar algún libro?

Opinions

I thought it was …	Creo que es …
boring	aburrido
entertaining	entretenido

I thought it was …	Me pareció …
badly-written	muy mal escrito
better/worse than the previous book	mejor/peor que su libro anterior
well-written	bien escrita/o

HOBBIES

Do you have any hobbies?	¿Tienes algun pasatiempo?

I like …	Me gusta …
gardening	la jardinería
travelling	viajar

I like to …	Me gusta …
cook	cocinar
draw	dibujar
paint	pintar
sew	coser
take photographs	hacer fotos

I make …	Hago …
pottery	cerámica
jewellery	joyería

I collect …	Colecciono …
books	libros
coins	monedas
comics	cómics
dolls	muñecas
miniature cars	coches miniatura
stamps	sellos

INTERESTS

TALKING ABOUT TRAVELLING

Have you travelled much?	¿Has viajado mucho?
How long have you been travelling?	¿Cuánto tiempo llevas viajando?
I've been travelling for (two) months.	Llevo (dos) meses viajando.
Where have you been?	¿Dónde has estado?
I've been to …	He estado en …
What did you think of (Athens)?	¿Qué te pareció (Atenas)?

I thought it was …	Me pareció …
boring	aburrida/o
great	fantástica/o
OK	normal
too expensive	demasiado cara/o
horrible	horrible

There are too many tourists there.	Hay demasiados turistas.
Not many people speak (English).	Poca gente habla (inglés).
I was ripped off in (Cairo).	Me estafaron en (El Cairo).
People are really friendly there.	Allí la gente es muy amable.
What is there to do in (Brussels)?	¿Qué se puede hacer en (Bruselas)?
There's a really good restaurant/hotel there.	Allí hay un restaurante/ hotel muy bueno.
I'll write down the details for you.	Ya te escribiré los detalles.
The best time to go is in (December).	La mejor época para ir es (diciembre).
Is it expensive?	¿Es caro?
Did you go alone?	¿Fuiste sola/o?
Is it safe for women travellers on their own?	¿Es seguro para mujeres que viajan solas?
Is it safe to hitch?	¿Es seguro hacer auto-stop?

STARS
Astrology

When's your birthday?	¿Cuándo es tu cumpleaños?
What star sign are you?	¿De qué signo eres?
I don't believe in astrology.	No creo en los signos del zodíaco.

I'm …   Soy …

Aries	aries
Taurus	tauro
Gemini	géminis
Cancer	cáncer
Leo	leo
Virgo	virgo
Libra	libra
Scorpio	escorpio
Sagittarius	sagitario
Capricorn	capricornio
Aquarius	acuario
Pisces	piscis

Ah, That explains it!
¡Ah, eso lo explica todo!

THEY MAY SAY …

Es importante.
It's important.

No importa.
It's not important.

(No) es posible.
It's (not) possible.

No es nada.
It's nothing.

No importa.
It doesn't matter.

(Leo's) are very …   (Los leo) son muy …

aggressive	agresivos
caring	bondadosos
charming	encantadores
crafty	habilidosos/ingeniosos
creative	creativos
emotional	emocionales
indecisive	indecisos
intense	intensos
interesting	interesantes
jealous	celosos
loyal	leales
outgoing	abiertos

INTERESTS

passive	pasivos
proud	orgullosos
self-centred	egoistos
sensual	sensuales
stingy	tacaños

I get on well with (Virgos).	Me llevo bien con los (virgo).

ascendent	el ascendente
chart	la carta astral
descendent	el descendiente
horoscope	el horóscopo
personality	la personalidad
zodiac	el zodíaco

Astronomy

Are you interested in astronomy?	¿Te interesa la astronomía?
I'm interested in astronomy.	Me interesa la astronomía.
Do you have a telescope?	¿Tienes un telescopio?
Is there a planetarium/ observatory nearby?	¿Hay algún observatorio por aquí cerca?
Where is the best place near here to see the night sky?	¿Cuál es el mejor lugar para observar el cielo de noche?
Will it be cloudy tonight?	¿Va a estar nublado esta noche?

When can I see …?	¿Cuándo puedo ver …?
Mercury	Mercurio
Mars	Marte
Uranus	Urano
Pluto	Plutón

What time does it rise?	¿A qué hora sale?
What time will it set?	¿A qué hora se pone?
Can I see it at this time of year from here?	¿Se puede ver en esta época del año desde aquí?
Which way is north?	¿Dónde está el norte?

Is that Orion?	¿Aquello es Orion?
It's the other way up in the southern/northern hemisphere.	Se ve al revés en el hemisferio sur/norte.

Earth	La Tierra
Milky Way	La Vía láctea
Ursa Major/The Great Bear/ The Big Dipper	La osa mayor
The Little Bear	La osa menor
The Plough	El carro

astronaut	una/un astronauta
astronomer	una/un astrónoma/o
atmosphere	la atmósfera
comet	el cometa
full moon	la luna llena
galaxy	la galaxia
meteor	el meteorito
moon	la luna
NASA	NASA
nebula	la nebulosa
planet	una planeta
shuttle	la lanzadera espacial
sky	el cielo
space	el espacio
space exploration	la exploración espacial
stars	las estrellas
sun	el sol
telescope	el telescopio
universe	el universo

INTERESTS

DID YOU KNOW ...	**el cometa** is a 'comet'
	la cometa means 'kite'

The Unexplained

Do you believe there's life out there?	¿Crees que hay vida ultraterrenal?
Do you believe in ...?	¿Crees en ...?
(black) magic	la magia negra
extraterrestrials	los extraterrestres
ghosts	fantasmas
life after death	la vida después de la muerte
mediums	las/los médiums
miracles	los milagros
Satan	Satanás
telepathy	la telepatía
UFOs	los ONVIs
witchcraft	la brujería
Have you ever seen one?	¿Alguna vez has visto alguna/o?
Are there haunted places in Spain?	¿Hay lugares embrujados en España?
People here/in my country tend (not) to be ...	La gente aquí/en mi país tiende a (no)ser ...
imaginative	imaginativa
realistic	realista
scientific	científica
superstitious	supersticiosa

WHAT ARE YA?

hortera	dag; jerk
pija/o	flash; nouveau riche type
siniestra/o	goth
heavy (jevi)	heavy
intelectual	intellectual type
progre	left-wing type
moderna/o	trendy
yupi	yuppie

INTERESTS

CROSSWORD – INTERESTS

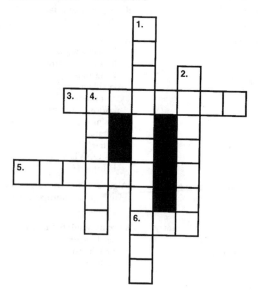

Across:

3. Queues, acceptance speeches, macroeconomics, all what you might call ...
5. bienestar ...
6. los ... hogar

Down:

1. Dali's lobster telephone is one example
2. Sometimes not as strange as the truth
4. A delight to the senses

Answers: page 366

POLITICS

Politics play a large part in daily Spanish life and are the topic of much conversation.

Did you hear about …?	¿Has oído que …?
	¿Te has enterado de que …?
I read in (*El Mundo*) today that …	Hoy he leído en (*El Mundo*) que …
What do you think of the current/new government?	¿Qué te parece el nuevo gobierno/el gobierno actual?

I (don't) agree with their policy on …

No estoy de acuerdo con su política sobre …

drugs	drogas
education	educación
the environment	el medio ambiente
military service	el servicio militar
privatisation	la privatización
social welfare	el estado del bienestar
the economy	la economía

I am …

Estoy …

against …	en contra de …
in favour of …	a favor de …

Who do you vote for?   ¿A quién votas?

DID YOU KNOW …

Propaganda in Spanish doesn't have the negative connotations that it does in English – it simply means 'publicity' or 'advertising'.

SOCIAL ISSUES

I support the … party.	Apoyo al partido …
I'm a member of the … party.	Soy miembro del partido …
communist	comunista
conservative	conservador
green	verde
social democratic	socialdemócrata
socialist	socialista
I'm an anarchist.	Soy anarquista.
I'm an abstainer.	Yo me abstengo; Yo voto en blanco.
In my country we have a (socialist) government.	En mi país tenemos un gobierno (socialista).
Politicians are all the same.	Todos los políticos son iguales.
Politicians can never be trusted.	No se puede confiar en los políticos.
How do you think Franco affected Spain?	¿Cuál crees que ha sido la influencia de Franco en España?
Do you support the royal family?	¿Apoyas a la familia real?

Useful Abbreviations

CNT	Anarchist Union
CCOO	Communist Union
UE	European Union
CIU	Conservative Catalan Nationalist Party
CEOE	Union of business leaders
IU	Spanish Left Coalition
ONG	Non-government organization
OTAN	NATO
PCE	Spanish Communist party
PNV	Conservative Basque Nationalist Party
PSOE	Spanish Labour Party
PP	Spanish Liberal Party
UGT	Left Union

candidate's speech	mitin
corrupt	corrupta/o
counting of votes	escrutinio
democracy	democracia
demonstration	manifestación
dole	paro

... elections	elecciones ...
local council	municipales
regional	autonómicas
general/national	generales
European	europeas

electorate	electorado
exploitation	explotación
legislation	legislación
legalisation	legalización
parliament	parlamento
policy	política
polls	sondeos
president	presidenta (f)
	presidente (m)
prime minister	primera
	ministra (f)
	primer
	ministro (m)

racism	racismo
rally	concentración
rip-off	estafa
sexism	sexismo
strike	huelga
term of office	mandato
trade union	sindicatos
unemployment	paro
vote	votar

WHICH PAST?

If you want to say something without a specific time reference, you would use the verb with the past participle, just as we do in English with the verb 'to have'. So 'We have bought the tickets' will be **Hemos comprado los billetes**.

Once you put a specific day or time to an event or action you use the simple past: 'We bought the tickets yesterday' – **Compramos billetes ayer**.

SOCIAL ISSUES

ENVIRONMENT

Does (Spain) have a pollution problem?	¿Hay un problema de contaminación en (España)?
Does (Barcelona) have a recycling program?	¿Hay algún programa de reciclaje en (Barcelona)?
Is this recyclable?	¿Esto es reciclable?

Are there any protected ... here?	¿Hay ... protegidas/os aquí?
Is this a protected ...?	¿Este ... está protegida/o?
park(s)	parque(s)
forest(s)	bosque(s)
species	especie(s)

Where do you stand on ...?	¿Qué piensas de ...?
pollution	la contaminación
deforestation	la deforestación
nuclear testing	las pruebas nucleares

antinuclear group	el grupo antinuclear
biodegradable	biodegradable
conservation	la conservación
disposable	desechable
drought	la sequía
ecosystem	el ecosistema
endangered species	los especies en peligro de extinción
hunting	la caza
hydroelectricity	la energía hidroeléctrica
industrial pollution	la contaminación industrial
irrigation	la irrigación
nuclear energy	la energía nuclear
ozone layer	la capa de ozono
pesticides	las pesticidas
recyclable	reciclable
recycling	reciclar
reservoir	el embalse
toxic waste	los residuos tóxicos
water supply	el suministro de agua

SOCIAL ISSUES

How do people feel about ...?	¿Qué piensa la gente de ...?
What do you think about ...?	¿Qué piensas de ...?

I'm in favour of ...	Estoy a favor de ...
I'm against ...	Estoy en contra de ...
abortion	el aborto
animal rights	los derechos de los animales
equal opportunity	la igualdad de oportunidades
euthanasia	la eutanasia
immigration	la inmigración
party politics	los partidos políticos
racism	el racismo
tax	los impuestos
unions	los sindicatos

What is the current policy on (immigration)?	¿Cuál es la política actual sobre (inmigración)?
Is there an (unemployment) problem here?	¿Existe un problema de (paro) aquí?

THEY MAY SAY ...

¡Estoy de acuerdo!	I agree!
¡Por supuesto!	Absolutely!
¡Exactamente!	Exactly!
¡Desde luego!	Of course!
¡Ni hablar!	No way!
¡Y una mierda!	
¡Para nada!	
¡No estoy de acuerdo!	I disagree!
¡Eso no es verdad!	That's not true!
¡Sí hombre!	Yeah, sure!
Sí pero ...	Yes, but ...
¡Anda ya!	In your dreams!
¡No me jodas!	Come off it!
Lo que sea.	Whatever.

SOCIAL ISSUES

Is there an adequate social welfare program?	¿Hay un buen programa de servicios sociales?
What assistance is there for ...?	¿Qué tipo de asistencia reciben ...?
the aged	los ancianos
homeless	los sin hogar
street kids	los jóvenes callejeros

activist	una/un activista
citizenship	la ciudadanía
class system	el sistema de clases
demonstration	una manifestación
dole	el paro
equality	la igualdad
human rights	los derechos humanos
inequality	la desigualdad
petition	la petición
protest	una protesta
race	la raza
social security	la seguridad social
strike	la huelga
unemployment	el desempleo
welfare	el bienestar social
political speech	un mitin

GRAFFITI

Nucleares, no gracias.
Nuclear power stations, no thanks.

PSOE GAL, todo es igual.
The PSOE (Socialist party) & GAL (militant anti-terrorist group) are linked.

Pujol, enano, habla castellano.
Pujol, you dwarf, speak in Castilian. (Pujol is President of the Autonomous Government of Catalonia)

¡Viva er Betil	Go, Betis! (Sevillian football club)
Tonto el que lo lea.	You're stupid for reading this.
Fachas hijos de puta.	Fascist bastards.

DRUGS

All drugs are illegal in Spain, although small amounts kept for discrete personal use may be tolerated. You may find yourself in a position where the issue is being discussed, and the following phrases may help you understand the conversation, but if referring to your own interests, use discretion.

I don't take drugs.	No consumo ningún tipo de drogas.
I'm not interested in drugs.	Las drogas no me interesan.
I take (cocaine) occasionally.	Tomo (cocaína) de vez en cuando.
I smoke regularly.	Fumo regularmente.
Do you want to have a smoke?	¿Nos fumamos un porro?
I'm a heroin addict.	Soy (heroinómana).
Where can I find clean syringes?	¿Dónde puedo conseguir jeringas sin usar?
Do you sell syringes?	¿Vende jeringas?
I'm stoned.	Estoy ciega/o.
I'm out of it.	Estoy colocada/o.
My friend has taken an overdose.	Mi amigo/a ha sufrido una sobredosis.
This drug is for personal use.	Esta droga es para consumo propio.
I'm trying to get off it.	Estoy intentando desintoxicarme.
Where can I get help with a drug problem?	Necesito ayuda, tengo un problema de drogadicción. ¿Dónde puedo acudir?
Do you have a methodone program in this country?	¿Hay algún programa de metadona en este país?
Can I register?	¿Me puedo inscribir?
I'm on a methadone program.	Estoy en un programa de metadona.

SOCIAL ISSUES

DOPE – COLLOQUIAL TERMS

One problem with being in another country is that it is often difficult to assess situations and people as easily as you can back home, especially when you are unfamiliar with the language. Here are some colloquial terms common amongst drug-users – if you hear them in use around you, you're probably in the wrong bar.

tripi	acid
coca	cocaine
mono	cold turkey
camello	drug dealer
chocolate	hash
jaco; caballo	heroin
yonki	heroin addict
chutarse	to inject
maría	marijuana
liar un porro	to roll a joint
chuta	syringe

acid	LSD; ácidos
addiction	la adicción
cocaine	la cocaína
cocaine addict	una/un cocainómana/o
cold turkey	el síndrome de abstinencia
drug addiction	la toxicomanía
drug dealer	un traficante de drogas
heroin addict	una/un heroinómana/o
to inject	inyectarse
overdose	una sobredosis
syringe	una jeringa
syringe disposal	la recogida de jeringuillas usadas

SHOPPING

LOOKING FOR ...

Where can I buy ...?   ¿Dónde puedo comprar ... ?

Where is the nearest ...?   ¿Dónde está la/el ... más
                                     cercana/o?

bakery	la panadería
bank	el banco
bookshop	la librería
cake shop	la pastelería
camera shop	la tienda de fotografía
clothing store	la tienda de ropa; boutique
craft shop	la tienda de artesanía
delicatessen	la charcutería
department store	los grandes almacenes
fish shop	la pescadería
general store; shop	la tienda de alimentación; el almacén
greengrocer	la verdulería; frutería
launderette	la lavandería
market	el mercado
newsagency	el quiosco
optician	la óptica
pharmacy	la farmacia
record shop	la tienda de discos
shoe shop	la zapatería
souvenir shop	la tienda de recuerdos
stationers	la papelería
supermarket	el supermercado
travel agency	la agencia de viajes

SHOPPING

MAKING A PURCHASE

I'm just looking.	Sólo estoy mirando.
How much is this?	¿Cuánto cuesta esto?; ¿Cuánto vale esto?
Can you write down the price?	¿Puede escribir el precio?
I'd like to buy ...	Quisiera comprar ...
Do you have others?	¿Tiene otros?
Can I look at it?	¿Puedo verla/o?
I don't like it.	No me gusta.
I'll buy it.	Me la/lo llevo.
Do you accept credit cards?	¿Aceptan tarjetas de crédito?
Can I have a receipt?	¿Podría darme un recibo?
Does it have a guarantee?	¿Tiene garantía?
Can I have it sent overseas?	¿Pueden enviarlo por correo a otro país?
I'd like to return this please.	Me gustaría devolver esto, por favor.
It's faulty.	Es defectuosa/o.
It's broken.	Está estropeada/o.
I'd like my money back.	Quiero que me devuelvan el dinero.

THEY MAY SAY ...

¿En qué puedo servirle? ¿Qué desea?	Can I help you?
¿Algo más?	Will that be all?
¿Se lo envuelvo?	Would you like it wrapped?
Lo siento, es el único que tenemos.	Sorry, this is the only one.
¿Cuánto/s quiere?	How much/many would you like?

BARGAINING

Really?	¡Venga, hombre!
That's very expensive!	¡Es carísimo!
The price is very high.	Cuesta demasiado.
Do you have something cheaper?	¿Tiene algo más barata/o?
I don't have much money.	No tengo mucho dinero.
Could you lower the price?	¿Podría bajar un poco el precio?
I'll give you (2500) pesetas.	Te doy (2500) pesetas.
No more than (3000).	No más de (3000).

Give me a ...   Póngame ...
    gram   un gramo
    kilogram   un quilo
    millimetre   un milímetro
    centimetre   un centímetro
    metre   un metro
    kilometre   un kilómetro
    half   un medio
    half a litre   medio litro
    quarter   un cuarto

SHOPPING

ESSENTIAL GROCERIES

Where can I find the ...?   ¿Dónde puedo encontrar ...?

I'd like ...   Quisiera ...
    batteries   pilas
    bread   pan
    butter   mantequilla
    cheese   queso
    chocolate   chocolate
    eggs   huevos
    flour   harina
    gas cylinder   cilindro de gas
    ham   jamón
    honey   miel

SHOPPING

margarine	margarina
marmalade	mermelada
matches	fósforos; cerillas
milk	leche
... olives	aceitunas ...
black	negras
green	verdes
stuffed	rellenas
olive oil	aceite de oliva
pepper	pimienta
salt	sal
shampoo	champú
soap	jabón
sugar	azúcar
sunflower oil	aceite de girasol
toilet paper	papel higiénico
toothpaste	pasta dentífrica
washing powder	jabón de lavar
yoghurt	yogur

SOUVENIRS

fan	un abanico
embroidery	bordado
handicrafts	la artesanía
jewellery	la joyería
leather wine bottle	una bota de vino
leathergoods	los artículos de cuero
poster	un póster
pottery	la alfarería; cerámica
silverware	la plata
T-shirt	una camiseta

DID YOU KNOW ...	Contestar means *to answer.*
	Assistir means *to attend.*

CLOTHING

clothing	la ropa
boots	las botas
coat	un abrigo
dress	un vestido
jacket	una chaqueta; chupa
jeans	los tejanos; vaqueros
jumper (sweater)	un jersey; pullover; suéter
shirt	una camisa
shoes	los zapatos
socks	los calcetines
stockings; pantyhose	las medias
swimsuit	un bañador
T-shirt	una camiseta
umbrella	las paraguas
underpants (men)	los calzoncillos
underpants (women)	las bragas

SHOPPING

Can I try it on?	¿Me la/lo puedo probar?
My size is …	Uso la talla …
It doesn't fit.	No me queda bien.

It's …	Es …
too big	demasiado grande
too small	demasiado pequeño
too short	muy corto
too long	muy largo
too tight	muy apretado
too loose	muy holgado

MATERIALS

ceramic	la cerámica
cotton	el algodón
handmade	hecho a mano
glass	el vidrio
leather	el cuero

lycra	la licra
metal	el metal
of brass	de latón
of gold	de oro
of silver	de plata
plastic	el plástico
silk	la seda
stainless steel	el acero inoxidable
synthetic	la fibra
wool	la lana
wood	la madera

COLOURS

dark …	… oscuro
light …	… claro
black	negra/o
blue	azul
brown	marrón
green	verde
grey	gris
orange	naranja
pink	rosa
purple	lila
red	roja/o
white	blanca/o
yellow	amarilla/o

NO NOT NEVER EVER

The easiest way to make a negative statement is to put **no** in front of the verb.

No va.
It doesn't go.

To say 'never', say **no + verb + nunca** or **¡jamás!**

Jamás also means 'ever':

¿Has estado en Nueva York jamás?
Have you ever been to New York?

No he estado en Nueva York nunca.
No, I've never been to New York.

TOILETRIES

See also page 192.

aftershave	la loción para después del afeitado
bath/shower gel	el gel de baño
comb	el peine

condoms	los preservativos; condones
dental floss	el hilo dental
deodorant	el desodorante
hairbrush	el cepillo (para el cabello; pelo)
moisturising cream	la crema hidratante
panty liner	una salva slip
pregnancy test kit	la prueba de embarazo
razor	la afeitadora
razor blades	las cuchillas de afeitar
sanitary napkins	las compresas
shampoo	el champú
shaving foam	la espuma de afeitar
soap	el jabón
scissors	las tijeras
sunblock cream	la crema solar
tampons	los tampones
tissues	los pañuelos de papel
toilet paper	el papel higiénico
toothbrush	el cepillo de dientes
toothpaste	la pasta dentífrica

SHOPPING

FOR THE BABY

baby food	la comida de bebé; potitos
baby powder	el talco
bib	el babero
disposable nappies	los pañales
dummy; pacifier	el chupete
feeding bottle	el biberón
nappy	el pañal
nappy rash cream	la crema para la irritación de los pañales
powdered milk	la leche en polvo
rubber duck	un juguete flotante
teat	la tetina

SHOPPING

STATIONERY & PUBLICATIONS

Is there an English-language bookshop nearby?	¿Hay alguna librería de libros en inglés por aquí cerca?
Where is the English-language section?	¿Dónde está la sección de libros en inglés?
Do you have the latest novel by ...?	¿Tienen el último libro de ...?
Do you have a copy of ...?	¿Tienen el libro ...?
Can you recommend a good Spanish book available in English?	¿Me puede recomendar un buen libro español traducido al inglés?
Do you know if this author is translated into English?	¿Sabe si esta/e escritora/ escritor está traducida/o al inglés?
Do you sell ...?	¿Venden ...?
magazines	revistas
newspapers	periódicos
postcards	postales
(El País), please.	¿Tienen (El País)?
Is there a local entertainment guide?	¿Tienen alguna guía del ocio local?
dictionary	un diccionario
envelope	un sobre
... map	un mapa de ...
city	la ciudad
regional	la zona
road	carreteras
newspaper in English	un periódico en inglés
paper	el papel
pen (ballpoint)	el bolígrafo
popular magazines (eg *Hola*)	las revistas del corazón
stamp	un sello

MUSIC

I'm looking for a (Loquillo) CD.

Quisiera un compact de (Loquillo).

Do you have any (Camarón de la Isla) records?

¿Tienen discos de (Camarón de la Isla)?

What is her/his best recording?

¿Cuál es su mejor disco?

Who is the best (ballad) singer?

¿Cuál es el mejor cantante de (baladas)?

Who is the best Spanish (rock) group?

¿Cuál es el mejor grupo de (rock) en castellano?

What's the latest record by ...?

¿Cuál es el último disco de ...?

What music can you recommend to take back to (Australia)?

¿Qué música me recomienda para llevar de recuerdo a (Australia)?

Can I listen to this CD here?

¿Puedo escuchar este compact aquí?

Do you have this on ...?
¿Tienen este en ...?

CD	compact
record	disco
cassette	casete

I need (a) ...
Necesito ...

blank tape
una cinta virgen
headphones
unos auriculares
batteries
unas pilas

SHOPPING

PHOTOGRAPHY

How much is it to process this film?	¿Cuánto cuesta revelar este carrete?
When will it be ready?	¿Cuándo estará listo?
I'd like a film for this camera.	Quiero un carrete para esta cámara.
Can you put the film in for me please?	¿Puede colocarme usted el carrete?
Do you have one-hour processing?	¿Tienen servicio de revelado en una hora?
I'd like to have some passport photos taken.	Me gustaría hacerme fotos de pasaporte.
The film is jammed.	El carrete está encallado.
This camera doesn't work.	Esta cámara no funciona.
Can you repair it?	¿Pueden arreglarla?

battery	la pila
B&W (film)	el blanco y negro
camera	la cámara (fotográfica)
colour (film)	(película) en color
film	el carrete
film speed	la sensibilidad
flash	la bombilla/flash
lens	el objetivo
light meter	el fotómetro
slides	las diapositivas
video tape	la cinta de vídeo

SMOKING

A packet of cigarettes, please.	Un paquete de cigarrillos, por favor.
Are these cigarettes strong/ mild?	¿Son fuertes/suaves estos cigarrillos?
Do you have a light?	¿Tiene fuego?
Do you mind if I smoke?	¿Le importa si fumo?
Please don't smoke here.	Por favor, no fume aquí.

Would you like one?	¿Quieres uno?
Could I have one?	¿Me das uno?
I'm trying to give up.	Estoy intentando dejar de fumar.

carton	cartón
cigarette machine	máquina de tabaco
cigarette papers	papel de fumar
cigarettes	los cigarrillos
filtered	con filtro
lighter	el encendedor/mechero
matches	los fósforos/cerillas
menthol	mentolado
pipe	la pipa
tobacco (pipe)	el tabaco de pipa
… tobacco	el tabaco …
dark	negro
light	rubio
rolling	de liar
without filter	sin filtro

SHOPPING

SOME ABBREVIATIONS

Cia.	Co.
C.P.	Postcode
Depto./Sede	Dept/HQ
DNI	ID
I	Information
IVA	VAT
Ptas/PTS.	Pesetas
PVP	RRP (recommended retail price)
S.A.	Ltd./Inc.
Sr./Sra./Srta.	Mr/Mrs/Ms
TVE	Spanish public broadcasting network
Ud. /Uds.	You (formal)/You (formal, plural)

SHOPPING

SIZES & COMPARISONS

small	pequeña/o
big	grande
as big as	tan grande como
heavy	pesada/o
light	leve; ligera/o
more	más
less	menos
too much/many	demasiado/s
many	muchos
some	algunas/os
few	pocas/os
also	también
neither	tampoco
enough	bastante; suficiente
a little bit	un poco; un poquito
a lot	mucho

FOOD

Breakfast in Spain is a light snack. Lunch is the principal meal (often soup, bread, a main course, fruit or dessert and coffee), taken between 2 and 4pm, and a light evening meal is eaten at about 10pm.

breakfast	desayuno
lunch	almuerzo/comida
tea	merienda
dinner	cena

VEGETARIAN & SPECIAL MEALS

Finding vegetarian food is a real headache in Spain once you've tired of tortillas. Vegetables are normally listed (and served) separately in Spanish menus, so you can always order them as separate courses. Look under **Legumbres** or **Entremeses** on the menu. Getting back to tortillas, visitors familiar with the Mexican tortilla (a kind of thin maize pancake) should be aware that the Spanish tortilla is quite different. It is, in fact, an omelette.

I'm a vegetarian.	Soy vegetariana/o.
I don't eat meat.	No como carne.
I don't eat chicken, fish or ham.	No como pollo, ni pescado, ni jamón.
Do you have any vegetarian dishes?	¿Tienen algún plato vegetariano?
Does this dish have meat?	¿Lleva carne este plato?
Can I get this without the meat?	¿Me puede preparar este plato sin carne?
Does it contain eggs/dairy products?	¿Lleva huevos/productos lácteos?
I'm allergic to (peanuts).	Soy alérgica/o a (los cacahuetes).
Is this kosher?	¿Es apto para los judíos?
Is this organic?	¿Es orgánico?

FOOD

BREAKFAST

Breakfast in Spain usually consists of a large bowl of coffee with bread, biscuits or cakes. Those used to more healthy or substantial fare can, however, find the following popular snacks in bars and cafes throughout the day:

bocadillo	sandwich
bollos	bread roll
churros con chocolate	fried pastry strips for dunking in hot chocolate
croissants	croissants, often with sweet or savoury fillings
magdalena	fairy cake, often dunked in coffee
pastas	small cakes, available in a variety of flavours

SNACKS

The most popular way to snack in Spain is to go for *tapas* (see page 149) in the early evening. Most bars have a few tapas available throughout the day. Another favourite snack in Spain is the bocadillo, a sandwich made with a long crusty roll. Fillings vary greatly and you will probably find:

atún	tuna
beicon con queso	cold bacon with cheese
jamón dulce	cooked ham
jamón serrano	cured ham
lomo	pork sausage
lomo con pimientos	pork sausage with peppers
longaniza	cooked sausage
tortilla de patata	potato omelette
queso	cheese
salchichón	peppery white sausage

Those with a sweet tooth will also enjoy Spain's pastelerías, which offer a fine range of cakes and biscuits.

EATING OUT

Table for ..., please.	Una mesa para ..., por favor.
Can I see the menu please?	¿Puedo ver el menú, por favor?
I'd like the set lunch, please.	Quisiera el menú del día, por favor.
What does it include?	¿Qué está incluido?; ¿Qué incluye?
Is service included in the bill?	¿El servicio está incluido en la cuenta?
Does it come with salad?	¿Viene con ensalada?
What is the soup of the day?	¿Cuál es la sopa del día?
What's the speciality here?	¿Cuál es la especialidad de este restaurante?
What do you recommend?	¿Qué me recomienda?
What are they eating?	¿Qué están comiendo ellas/os?
I'll try what she's having.	Probaré lo que ella está comiendo.
What's in this dish?	¿Qué ingredientes tiene este plato?
I'd like something to drink.	Quiero algo para beber.
Do you have a highchair for the baby?	¿Tienen una sillita para el bebé?
Can you please bring me ...?	¿Me puede traer ... por favor?
some salt	la sal
more water	más agua
more wine	más vino
some pepper	la pimienta
more bread	más pan
Can you please bring me the complaints book?	¿Me puede traer el libro de reclamaciones, por favor?
The bill, please.	La cuenta, por favor.
Thank you, that was delicious.	Muchas gracias, estaba buenísimo.

FOOD

FOOD

ashtray	cenicero
the bill	cuenta
cup	taza
dessert	postre
a drink	una bebida
first course/entrée	primer plato
fork	(un) tenedor
fresh	fresca/o
a glass	un vaso (una copa for wine or spirits)
house wine	vino de la casa
knife	(un) cuchillo
plate	(un) plato
second/main course	segundo plato
set menu	menú del día
spicy	picante
spoon	cuchara
stale	pasado/rancio
stale (bread)	(pan) duro
sweet	dulce
teaspoon	cucharita
toothpick	palillo

MENU DECODER

a la plancha	grilled	berberechos	cockles
a la vasca	a Basque green sauce	berenjena	aubergine; eggplant
aceite	oil	besugo	bream
aceituna	olive	bistec	steak
aceitunas rellenas	stuffed olives	bistec con patatas	steak & chips
acelgas	chard (a variety of beef)	blanco	white (wine)
		bocadillo	tapa in a sandwich
adobo	battered	bollos	bread rolls
agua	water	boquerones	anchovies
agua del grifo	tap water	boquerones en vinagre	anchovies in vinaigrette
agua mineral	mineral water	boquerones fritos	fried anchovies
sin gas	plain	una botella	bottle
con gas	fizzy	un botellín	small bottle (¼ litre)
aguacate	avocado		
ahumado/a	smoked	brasa	chargrilled
ajo	garlic	buey	ox
al ajillo	in garlic	butifarra	thick sausage (to be cooked)
al horno	baked		
albaricoque	apricot	cabra	goat
albóndigas	meatballs	cacahuete	peanut
alcachofa	artichoke	café	coffee
allioli	garlic sauce	con leche	with milk
almejas	clams	cortado	with a little milk
almendra	almond		
alubias	kidney beans	descafeinado	decaffeinated
anchoas	anchovies	helado	iced
anguila	eel	solo	black
un anís	anise	calabacín	zucchini; courgette
apio	celery		
arroz	rice	calabaza	pumpkin
arroz con leche	rice pudding	calamares	calamari; squid
asado	roasted	calamares a la romana	squid rings fried in butter
atún	tuna		
bacalao	salted cod		
una bebida	a drink		
beicon con queso	cold bacon with cheese		

FOOD

FOOD

MENU DECODER

caldereta	stew	chorizo	red sausage
caldo	broth; stock; consommé	chorizo al horno	spicy baked sausages
callos	tripe	chorizo	spicy red/white sausage
camarón	small prawn; shrimp	chuleta	chop, cutlet
una caña	small glass ($^1/_4$ litre)	churrasco	grilled meat or ribs in a tangy sauce; a Galician meat dish
canelones	cannelloni		
cangrejo	crab		
cangrejo de río	crayfish		
carabinero	large prawn	churro	long, deep-fried doughnut
caracol	snail		
carajillo	with liqueur	churros con chocolate	fried pastry strips for dunking in hot chocolate
carne	meat		
caza	game (meat)		
cazuela	casserole	ciruela	plum
cebolla	onion	cochinillo	suckling pig
cenicero	ashtray	cocido	cooked; also stew made with chickpeas, pork and chorizo
cerdo	pig, pork		
cereales	cereal		
cereza	cherry		
una cerveza	a beer		
un champán; un cava	champagne	cocina	kitchen
champiñones	mushrooms	coco	coconut
champiñones al ajillo	garlic mushrooms	col	cabbage
		coles de bruselas	Brussels sprouts
chanquetes	whitebait (illegal, but still served up on coasts)	coliflor	cauliflower
		un combinado	cocktail
		un coñac	brandy
		conejo	rabbit
charcutería	cured pork meats, or a shop selling them	una copa (de ...)	a glass (of ...)
		cordero	lamb
		costillas	ribs
chipirón	small squid	croquetas	fried croquettes, often filled with ham or chicken
chivo	kid, baby goat		
choco	cuttlefish		

MENU DECODER

crudo	raw	frambuesa	raspberry
cuajada	milk junket with honey	fresa	strawberry
		fresca/o	fresh
una cuchara	a spoon	frijol	dried bean
cucharita	teaspoon	frita(s)/o(s)	fried
un cuchillo	a knife	fruta	fruit
doble	long black	fuerte	strong
dorada	sea bass	gachos	type of porridge
dulce	sweet	galleta	biscuit; cookie
(pan) duro	stale (bread)	gamba	prawn; shrimp
empanada	pie	gambas a la plancha	grilled prawns
ensaimada	sweet bread (made of lard)	garbanzo	chickpea
ensalada	salad	gazpacho	cold soup made with garlic, tomato and vegetables
ensaladilla rusa	vegetable salad with mayonnaise		
		gazpachos	game dish with garlic and herbs
entremeses	hors-d'oeuvres		
escabeche	pickled or marinated fish		
		girasol	sunflower
espárragos	asparagus	granada	pomegranate
espagueti	spaghetti	gratinada	au gratin
espinacas	spinach	guindilla	hot chilli pepper
espumoso	sparkling	guisantes	peas
estofada(s)/o(s)	braised	un güisqui	whisky
estofado	stew	hígado	liver
faba	type of dried bean	haba	broad bean
		hamburguesa	hamburger
faisán	pheasant	harina	flour
fideos	thin pasta noodles with sauce	helado	ice cream
		hervida(s)/o(s)	boiled
		hierba buena	mint
filete	fillet	higo	fig
filete empanado	pork, cheese and ham wrapped in breadcrumbs and fried	hongo	wild mushroom
		horchata	almond drink
		horneado	baked
		horno	oven
flan	crème caramel		

FOOD

FOOD

MENU DECODER

hortalizas	vegetables	manzanilla	camomile; also a type of sherry and a type of olive
huevo	egg		
huevos revueltos	scrambled eggs		
infusión	herbal tea		
jabalí	wild boar	marinado	marinated
jamón	ham	marisco	shellfish
jamón dulce	boiled ham	un martini	martini
jamón serrano	cured ham	mayonesa	mayonnaise
una jarra	jug	una mediana	bottle (¹/₃ litre)
jengibre	ginger	mejillones	mussels
un jerez	sherry	mejillones al vapor	steamed mussels
judías (verdes)	(green) beans		
judías blancas	butter beans	melocotón	peach
la cuenta	the bill	melón	melon
langosta	spiny lobster	membrillo	quince
langostino	large prawn	menta	mint
lechuga	lettuce	menú del día	set menu
legumbre	pulse	merluza	hake
lengua	tongue	merluza a la plancha	fried hake
lenguado	sole		
lentejas	lentils	miel	honey
lima	lime	migas	fried breadcrumb dish
limón	lemon		
una litrona	a litre bottle	mojama	cured tuna
lomo	pork loin; sausage	montado	tiny tapas sandwich
lomo con pimientos	pork sausage with peppers	morcilla	blood sausage, ie black pudding
longaniza	dark pork sausage	muy hecho	well done (steak)
		naranja	orange
macarrones	macaroni	nata	cream
magdalena	fairy cake, often dunked in coffee	natillas	creamy milk dessert
		nuez	nut; walnut; plural nueces
maíz	sweet corn		
mandarina	tangerine	olla	pot
mango	mango	orejón	dried apricot
manzana	apple	ostras	oysters

MENU DECODER

paella	rice & seafood dish. Some varieties contain meat.	picante	spicy
		pil pil	garlic sauce sometimes spiked with chilli
pajarito	small bird		
palillo	toothpick	pimienta	pepper
paloma	pigeon	pimiento rojo/ verde	red/green capsicum
pan	bread		
parrilla	grilled	pinchitos	Moroccan-style kebabs
pasa	raisin		
pasado; rancio	stale	pincho	a small tapas serving, often on a toothpick
pastas	small cakes, available in a variety of flavours		
		piña	pineapple
		piñón	pine nut
pastel	pastry, cake	pistacho	pistachio
patata	potato	plancha	grill; grilled; on the hot plate
patatas alioli	potatoes in garlic sauce		
		plátano	banana
patatas bravas	spicy, fried potatoes in tomato sauce	platija	flounder
		un plato	a plate
		poco hecho	rare (steak)
patatas fritas	chips; French fries	pollo	chicken
		postre	dessert
patisería	cake shop	potaje	stew
pato	duck	primer plato	first course; entrée
pavía	battered	puerros	leeks
pavo	turkey	pulpo	octopus
pechuga	chicken breast	pulpo a la gallega	octopus in sauce
pepino	cucumber		
pera	pear	queso	cheese
perdiz	partridge	un quinto	very small bottle ($^1/_5$ litre)
peregrina	scallop		
pescadilla	whiting	rabo	tail
pescado	fish	ración	small tapas plate or dish
pescaíto frito	tiny fried fish		
pez espada	swordfish	rape	monkfish
picadillo	minced meat	rebozado/a	battered & fried

FOOD

FOOD

MENU DECODER

refrescos	soft drinks	una taza	a cup
relleña(s)/o(s)	stuffed	té	tea
remolacha	beet	un tenedor	a fork
riñón	kidney	ternera	beef; veal
un ron	rum	tinto	red
rosada	ocean catfish, wolf-fish	tocino	bacon
		tomate	tomato
rosado	rosé	torta	round flat bun, cake
sal	salt		
salado	salted; salty	tortilla	omelette
salchicha	fresh pork sausage	tortilla de patata	egg & potato omelette
salchichón	peppery white sausage	tortilla española	potato omelette
salmón	salmon	tostada	toast
sandía	watermelon	trigo	wheat
una sangría	sangría (red wine punch)	trucha	trout
		trufa	truffle
sardina	sardine	un tubo	tall glass ($^1/_4$ litre)
seco	dry; dried		
segundo plato	second/main course	turrón	almond nougat
		uva	grape
sepia	cuttlefish	vaca, carne de	beef
serrano	mountain-cured ham	un vaso; una copa	glass
sesos	brains	vegetal	vegetable
seta	wild mushroom	vegetariano/a	vegetarian
una sidra	cider	venera	scallop
sobrasada	soft pork sausage	verdura	green vegetable
		vieira	scallop
soja	soy	vino	wine
solomillo	sirloin	vino de la casa	house wine
sopa	soup	yema	candied egg yolk
tapa	bite-sized snack	zanahoria	carrot
		zarzuela	fish stew
tarta	cake	zarzuela de marisco	shellfish stew
		zumo	fruit juice

TYPICAL DISHES
Starters — Primer Plato

ensalada	salad
fideos	thin pasta noodles with sauce
tortilla de patatas	egg & potato omelette

Soups — Sopas

caldo gallego	white bean and potato soup with turnip, greens and chorizo sausage
crema de cangrejos de segovia	freshwater crab and fish soup
fabada asturiana	broad bean soup with Spanish sausages and serrano ham
garbanzos con carne	chickpea, pork, chorizo and vegetable soup; can be served as a main course
gazpacho	cold soup made with garlic, tomato and other vegetables
olla podrida	vegetable and meat stew served with fried slices of bread
sopa al cuarto de hora	'fifteen-minute soup'; clam, shrimp, ham and rice soup served with chopped hard-boiled egg
sopa de ajo	garlic soup

Main Course — Segundo Plato

albóndigas	meatballs in onion and chicken sauce
almejas a la marinera	clams in white wine with garlic, onions and parsley
bacalao al ajo arriero	salt cod cooked in olive oil with tomatoes, onions and garlic
besugo al horno	red snapper, baked with sliced potatoes in olive oil, onions and tomatoes
bistec con patatas	steak & chips
calamares en su tinta	squid fried with onions, garlic and parsley, with a sauce made from the squids ink

FOOD

callos a la madrileña	tripe stew with ham, chorizo and sometimes calves' feet
cocido	stew made with chickpeas, pork and chorizo
cochifrito	lamb fricassee in lemon and garlic sauce
cordonices a la cazadora	quail stew with onions, leeks, tomatoes, turnips and carrots
croquetas	fried croquettes, often filled with ham or chicken
changurro	crab meat with sherry and brandy baked and served in individual ramekins
charcutería	cured pork meats
chorizo al horno	spicy baked sausages
chuletas de cordero a la navarra	lamb chops and chorizo sausage baked with onion and tomato
churrasco	slabs of grilled meat or ribs in a tangy sauce; a Galician dish
empanada	meat pie; a Galician dish
filete empanado	pork, cheese and ham wrapped in breadcrumbs and fried
filete de ternera	veal steak
habas a la catalana	casserole of broad beans with chorizo sausage, parsley and mint
liebre a la cazadora	hare casserole in red wine and garlic
lomo de cerdo a la zaragozana	pork loin chops with tomato sauce and black olives
merluza a la plancha	fried hake
merluza/mero en salsa verde	hake/pollock cutlets fried in olive oil with parsley and green pea sauce
morcilla	blood sausage (black pudding)
paella	Spain's best-known dish: saffron rice with seafoood, chicken pieces, chorizos and vegetables. In the Valencian paella the shellfish may be lobster, shrimps, prawns, clams and/or mussels. The Castillian paella is likely to have only

clams, but veal, beef or pork cubes
may be added as well as chicken. The
vegetables are normally peas and
peppers. The paella is traditionally
cooked out-of-doors on wood fires.

perdices estofadas	partridges braised in white wine with vegetables and garlic
pinchitos	Moroccan-style kebabs (Andalucía)
pollo a la chilindrón	sautéed chicken, with green and red peppers, tomatoes, serrano ham and green and black olives
pollo en pepitoria	casserole of chicken pieces braised in white wine with ground almonds, garlic and saffron
zarzuela de marisco	shellfish stew

FOOD

Desserts — Postres

arroz con leche	rice pudding
bartolillos de madrid	small pastry fritters with custard filling
bizcocho borracho	squares of sponge cake soaked in a syrup of sweet wine and cinnamon
brazo de gitano	sponge cake roll with rum cream filling
buñuelos de plátano	banana fritters
buñuelos de viento	pastry fritters sprinkled with sugar and cinnamon
cuajada	milk junket with honey
churros madrileños	crisp fried crullers, sprinkled with sugar (similar to doughnuts)
flan	crème caramel
helado	ice cream
leche frita	custard squares fried in olive oil and sprinkled with sugar and cinnamon
natillas	soft custard served in individula dishes, topped with egg white or with a ladyfinger biscuit

SELF-CATERING

In the Delicatessen

Look for the delicatessen counter in the local market or supermarket. Shops which only sell deli fare are not common in Spain, although you will find some highly specialised stores which just sell ham or cheese.

When you join a queue at a food counter, it is usual to ask 'Who's last?', ¿Quién es la última/el último?, so that you'll know when it's your turn to be served.

How much is (a kilo of cheese)?	¿Cuánto vale (un quilo de queso)?
Do you have anything cheaper?	¿Tiene algo más barato?
What is the local speciality?	¿Cuál es la especialidad de la zona?
Give me (half) a kilo, please.	Póngame (medio) quilo, por favor.
I'd like (six slices of ham).	Póngame (seis lonchas de jamón).
Can I taste it?	¿Puedo probarla/lo?

Making Your Own Meals

Where can I find the (sugar)?	¿Dónde puedo encontrar (el azúcar)?
I'd like some …	Quisiera un poco de …
bread	pan
butter	mantequilla
cheese	queso
chocolate	chocolate
eggs	huevos
flour	harina
ham	jamón
honey	miel

FOOD

margarine	margarina
marmalade	mermelada
milk	leche
… olives	aceitunas …
black	negras
green	verdes
stuffed	rellenas
olive oil	aceite de oliva
pepper	pimienta
salt	sal
sugar	azúcar
sunflower oil	aceite de girasol
yoghurt	yogurt

> **TIP BOX**
>
> **El chocolate**
> means 'chocolate' as
> one might guess; but
> it's also a word for
> 'hashish'.

FOOD

AT THE MARKET
Meat & Poultry

beef	vaca
chicken	pollo
chop	chuleta
boiled ham	jamón dulce
cured ham	jamón serrano
hamburger	hamburguesa
lamb	cordero
loin	lomo
meatballs	albóndigas
ox	buey
pork	cerdo
ribs	costillas
sausage	salchicha
spicy red/white sausage	chorizo/salchichón
cooked Spanish sausage	longaniza
steak	bistec
turkey	pavo
veal	ternera

FOOD

Fish & Seafood

anchovies	anchoas	oysters	ostras
bream	besugo	lobster	langosta
calamari	calamares	mussels	mejillones
cod	bacalao	prawns	langostinos
crab	cangrejo	salmon	salmón
hake	merluza	trout	trucha
octopus	pulpo	tuna	atún

Vegetables

artichoke	alcachofa
asparagus	espárragos
aubergine/eggplant	berenjena
(green) beans	judías (verdes)
beetroot	remolacha
Brussel sprouts	coles de bruselas
cabbage	col
carrot	zanahoria
red/green capsicum	pimiento rojo/verde
cauliflower	coliflor
celery	apio
chard (a variety of beef)	acelgas
courgette/zucchini	calabacín
cucumber	pepino
garlic	ajo
leeks	puerros
lettuce	lechuga
mushroom	champiñón
onion	cebolla
peas	guisantes
potato	patata
spinach	espinacas
spring onion	cebolla larga
tomato	tomate

Pulses

broad beans	habas
cereal	cereales
chickpeas	garbanzos
kidney beans	alubias
lentils	lentejas
rice	arroz

IN THE MORNING

In the morning is **por la mañana**;
at night is **por la noche**

Fruit & Nuts

apple	manzana	mango	mango
apricot	albaricoque	melon	melón
avocado	aguacate	orange	naranja
banana	plátano	peach	melocotón
cherry	cereza	pear	pera
coconut	coco	pineapple	piña
fig	higo	plum	ciruela
grape	uva	quince	membrillo
kiwifruit	kiwi	strawberry	fresa
lemon	limón	watermelon	sandía

almond	almendra	peanut	cacahuete
nut	nuez	pinenut	piñón
hazelnut	avellana	pistachio	pistacho

FOOD

DRINKS
Non-Alcoholic

almond drink	horchata
fruit juice	zumo
soft drinks	refrescos
water	agua
fizzy mineral water	agua mineral con gas
plain mineral water	agua mineral sin gas
tap water	agua del grifo

FOOD

coffee ...	café ...
with liqueur	carajillo
with a little milk	cortado
with milk	con leche
iced coffee	café helado
black coffee	café solo
long black	doble
decaffeinated	café descafeinado
tea	té

Alcoholic

anise	un anís
beer	una cerveza
champagne	un champán/un cava
cider	una sidra
cocktail	un combinado
brandy	un coñac
rum	un ron
sangría (red wine punch)	una sangría
sherry	un jerez
whisky	un güisqui

glass of ...wine	un vino ...
red	tinto
white	blanco
rosé	rosado
sweet	dulce
sparkling	espumoso

DID YOU KNOW ...

Simpática/o is a word that is used a lot in Spanish. It is hard to translate but it has the sense of 'nice, kind, easy to get along with'.

A beer	una cerveza
A ... of beer.	... de cerveza
small glass ($1/4$ litre)	una caña
tall glass ($1/4$ litre)	un tubo
very small bottle ($1/5$ litre)	un quinto
small bottle ($1/4$ litre)	un botellín
bottle ($1/3$ litre)	una mediana
a litre bottle	una litrona

A ... of whiskey/rum.	... de güisqui/ron.
A ... of wine/sherry.	... de vino.
glass	un vaso/una copa
bottle	una botella
jug	una jarra
shot	un chupito

FOOD

TAPAS

Almost every bar in Spain offers a selection of tapas, or snacks, with a great variation in style, size and quality. Tapas are usually cheap, and you may even be offered bite-sized portions free with your drink. The best way to discover these delicious snacks is to experiment by pointing at any interesting dish and asking for
un pincho de esto

> ### THEY MAY SAY ...
>
> *Te invito*
> This commonly heard Spanish phrase literally means 'I invite you', but is commonly understood to mean 'My shout', 'I'll pay'.

Serving Sizes

pincho	a small serving, often on a toothpick
tapa	standard bite-sized portion
ración	small plate or dish
montado	tiny sandwich
bocadillo	tapa in a sandwich

Common Tapas

aceitunas rellenas	stuffed olives
berberechos	cockles
boquerones en vinagre	anchovies in vinaigrette
boquerones fritos	fried anchovies
calamares a la romana	squid rings fried in butter
callos	tripe
champiñones al ajillo	garlic mushrooms
ensaladilla rusa	vegetable salad with mayonnaise
gambas a la plancha	grilled prawns
mejillones al vapor	steamed mussels.
patatas alioli	potatoes in garlic sauce
patatas bravas	potatoes in tomato sauce
pescaíto frito	tiny fried fish
pulpo a la gallega	octopus in sauce
tortilla de patata	potato omelette

IN THE BAR

Bar-hopping is a favourite pastime in Spain. Every residential street will have at least one local bar and town centres have a whole range of different types of bars. Mesones and tabernas are old-style inns with atmosphere. Cervecerías, champañerías and sidrerías specialise in beer, champagnes and cider respectively. Drinking and eating always go together in Spain, so join the locals in selecting a different morsel from the tapas bar each time you order.

In most bars in Spain you will not be expected to pay when ordering. Instead, you can pay when you are ready to leave.

Shall we go for a drink?	¿Vamos a tomar una copa?
Do you want to go for a drink?	¿Quieres ir a tomar algo?

FOOD

Getting Attention

Bars in Spain are often crowded and busy, and you usually have to be a bit pushy to get served.

Excuse me!	¡Por favor!
	¡Oiga!
I'm next!	Yo soy la/el siguiente.
	¡Ahora voy yo!
I was here before him!	¡Yo estoy antes que este señor!

Your Shout, My Shout

I'll buy you a drink.	Te invito a una copa.
What would you like?	¿Qué quieres tomar?
What will you have?	¿Qué va a ser?
I'll have …	Me apetece …
	Para mí, …
	Yo tomaré …
It's my round.	Es mi ronda.
It's on me.	Pago yo.
You can get the next one.	La próxima la pagas tú.
Same again, please.	Otra de lo mismo.

One Too Many?

Thanks, but I don't feel like it.	Lo siento, pero no me apetece.
I don't drink (alcohol).	No bebo.
This is hitting the spot.	Me lo estoy pasando muy bien; bomba.
I'm a bit tired, I'd better get home.	Estoy cansada/o, quiero irme a casa.
Where is the toilet?	¿Dónde está el lavabo?
Is food available here?	¿Sirven comida aquí?
I'm feeling drunk.	Esto me está subiendo mucho.
I think I've had one too many.	Creo que he tomado demasiadas copas.
I'm pissed.	Estoy borracha/o; bolinga; pedo.
I feel ill.	Me siento mal.
I want to throw up.	Tengo ganas de vomitar.
S/he's passed out.	Está durmiendo la mona.
I'm hung over.	Tengo resaca.

FOOD

IN THE COUNTRY

CAMPING

Is there a campsite nearby?	¿Hay algún camping cerca?
Where's the nearest campsite?	¿Dónde está el camping más cercano?
Do you have any sites available?	¿Tiene parcelas libres?
How much is it ...?	¿Cuánto vale ...?
per person	por persona
per tent	por tienda
per vehicle	por vehículo
Where are the ...?	¿Dónde están las ...?
showers	duchas
washing facilities	instalaciones

SIGNS

CAMPING	CAMPING GROUND
PROHIBIDO ACAMPAR	NO CAMPING

Can I camp here?	¿Se puede acampar aquí?
Who owns this land?	¿Quién es el propietario de este terreno?
Can I talk to her/him?	¿Puedo hablar con ella/él?
backpack	la mochila
can opener	el abrelatas
canvas	el sobretoldo
compass	la brújula
crampons	loscrampones
firewood	la leña
gas cartridge	el cartucho de gas

153

hammer	el martillo
hammock	la hamaca
ice axe	el pico; la pica; el piolet
mat	la esterilla
mattress	el colchón
penknife	la navaja
rope	la cuerda
sleeping bag	el saco de dormir
stove	la estufa; cocina
tent	la tienda (de campaña)
tent pegs	las piquetas
torch (flashlight)	la linterna
water bottle	la cantimplora

IN THE COUNTRY

WEATHER

What's the weather like?	¿Qué tiempo hace?
The weather is fine/bad today.	Hace buen/mal tiempo hoy.
It's raining.	Llueve.
It's hot (today).	Hace calor (hoy).
It'll be hot (tomorrow).	Hará calor (mañana).

	Today	Tomorrow
cloudy	Está nublado.	Estará nublado.
cold	Hace frío.	Hará frío.
foggy	Hay niebla.	Habrá niebla.
frosty	Está helando.	Helará.
hot	Hace calor.	Hará calor.
raining	Llueve.	Lloverá.
snowing	Nieva.	Nevará.
sunny	Hace sol.	Hará sol.
windy	Hace viento.	Hará viento.

HIKING & MOUNTAINEERING

There is plenty of walking, hiking and mountaineering to do in Spain. A recognised cross-country walking trail is known as a Gran Recorrido (GR), while the shorter walking paths scattered throughout the country are called Pequeños Recorridos (PR).

Getting Information

Where can I find out about hiking routes in the region?	¿Dónde hay información sobre caminos rurales de la zona?
Are there guided treks/climbs?	¿Se organizan excursiones/ escaladas guiadas?
I'd like to talk to someone who knows this area.	Quisiera hablar con alguien que conozca este sector.
How long is the trail?	¿Cuántos kilómetros tiene el camino?
Is the track (well-)marked?	¿Está (bien) marcado el sendero?
How high is the climb?	¿A qué altura se escala?
Which is the shortest/easiest route?	¿Cuál es el camino más corto/ fácil?
Is the path open all year?	¿Está la ruta abierta todo el año?
When does it get dark?	¿A qué hora oscurece?
Is it very scenic?	¿Tiene vistas?
Where can I rent mountain gear?	¿Dónde se alquila el material de montaña?
Where can we buy supplies?	¿Dónde podemos comprar comida?

On the Path

Where have you come from?	¿De dónde vienes?
How long did it take you?	¿Cuánto has tardado?
Does this path go to …?	¿Este camino va a …?
I'm lost.	Me he perdido/a.

Where can I spend the night?	¿Dónde puedo pasar la noche?
Can I leave some things here for a while?	¿Puedo dejar algunas cosas aquí durante un rato?
May I cross your property?	Pudeo cruzar su propiedad?
Is the water OK to drink?	¿Se puede beber el agua?

altitude	la altura
backpack	la mochila
binoculars	los prismáticos
cable car	el teleférico
candles	las velas
cave	una cueva; caverna
cliff	un acantilado; barranco
to climb	subir
compass	la brújula
cross-country trail	el camino
downhill	la cuesta abajo
first-aid kit	el maletín de primeros auxilios
forest	el bosque
gap; narrow pass	un portillo; una pasada
glacier	el glaciar
gloves	los guantes
guide	la/el guía
guided trek	la excursión guiada
harness	el arnés
to hike	ir de excursión
hiking boots	las botas de montaña
itinerary	el itinerario
ledge	el saliente
lookout	el mirador
map	el mapa
mountain	la montaña
mountaineering	alpinismo
mountain hut	el refugio de montaña
mountain path	el sendero
pass	el paso
peak	la cumbre

pick	la piqueta
provisions	los víveres; el abastecimiento
rock climbing	escalar
rope	la cuerda
to scale	trepar
signpost	un cartel indicator
steep	escarpada/o
trek	la excursión
uphill	cuesta arriba
view	la vista
to walk	caminar

AT THE BEACH

SIGN	
PROHIBIDO BAÑARSE	NO BATHING

Can we swim here?	¿Podemos nadar aquí?
Is it safe to swim?	¿Es seguro nadar aquí?
What time is high/low tide?	¿A qué hora es la marea alta/baja?

coast	la costa
rock	el peñón
sand	la arena
sea	el mar
sunblock	la crema solar
sunglasses	las gafas de sol
towel	la toalla
wave	la ola

See also Aquatic Sports, page 170.

IN THE COUNTRY

IN THE COUNTRY

GEOGRAPHICAL TERMS

agriculture	la agricultura
beach	la playa
bridge	el puente
cave	la cueva
city	la ciudad
cliff	el acantilado
the country	el campo
desert	el desierto
earth	la tierra
farm	la granja
field	el campo
footpath	el camino
forest	el bosque
harbour	el puerto
hill	la colina
island	la isla
lake	el lago
mountain	la montaña
mountain range	la cordillera
national park	el parque nacional

plain	la llanura
plateau	la meseta
river	el río
road	la carretera
rock	la roca
sea	el mar
spring	la primavera
stone	la piedra
stream	el arroyo
tide	la marea
trail	el sendero
valley	el valle
vegetation	la vegetación
village	el pueblecito
vineyard	el viñedo
waterfall	la cascada

SEASONS

summer	el verano
autumn	el otoño
winter	el invierno
spring	la primavera

FAUNA
Farm Animals

bull	el toro
calf	el ternero
chicken	el pollo
cockerel	el gallito
cow	la vaca
donkey	el burro
duck	el pato
goat	la cabra

goose	el ganso
hen	la gallina
lamb	el cordero
horse	el caballo
ox	el buey
pig	el cerdo
sheep	la oveja

See also Pets, page 90.

Wildlife

What's that animal/bird/
  insect called?

wild animal

ant	la hormiga
badger	el tejón
bear	el oso
brown bear	el oso pardo
boar	el jabalí
butterfly	la mariposa
deer	
red	el ciervo
roe	el corzo
fallow	el gamo
fly	la mosca
fox	el zorro
genet	la gineta
(small feline)	

¿Cómo se llama este animal/
  pájaro/insecto/bicho?

animal salvaje

hare	la liebre
ibex	la cabra
(mountain	montés
goat)	
lynx	el lince ibérico
mongoose	la mangosta
monkey	el mono
otter	la nutria
rabbit	el conejo
snake	la serpiente
spider	la araña
squirrel	la ardilla
toad	el sapo
wolf	el lobo

Birds

bird	el pájaro
buzzard	el ratonero
crane	la grulla
eagle	el águila
Egyptian	el acantilado
vulture	alimoche
harrier	el aguilucho
kestrel	el cernícalo
kite	el milano
owl	el búho
sparrowhawk	el gavilán
stork	la cigüeña
vulture	el buitre
black	negro
griffon	leonardo
woodpecker	el pajaro
	carpintero

STRESS

If a word ends in a
vowel, -n or -s, the
stress is on the second-
last syllable.

sombre**ro, tie**nen
muchos

If a word ends in a
consonant (except -n
and -s) the stress falls
on the last syllable.

ha**blar**, ciu**dad**

FLORA

conifer	la conífera	juniper	el enebro
eucalyptus	el eucalipto	oak	el roble
fir	el abeto	cork oak	el alcornoque
gorse	la aulaga	pine	el pino
heather	el brezo	scrub	la maleza

Herbs, Flowers & Crops

almond tree	el almendro	orange tree	el naranjo
carnation	el clavel	orchid	la orquídea
crops	el cultivo	rice	el arroz
harvest	la cosecha	rose	la rosa
iris	el lirio	rosemary	el romero
lavendar	la lavanda	sunflower	el girasol
lemon tree	el limonero	thyme	el tomillo
market garden/ orchard	la huerta	vineyard	la viña
		grapevine	la vid; parra
olive tree	el olivo	wheat	el trigo

TYPES OF SPORT

What sport do you play?	¿Qué deporte practicas?
I play/practise …	Practico …
American football	el fútbol americano
athletics	el atletismo
Australian Rules Football	el fútbol australiano
baseball	el béisbol
basketball	el baloncesto
boxing	el boxeo
cricket	el críquet
cycling	el ciclismo
diving	el submarinismo
fencing	la esgrima
football	el fútbol
handball	el balonmano
hockey	el hockey
indoor soccer	el fútbol sala
judo	el judo
pelota	la pelota vasca
rowing	el remo
rugby	el rugby
skiing	el esquí
soccer	el fútbol
surfing	el surf
swimming	la natación
tennis	el tenis
gymnastics	la gimnasia rítmica
weightlifting	el levantamiento de pesas

Although most international sports, especially football (soccer), are played and have a strong following in Spain, national and local sports are also very popular, especially the Basque game of pelota.

ball	la pelota
pelota	la pelota vasca
pelota player	pelotari
striker	delantera/o
wall	el frontón

See the Basque chapter, page 226, for more about pelota

TALKING ABOUT SPORT

Do you like sport?	¿Te gustan los deportes?
Yes, very much.	Me encantan.
No, not at all.	No me gustan nada.
I like watching rather than particpating.	Me gusta verlos pero no practicarlos.
What sport do you follow?	¿A qué deporte eres aficionada/o?
I follow …	Soy aficionada/o a …
Who's your favourite …?	¿Quién es tu … favorita/o.
player	jugadora/jugador
sportsperson	deportista
What's your favourite team?	¿Cuál es tu equipo favorito?
How do you play (basketball)?	¿Cómo se juega a (baloncesto)?
Can you play (rugby)?	¿Sabes jugar al (rugby)?
Yes, I know how to play.	Sí, sé jugar.
No, I don't know how to play.	No, no sé jugar.
Do you feel like (going for a swim)?	¿Te apetece (nadar)?
Yes, that'd be great.	Me apetece muchísimo.
Not at the moment, thanks.	No gracias, ahora no.
Do you want to go (skiing) this weekend?	¿Quieres ir a (esquiar) este fin de semana?
Yes, why not?	¡Por supuesto!
I'm sorry, I can't.	Lo siento, pero no puedo.

ACTIVITIES

GOING TO THE MATCH

Would you like to go to a (basketball) game?	¿Te gustaría ir a un partido de (baloncesto)?
Where is it being held?	¿Dónde se juega?
How much are the tickets?	¿Cuánto valen las entradas?
What time does it start?	¿A qué hora empieza?
Who's playing?	¿Quién juega?
Who do you think will win?	¿Quién crees que va a ganar?
Who are you supporting?	¿Con qué equipo vas?
I'm supporting …	(Voy) con …
Who's winning?	¿Quién gana?
Which team is winning/losing?	¿Qué equipo/quién va ganando/va perdiendo?
What's the score?	¿Cómo van?

What a …!	¡Qué; Vaya …!
goal	gol
hit	tiro
kick	chute
pass	pase

What a great performance!	¡Qué bien esta jugada!
The referee has disallowed it.	El árbitro lo ha anulado.
How much time is left?	¿Cuánto tiempo queda de partido?
That was a really good game!	¡Qué partidazo!
What a boring game!	¡Qué partido màs aburrido!
What was the final score?	¿Cómo han quedado?
It was a draw.	Empate.

international championships	los campeonatos internacionales
medal	la medalla
national championships	los campeonatos nacionales
Olympic Games	los juegos olímpicos
referee	el árbitro
seat (actual seat)	el asiento

seat (place)	la localidad
ticket	la entrada
ticket office	la taquilla

THEY WILL SAY ...

¡Venga!/¡Aupa!	Come on!
¡Goooooooool!	Goal!
¡Penalty clarísimo!	That was clearly a penalty!
¡Árbitro casero!	The ref's an amateur!
¡Ha sido falta!	That was a foul!
¡Eso es fuera de juego!	Offside!

¡Campeones, campeones, eo eo eo eo!
   (Common football chant)

SOCCER

Do you follow soccer?	¿Eres aficionada/o al fútbol?
Who do you support?	¿De qué equipo eres?
I support (Liverpool).	Soy del (Liverpool).
What a terrible team!	¡Vaya equipo más malo!
(Everton) are much better.	(Everton) es mucho mejor.

ACTIVITIES

Common Soccer Teams	Their Nicknames
Atlétic de Bilbao	Leones
Atlético de Madrid	Colchoneros
Betis	—
Deportivo de la Coruña	Depor
Español	Periquitos
Barça/Barcelona	Culés
Real Madrid	Merengues
Sevilla	—
Valencia	Chés

Who's the best team?	¿Cuál es el mejor equipo?
Who's at the top of the league?	¿Quién va primero en la liga?
Who plays for (Real Madrid)?	¿Quién juega en el (Real Madrid)?
My favourite player is ...	Mi jugador favorito es ...
He's a great player.	Es un gran jugador.
He played brilliantly in the match against (Italy).	Jugó un partidazo contra (Italia).

coach	entrenadora (f)	kick off	el saque inicial
	entrenador (m)	league	la liga
corner	córner	manager	el mánager
cup	la copa	offside	fuera de juego
fans	la afición	penalty	el penalty
free kick	el tiro libre	player	el jugadora
foul	la falta	to score	marcar
goal	el gol	to shoot	chutar
goalkeeper	portera/o	supporters	hinchas

Important Spanish Tournaments

Liga	National League
Copa del Rey	King's Cup
Copa de la UEFA	UEFA Cup
Copa de Europa	European Cup
Recopa	Cup-winner's Cup
Mundiales	World Cup

FOOTBALL & RUGBY

I play ...	Juego al ...
Have you ever seen ...?	¿Has visto alguna vez ...?
Are you familiar with ... ?	¿Sabes lo que es el ...?
American football	fútbol americano
Aussie Rules	fútbol australiano
rugby	rugby

If you're interested, you can see it on Canal Plus.	Si quieres verlo, a veces dan los partidos en el Canal Plus.
It's a contact sport.	Es un deporte de contacto.
Do you want me to teach you to play?	¿Quieres que te enseñe a jugar?

field goal	el gol de campo
forward	el delantero
fullback	el defensa
to kick for touch	intentar mandar el balón fuera del campo de juego
kick-off	el saque (inicial)
pass	el pase
scrum	melée
tackle	el placaje
to touch down	poner el balón en el suelo
try	un ensayo
winger	el extremo

KEEPING FIT

Where's the best place to jog/run around here?	¿Cuál es el mejor sitio para hacer footing por aquí cerca?
Where's the nearest …?	¿Dónde está … más cercana/o?
gym	el gimnasio
swimming pool	la piscina
tennis court	la pista de tenis
What is the charge per …?	¿Cúanto cobran por …?
day	día
game	partida
hour	hora
Can I hire …?	¿Es posible alquilar …?
a bicycle	una bicicleta
a racquet	una raqueta
shoes	zapatillas/zapatos
Do I have to be a member to attend?	¿Hay que ser socia/o para entrar?
Is there a women-only session/pool?	¿Hay alguna clase de gimnasia/piscina sólo para mujeres?
Where are the changing rooms?	¿Dónde están los vestuarios?
May I see the gym?	¿Puedo ver el gimnasio?
Is there a crèche?	¿Tienen servicio de guardería?
Can you give me a list of aerobic sessions please?	¿Me puede dar un horario para las clases de aeróbic, por favor?

ACTIVITIES

DID YOU KNOW … A letter you write to someone is *una carta*; a letter of the alphabet is *una letra*

exercise bicycle	la bicicleta aeroestática
jogging	footing
massage	el masaje
rowing machine	la máquina de remar
sauna	el sauna
shower	la ducha
towel	la toalla
weights	las pesas
workout	entreno

WALKING & MOUNTAINEERING

See In the Country chapter, pages 155 to 157, for trekking terms.

TENNIS

Do you like tennis/table tennis?	¿Te gusta jugar a tenis/ ping pong?
Do you play tennis?	¿Sabes jugar a tenis?
I play tennis.	Juego a tenis.
Would you like to play tennis?	¿Quieres jugar a tenis?
Is there a tennis court near here?	¿Hay alguna pista de tenis aquí cerca?
How much is it to hire the court?	¿Cuánto vale alquilar la pista de tenis?
Can you play at night?	¿Se puede jugar de noche?
Is there racquet and ball hire?	¿Se alquilan raquetas y pelotas?
Are there instructors?	¿Tienen monitoras/es?
What type of surface does the court have?	¿Qué tipo de superficie tiene la pista de tenis?

tennis court	la pista de tenis
tournament	el torneo
ace	ace
advantage	ventaja
deuce	iguales
fault	falta

ACTIVITIES

game	el juego
game ball	la pelota de juego
grass court	la pista de hierba
hard court	la pista dura
line	la línea
love	cero a cero
match	el partido
match ball	el peloto de partido
net	la red
ping pong ball	la pelota de ping pong
play doubles (v)	jugar dobles
point	el punto
racquet	la raqueta
serve	el servicio
set	el set
set ball	la pelota de set
table tennis	el ping pong
table tennis table	la mesa de ping pong
table tennis bat	la pala

CYCLING

Where does the race pass through?	¿Por dónde pasa la carrera?
Who's winning?	¿Quién va ganando?
Is today's leg very hard?	¿Es muy dura la etapa de hoy?
How many kilometres is today's race?	¿Cuántos quilómetros tiene la etapa de hoy?
Where does it finish?	¿Dónde termina?
My favourite cyclist is ...	Mi ciclista favorito es ...

cyclist	ciclista
leg (in race)	etapa
winner/winner of a leg	vencedora/vencedor de etapa
(yellow) jersey	maillot (amarillo)
hilly stage of the race	etapa de montaña
race against the clock	contrareloj
Vuelta ciclista	Spanish national cycle race

SKIING

How much is a pass for these slopes?	¿Cuánto vale el forfait para estas pistas?
What are the skiing conditions like at …?	¿Cuáles son las condiciones de las pistas de esquí en …?
Is it possible to go cross-country skiing at …?	¿Es posible hacer esquí de fondo en …?
At what levels are the different slopes?	¿De qué nivel son las pistas?
Where are the (black) level slopes?	¿Dónde están las pistas (negras)?

cross-country	la carrera de fondo
downhill	el descenso
instructor	la/el profesora/profesor
safety binding	la fijación de seguridad
skis	los esquíes
ski-boots	las botas
ski-lift	el tele-arrastre
ski-pass	forfait
ski slope	la pista
ski-suit	el traje de esquí
stock	el bastón de esqui
sunblock	la crema solar

AQUATIC SPORTS

diving	el salto de trampolín
diving equipment	el equipo de inmersión
motorboat	la motora
surfboard	la tabla de surf
surfing	el surf
swimming	la natación
water-skiing	el esquí acuático
water-skis	los esquís para el agua
wave	la ola
windsurfing	el windsurf

See also At the Beach, page 157.

ACTIVITIES

BULLFIGHTING

The corrida (bullfight) is a spectacle with a long history and many rules. It is not, as many would suggest, simply a ghoulish alternative to the slaughterhouse (itself no pretty sight). Aficionados will say that the bull is better off dying at the hands of a matador than in the matadero (abattoir). The corrida is about many things – death, bravery, performance. No doubt, the fight is bloody and cruel, and about that hackles will always rise. To witness the fight is not necessarily to understand it, but it might clue you in to some of the thought and tradition behind it. Although many Spaniards themselves consider it a cruel and 'uncivilised' activity (no-one would call it a sport), there is no doubting its popularity. If on a bar-room TV there is football on one channel and a corrida on another, the chances are high that football fever will cede to the fascination of the fiesta.

If you'd like to state your opinion, or if you feel it may be more prudent not to enter a discussion but simply to decline politely, see below and pages 47 and 115.

Do you like bullfighting?	¿Te gustan los toros?
Is bullfighting popular in this area?	¿Son los toros populares en esta región?
Would you like to go to a bullfight?	¿Quieres ir a una corrida?
I'd like to go to a bullfight.	Me gustaría ir a una corrida de toros.
Do you agree with bullfighting?	¿Estás de acuerdo con los toros?
I don't agree with bullfighting.	No estoy de acuerdo con los toros.
Is there a bullfight today/soon?	¿Hay alguna corrida de toros hoy/pronto?
Where is the bullring?	¿Dónde está la plaza de toros?
Who's appearing tonight?	¿Quién torea esta tarde?
Where can I get tickets for the bullfight?	¿Dónde se compran las entradas para los toros?

THEY MAY SAY ...

¡Olé!
¡Torero, torero!

Es tan bueno que le han concedido ...
He's so good they've given him ...

una oreja	an ear
las dos orejas	both ears
el rabo	the tail

ACTIVITIES

What's the bullfighter called?	¿Cómo se llama el torero?
What's that music?	¿Qué es esa música?
What's happening now?	¿Qué pasa ahora?
What does this mean?	¿Qué significa esto?
Why are people shouting?	¿Por qué grita la gente?

Bullfighting Terms

las almohadillas	cushions, thrown at a poorly performing bullfighter
las banderillas	short prods with decorated harpoon-style ends
los banderilleros	those who place the coloured banderillas into the bull's neck
la capa	cape
el capote	cloak
la corrida	bullfight
la cuadrilla	the torero's team
los cuernos	horns
la espada	sword
la estocada	the final (and fatal) plunge of the sword into the bull's neck
las faenas	moves of the matador in the ring
la lidia	the art of bullfighting
el matador	the bullfighter who kills the bull
la montera	the bullfighter's hat
las orejas	ears
los peones	junior bullfighters under the orders of the matador
los picadores	those on horseback who try to weaken the bull with their lances
las plaza de toros	bullring
el rabo	tail
el ruedo	arena
el sol/la sombra	sun/shade
el tendido	section of the stand in which you are seated

ACTIVITIES

el torero	name generally given to different types of bullfighters
el toro	bull
el toro bravo	fighting bull
el traje de luces	'suit of lights' — the specially decorated suit made for bullfighters
la vuelta al ruedo	lap of honour

HORSE RACING

Horse racing isn't very popular in Spain, where people are more likely to bet on the lottery. However, all the major cities have courses, and enthusiasts should be able to get a meeting or two in during their trip.

Where are horse races held?	¿Dónde hay carreras de caballos?
Where is the [horse] racetrack?	¿Dónde está el hipódromo?
Shall we have a bet?	¿Apostamos algo?
How much do you want to put on?	¿Cuánto quieres apostar?
Which horse is favourite?	¿Qué caballo es el favorito?
Which horse should I back?	¿A qué caballo apuesto?
At what odds is this horse?	¿Qué dan los corredores por este caballo?
This horse is five to one.	Este caballo está cinco a uno.
What weight is the horse carrying?	¿Qué peso lleva el caballo?

bet	la apuesta
bookmaker	el corredor de apuestas
horse	el caballo
jockey	la/el jockey
photo finish	el foto finish
race	la carrera
ride (v)	montar a caballo

HORSE RIDING

Is there a horse-riding school around here?	¿Hay alguna escuela de equitación?
Are there rides available?	¿Es posible dar un paseo a caballo?
How long is the ride?	¿Cuánto dura el paseo?
How much does it cost?	¿Cuánto vale?
Do you offer rides for beginners?	¿Ofrecen paseos para principiantes?
I'm an experienced rider.	Soy una/un jinete experimentada.
Can I rent a hat and boots?	¿Se pueden alquilar el casco y las botas de montar?

THE HORSES MAY HEAR ...

¡Arreeee!	Gee up!
¡Soooo!	Whoah!

canter	el medio galope	gallop	el galope
crop	la fusta	stables	la cuadra
horse	el caballo	stallion	el semental
mare	la yegua	trot	el trote

CAR RACING

a crash	un accidente
to crash; collide	chocar
driver	la corredora/el corredor; la/el piloto
to fall behind	quedarse atrás; rezagarse
Formula One	Fórmula Uno
helmet	el casco
... kilometers an hour	... kilómetros por hora
lap	una vuelta

ACTIVITIES

to overtake; pass	pasar; adelantar
racetrack	el autódromo; la pista de carreras
racing car	el coche de carreras
to skid	patinar
to take the lead	llevar la delantera

GOLF

bunker	el búnker
flagstick	la banderola
follow-through	el impulso
golf course	el campo de golf
golf trolley	el carrito de golf
golfball	la pelota de golf
hole	el hoyo
iron	el bastón de hierro; el iron
teeing ground	la salida; el 'tee'
wood	el bastón de madera; un driver

GAMES

Do you play …	¿Te gusta jugar …?
billiards	al billar español
bingo	al bingo
cards	a las cartas
chess	al ajedrez
computer games	con juegos de ordenador
dominoes	al dominó
draughts	a los damas
ludo	al parchís
noughts and crosses	tres en raya
pinball	al millón
pool	el billar americano
roulette	a la ruleta
table football	alfutbolín

| Shall we play (ludo)? | ¿Jugamos al (parchís)? |
| I'm sorry, I don't know how to play (chess). | Lo siento, pero no sé jugar al (ajedrez). |

ACTIVITIES

How do you play (dominoes)?	¿Cómo se juega al (dominó)?
What are the rules?	¿Cuáles son las reglas?
Whose turn is it?	¿A quién le toca tirar ahora?
It's my turn.	Es mi turno.
I'm winning/losing.	Estoy ganando/perdiendo.
Stop cheating!	¡Deja de hacer trampas!

THEY MAY SAY ...

¡Afortunada/o!	Lucky!
¡Bingo!	Bingo!
¡Línea!	Line! (in bingo)
¡Qué mala suerte!	Hard luck!
¡Qué suerte tengo!	I'm on a roll!
¡Tramposa/o!	Cheat!
Tengo gafe.	I'm jinxed.

Cards

Do you want to play ...?	¿Quieres jugar ...
cards	a las cartas
bridge	al bridge
poker	al póquer

I don't know how to play.	No sé jugar.
I'll teach you.	Yo te enseño.
It's your turn to pick up a card.	Te toca coger una carta.
I can't go.	No voy.
I'll bet (200) pesetas.	Apuesto (200) pesetas.
I'll see you.	Te igualo.
I'll raise you 100 pesetas.	Y (100) más.

BAD SPANISH – INSULTS

¡Eres una ...!	You're a ...!
¡Qué ... eres!	You're so ...!
¡Mira que llegas a ser ...!	You're such a ...!
¡No seas ...!	Don't be ...!
¡Juan es un ...!	Juan is a ...!

hijo de puta	son of a bitch
cabrona/cabrón	fag
cabronaza/o	bastard
puta	slag
capulla/o	nob
gilipollas	dickhead
mierda	shit
jodida/o	arsehole
idiota	idiot
subnormal/anormal	retard
imbécil	imbecile
estúpida/o	cretin
desgraciada/o	creep
cerda/o	pig
plasta	pain in the neck
boba/o	wally
corta/o	halfwit

ACTIVITIES

ace	el as	
king	el rey	
queen	el caballo	– in a Spanish deck the Queen is replaced by a knight
jack	la sota	
spades	las espadas	– appear as swords
clubs	los bastones	– appear as a club or baton
diamonds	los oros	– appear as a gold coin
hearts	las copas	– appear as a goblet

to deal	repartir
deck	la baraja
hand	la mano
joker	el comodín
to shuffle	barajar

Poker

four of a kind	póquer
full hand	ful
pair	pareja
poker	póquer
royal flush	escalera de color
straight	escalera
three of a kind	trío
two pairs	doble pareja

> ### HARD G
>
> When u is added to g it makes the g hard. When gu is followed by e or i, the u is not pronounced:
>
> guerra (war) is said as gerra not gwerra.
>
> However when the gu is followed by a or o it is pronounced as gw:
>
> guapa (attractive) is said as gwapa.

Chess

Do you like chess?	¿Te gusta jugar al ajedrez?
Shall we play chess?	¿Jugamos al ajedrez?
White starts.	Las blancas empiezan.
It's my move.	Ahora muevo yo.
Hurry up and make a move!	¡Mueve de una vez!

Check!	¡Jaque!
Check to the king!	¡Jaque al rey!
Checkmate!	¡Jaque mate!
Cheat!	¡Tramposa/o!

bishop; rook	el álfil
black pieces	las negras
castle	la torre
chess board	el tablero de ajedrez
chess tournament	el campeonato de ajedrez
king	el rey

knight	el caballo
pawn(s)	el peón(es)
pieces	las fichas
queen	la reina
white pieces	las blancas
stalemate	quedar tablas

THE LOTTERY

Spain's major national lottery is administered by ONCE, the organisation for blind people. Playing the lottery is one of the most popular Spanish pastimes.

| I'd like a lottery ticket please. | ¿Me da un décimo de lotería por favor? |
| Which number do you want? | ¿Qué número desea? |

Major Draws
Bonoloto
El gordo
El niño
Lotería primitiva

> **EL IDIOMA**
>
> **El idioma** means *language*, as does **la lengua**.

TV & VIDEO

Do you mind if I put the TV on?	¿Te importa si enciendo la tele?
Turn the TV off!	¡Apaga la tele!
Do you mind if I turn the volume up/down?	¿Te importaría subir/bajar el volumen?
Can I change the channel?	¿Puedes cambiar de canal?
Which channel do you want to watch?	¿Qué canal quieres ver?
I feel like watching …	Me apetece ver …
cartoons	los dibujos animados
current affairs	un informativo

a documentary	un documental
a film	una película
a game show	un concurso
kids' programs	la programación infantil
news	las noticias
a series	una serie de televisión
a soap opera	una telenovela
a Latin American soap opera	una culebrón
sport	la programación deportiva
a variety program	un programa de variedades
the weather	el tiempo

Does this TV have the 'dual system'?	¿Esta tele tiene sistema dual?
Can we watch the English-language TV?	¿Podemos poner la tele en inglés?
I prefer to watch in Spanish.	Yo prefiero el castellano.
Where's the remote control?	¿Dónde está el mando a distancia?
It's over there/here.	Está allí/aquí.
The TV isn't working.	La televisión no funciona.

antenna	la antena	satellite dish	la antena parabólica
buttons	los botones		
cable TV	el cable	television	la televisión
channel	el canal	TV	tele
remote control	el mando a distancia	TV set	el televisor
		volume	el volumen

ACTIVITIES

DID YOU KNOW ...   Sistema dual is a special piece of equipment which allows you to view programs in their original language.

Video

It's possible to hire films on video in Spain, but it's not popular. Rather than hiring videos, people prefer to buy copies of their favourite films, to watch or record films on TV, or to enjoy themselves out of the house. That said, here are a few useful phrases:

Where can I hire videos?	¿Dónde alquilan películas de vídeo?
Do you loan videos here?	¿Alquilan películas aquí?
Yes, we loan them.	Sí, alquilamos películas.
No, I'm sorry, we only sell them.	No, lo siento, sólo las vendemos.
Do I have to be a member to borrow videos?	Para alquilar una película, hay que ser socio de este video club?
How much is it to hire this video?	¿Cuánto vale alquilar esta película?
Is this film for daily or weekly hire?	¿Esta película es de alquiler diario o semanal?
How long can I borrow this for?	¿Por cuántos días se alquila esta película?
Do you have ...?	¿Tienen ...?

FESTIVALS & HOLIDAYS

champagne	el cava; el champán
to celebrate (an event)	celebrar
to celebrate (in general)	festejar
church	la iglesia
to exchange gifts	regalar
gift	el regalo
holiday	el día festivo
party	la fiesta

BIRTHDAYS & SAINT'S DAYS

When is your …?	¿Cuándo es tu …?
birthday	cumpleaños
saint's day	santo

My … is on (25 January).	Mi … es el día (25 de enero).

Congratulations!	¡(Muchas) felicidades!
Happy birthday!	¡Feliz cumpleaños!
Happy saint's day!	¡Feliz santo!
Many happy returns!	¡Que cumplas muchos más!
Blow out the candles!	¡Sopla las velas!

birthday cake	pastel de cumpleaños
candles	velas

HAPPY BIRTHDAY TO YOU …

¡Cumpleaños feliz!
¡Cumpleaños feliz!
¡Todas/os te deseamos!
¡Cumpleaños feliz!

CHRISTMAS & NEW YEAR

Christmas in Spain begins on 24 December but gifts aren't usually exchanged until 6 January (Epiphany).

Christmas Day	la Navidad	25 December
Christmas Eve	la Nochebuena	24 December
New Year's Eve	el fin de año	31 December
New Year's Day	el año nuevo	1 January
Epiphany	día de los reyes magos	6 January

Happy Christmas!	¡Feliz navidad!
Happy New Year!	¡Feliz año nuevo!
	¡Próspero año nuevo!

Christmas Delicacies

mazapán	marzipan
polvorones	soft Christmas biscuits
roscón de reyes	special ring-shaped cake eaten at Epiphany
turrón	Christmas candy

Christmas & New Year Traditions

Poner el belén

Literally meaning 'to place the nativity scene', this Spanish tradition involves placing figures of the three Kings at a distance from a set of nativity figures on 24 December and moving them a little closer each day, culminating on 6 January, 'el día de los reyos magos', 'the day of the Three Wise Men'.

Cotillón

On New Year's Eve you can go from party to party, collecting a cotillón at each one, which is a kind of party bag containing sweets, party whistles and other goodies.

Las uvas

A much-loved Spanish tradition is the eating of twelve grapes (**uvas**) at midnight on New Year's Eve. They must be eaten in rapid succession, one for each consecutive strike of the clock. It's not as easy as it sounds!

Cabalgata de reyes

In villages, towns and cities throughout Spain on the evening of 5 January you can see a special Christmas procession featuring the Three Wise Men and other Christmas and popular characters.

EASTER

Happy Easter!	¡Felices pascuas!
chocolate eggs	los huevos de chocolate
chocolate figures	la mona de pascua
easter cake	el roscón de pascua
Holy Week	la Semana santa
religious procession	la procesión religiosa

CHRISTENINGS & WEDDINGS

Congratulations!	¡Felicidades!
To the bride & groom!	¡Vivan los novios!
baptism	el bautizo
engagement	el compromiso
honeymoon	la luna de miel
wedding	la boda
wedding anniversary	el aniversario de bodas
wedding cake	la tarta nupcial
wedding present	el regalo de bodas

TOASTS & CONDOLENCES

> **YOU MAY SAY ...**
>
> Good health!; Cheers!
>
> ¡Salud!
> ¡A tu/su salud!
> ¡Chin chin!
> ¡Toda la suerte!
> ¡Por ti/vosotros/
>   nosotros!

And the most popular of all, accompanied by arm movements forming the shape of the cross:

¡Arriba, abajo, al centro y ...
pa'dentro!
(lit: 'up, down, in the centre
and inside')

Bon apétit!   ¡Buen provecho!
              ¡Que aproveche!
Bon voyage!   ¡Buen viaje!

Sickness

Get well soon!	¡Que te mejores!
Bless you! (after sneezing)	¡Jesús!; ¡Salud!

Death

I'm very sorry.	Lo siento muchísimo.
My deepest sympathy.	Mi más sentido pésame.
My thoughts are with you.	Te acompaño en el sentimiento.

Luck

Good luck!	¡Buena suerte!
Hope it goes well!	¡Qué te vaya bien!
What bad luck!	¡Qué mala suerte!
Never mind!	No te preocupes

HEALTH

AT THE DOCTOR

I am sick.	Estoy enferma/o.
My friend is sick.	Mi amiga/o está enferma/o.
I need a doctor (who speaks English).	Necesito una doctora/un doctor (que hable inglés).
Could the doctor come here?	¿Puede visitarme la doctora/ el doctor?

Where is the nearest ...?	¿Dónde está ... más cercano?
doctor	el doctor/el médico
hospital	el hospital
chemist	la farmacia
dentist	el dentista

THEY MAY SAY ...

¿Qué le pasa?	What's the matter?
¿Le duele?	Do you feel any pain?
¿Dónde le duele?	Where does it hurt?
¿Tiene la regla?	Are you menstruating?
¿Tiene fiebre?	Do you have a temperature?
¿Desde cuándo se siente así?	How long have you been like this?
¿Ha tenido esto antes?	Have you had this before?
¿Se encuentra bajo medicación?	Are you on medication?
¿Fuma?	Do you smoke?
¿Bebe?	Do you drink?
¿Toma drogas?	Do you take drugs?
¿Es alérgica/o a alguna medicina?	Are you allergic to anything?
¿Está embarazada?	Are you pregnant?

187

HEALTH

AILMENTS

I'm ill.	Estoy enferma/o.
I've been vomiting.	He estado vomitando.
I feel under the weather.	Tengo malestar general.

I feel …	Me siento …
dizzy	mareada/o
shivery	destemplada/o
weak	débil

I feel nauseous.	Tengo náuseas.
I can't sleep.	No puedo dormir.

I have …	Tengo …
an allergy	alergia
anaemia	anemia
a blister	una ampolla
bronchitis	bronquitis
a bruise	un cardenal
a burn	una quemadura
cancer	cáncer
a cold	un resfriado; catarro
cystitis	cistitis
constipation	estreñimiento
a cough	tos
diarrhoea	diarrea
fever	fiebre
glandular fever	mononucleosis
a headache	dolor de cabeza
hayfever	alergia al polen
hepatitis	hepatitis
indigestion	indigestión
an infection	una infección
an inflammation	una inflamación
influenza	gripe
lice	piojos

a lump	un bulto
a migraine	migraña
a pain	dolor
a rash	irritación
sore throat	dolor de garganta
sprain	una torcedura
an STD	una enfermedad de transmisión sexual
a stomachache	dolor de estómago
sunburn	una quemadura de sol
sunstroke	una insolación
thrush	afta
travel sickness	mareo
worms	lombrices

HEALTH

USEFUL PHRASES

I feel better/worse.	Me siento mejor/peor.
This is my usual medicine.	Éste es mi medicamento habitual.
I have been vaccinated.	Estoy vacunada/o.
I don't want a blood transfusion.	No quiero que me hagan una transfusión de sangre.
Do you have a student/ pensioner discount?	¿Hay algún descuento para estudiantes/pensionistas?
Can I have a receipt for my health insurance?	¿Puede darme un recibo para mi seguro médico?

WOMEN'S HEALTH

Could I see a female doctor?	¿Puede examinarme una doctora?
I'm on the Pill.	Tomo la píldora.
I think I'm pregnant.	Creo que estoy embarazada.
I haven't had my period for ... weeks.	Hace ... semanas que no me viene la regla.
I'd like to get the morning-after pill.	Quisiera tomar la píldora del día siguiente.

HEALTH

I'd like to have a pregnancy test.	¿Puede hacerme la prueba del embarazo?
I'm pregnant.	Estoy embarazada/encinta.
I'd like to terminate my pregnancy.	Quisiera interrumpir mi embarazo.
I'd like to use contraception.	Quisiera usar algún método anticonceptivo.

abortion	el aborto
cystitis	la cistitis
diaphragm	eldiafragma
IUD	el DIU
mamogram	la mamografía
menstruation	la menstruación; regla
miscarriage	el aborto natural
pap smear	la citología
period pain	el dolor menstrual
the Pill	la píldora
premenstrual tension	la tensión pre-menstrual
thrush	la afta
ultrasound	el ultrasonido

SPECIAL HEALTH NEEDS

I'm …	Soy …
asthmatic	asmática/o
diabetic	diabética/o
epilectic	epiléptica/o

I have high/low blood pressure.	Tengo la presión baja/alta.
I have a weak heart.	Tengo el corazón débil.
I'm on regular medication for …	Estoy bajo medicación para …
I'm on a special diet.	Sigo una dieta especial.
I have a skin allergy.	Tengo un alergia en la piel.
I have my own syringe.	Tengo mi propia jeringa.

I'm allergic to …	Soy alérgica/o …
antibiotics	a los antibióticos
aspirin	a la aspirina
bees	a las abejas
codeine	a la codeína
dairy products	a los productos lácteos
penicillin	a la penicilina
pollen	al polen

HEALTH

¿ES ALÉRGICO A ALGUNA MEDICINA?

inhaler	el inhalador
pacemaker	marcapasos

ALTERNATIVE TREATMENTS

aromatherapy	la aromaterapia
herbalist	el herborista
homeopathy	la homeopatía
massage	el masaje
massage therapist	la masajista
meditation	la meditación
naturopath	el naturópata
reflexology	la reflexología
yoga	el yoga

HEALTH

PARTS OF THE BODY

My ... hurts.
I have a pain in my ...
I can't move my ...

Me duele ...
Siento dolor en ...
No puedo mover ...

ankle	el tobillo	jaw	la mandíbula
appendix	el apéndice	knee	la rodilla
arm	el brazo	leg	la pierna
back	la espalda	mouth	la boca
bladder	la vejiga	muscle	el músculo
blood	el sangre	nose	la nariz
bone	el hueso	penis	el pene
breast	el pecho	ribs	las costillas
chest	el pecho	shoulders	los hombros
ear	la oreja	skin	la piel
eye	el ojo	spine	la columna
finger	el dedo		(vertebral)
foot	el pie	stomach	el estómago
hand	la mano	teeth	los dientes
head	la cabeza	throat	la garganta
heart	el corazón	vein	la vena

AT THE CHEMIST

Where is the nearest all-night
    chemist?
I need something for ...
I have a prescription.
How many times a day?
Take (two) tablets (four)
    times a day.
before/after meals

Could I please have ...?
    antibiotics
    aspirin

¿Dónde está la farmacia
    de guardia más cercana?
Necesito algo para ...
Tengo receta médica.
¿Cuántas veces al día?
Tome (dos) píldoras (cuatro)
    veces al día.
antes/después de la comidas

¿Me pone ... por favor?
    antibióticos
    las aspirinas

contraceptives	los anticonceptivos
cough medicine	algo para el catarro
laxatives	los laxantes
painkillers	los analgésicos
sleeping pills	las pastillas para dormir

AT THE DENTIST

I have a toothache.	Me duele una muela.
I have a cavity.	Tengo una caries.
I've lost a filling.	Se me ha caído un empaste.
I've broken a tooth.	Se me ha roto un diente.
My gums hurt.	Me duelen las encías.
I don't want it extracted.	No quiero que me lo arranque.
Please give me an anaesthetic.	Por favor, póngame anestesia.
Ouch!!	¡¡Ay!!

HEALTH

CROSSWORD – HEALTH

HEALTH

Across:
1. Healer using herbs
5. Digit
7. Often the first stop for health care

Down:
2. The whooping variety can be dangerous
3. Feminine contraceptive
4. Home of haemoglobin
6. Not feeling too strong

Answers: page 366

SPECIFIC NEEDS

DISABLED TRAVELLERS

Is there a special service for disabled people?
¿Tienen servicios para minusválidos?

What services are available for disabled people?
¿Qué servicios tienen para minusvalidos?

I need assistance,
I'm …
    disabled
    blind
    deaf
    mute
Necesito asistencia, porque soy …
    minusválida/o
    ciega/o
    sorda/o
    muda/o

Is there wheelchair access?
¿Hay acceso para la silla de ruedas?

I might be in a wheelchair, but I'm not stupid/ hard of hearing.
Puede que vaya en silla de ruedas, pero tonta/o; sorda/o no soy.

Are guide dogs allowed?
¿Se permite la entrada a los perros guía?

Is there a guide service for blind people?
¿Hay algún servicio de guía para personas ciegas?

Will there be a guide to describe things?
¿Es una excursión guiada?

Is there information in Braille?
¿Tienen algún tipo de información en braille?

Could you please speak more slowly/clearly?
Por favor hable más despacio/claro.

I'm deaf but I can lip-read.
Soy sorda/o pero puedo leer los labios.

Is there anyone here who speaks sign language?
¿Hay alguien aquí que pueda hablar el lenguaje de los signos?

I am hard of hearing.	Tengo problemas de oído.
Speak into my other ear please.	Hábleme por el otro oído, por favor.
I wear a hearing aid.	Llevo audífono.

guidedog	perro lazarillo
disabled	minusválida/o
hearing aid	audífono
paraplegic	parapléjica/o
wheelchair	silla de ruedas

GAY TRAVELLERS

The words for 'gay, lesbian, heterosexual', etc are more or less the same in Spanish as they are in English — though with Spanish pronunciation of course!

Are there any gay bars around here?	¿Hay algún bar gay/de ambiente por aquí?
Is there a gay telephone hotline?	¿Hay alguna línea telefónica de información gay?
Is there a local gay publication?	¿Conoces alguna revista de tema homosexual?
Is there a gay bookshop?	¿Hay alguna librería homo- sexual?
Am I likely to be harassed for being gay?	¿Me van a molestar por ser homosexual?

TRAVELLING WITH A FAMILY

| I'm travelling with my family. | Viajo con toda mi familia. |
| Are there facilities for babies? | ¿Hay facilidades para bebés? |

Are there other families in the …?	¿Hay otras familias en …?
hotel	el hotel
tour group	la excursión

Is there a childminding service in the hotel?	¿Tienen guardería en el hotel?
Can you provide an English-speaking babysitter?	¿Disponen de un servicio de canguros que hablen inglés?
Can you add an extra bed to the room?	¿Pueden añadir una cama en la habitación?
Do you hire out family cars?	¿Alquilan coches familiares?
Does this car have a child seat?	¿Este coche tiene sillita para niños?
Is it safe for babies/children?	¿Es seguro para bebés/niños?
Is there family entertainment?	¿Hay alguna diversión para toda la familia?
Is there children's entertainment here?	¿Hay algún espectáculo para niños aquí?
Is it for all ages?	¿Es para todos los públicos?
Is it suitable for all the family?	¿Es adecuado para toda la familia?
Is there a family price?	¿Hay un precio especial para familias?
Are children allowed?	¿Se admiten niños?
Is there a children's menu?	¿Tienen menú infantil?
Could you make it a child's portion?	¿Puede prepararme una ración para niños?
What time is the children's program on?	¿A qué hora dan el programa infantil?
Is there a playground around here?	¿Hay algún parque infantil por aquí cerca?

SPECIFIC NEEDS

DID YOU KNOW ... To speak of the future is to speak of **el porvenir**. The word **el futuro** is kept only to grammatical terms.

SPECIFIC NEEDS

LOOKING FOR A JOB

I'm looking for work.	Estoy buscando trabajo.
I'd like to find work.	Me gustaría encontrar trabajo.
Where is the best place to look for a job?	¿Cuál es el mejor sitio para buscar trabajo?
Do you have any vacancies for a …?	¿Hay algún puesto de trabajo para una/un …?

I have experience in …	Tengo experiencia …
acting	como actriz/actor
cleaning	en trabajos de limpieza
construction work	en la construcción
design	en el diseño
fruit picking	en la recolección de fruta
looking after children	como canguro; en cuidar niños
photography	en la fotografía
office work	en trabajo de oficina
sales	como vendedora/ vendedor
secretarial work	como secretaria/o
teaching	en la enseñanza
using computers	en ordenadores
waiting	como camarera/o
writing	como escritora/escritor

I have a qualification	Estoy cualificada para …

I can …	Puedo …
cook	cocinar
draw	pintar
drive	conducir
type	escribir a máquina

I'm looking for …	Estoy buscando trabajo …
part-time	a tiempo parcial
full-time	a tiempo completo
casual work	esporádico

What's the salary?	¿Cuál es el salario?
How is the salary paid?	¿Cómo me van a pagar?
How often would I get paid?	¿Cada cuánto me van a pagar?
Do I have to pay tax?	¿Tengo que pagar impuestos?
What are the working hours?	¿Cuál es el horario?
Is this a live-in job?	¿Es un trabajo que requiere vivir en la casa?
I'd like to apply for the position.	Me gustaría presentar una solicitud.
Here is my resumé.	Aquí está mi currículum.
I can provide references.	Puedo presentarle mis referencias.
I have a valid work permit.	Tengo permiso de trabajo.
I would be pleased to attend an interview.	Me gustaría tener una entrevista.
I will be able to work for three months/until (May).	Puedo trabajar aquí durante tres meses/hasta (mayo).

amateur	amateur; aficionada/o
certificate	certificado
college	residencia de estudiantes
company	compañía
contract	contrato
degree	título
dismissal	despido
dole	paro
employer	jefa/e
exploitation	explotación
harrassment	acoso
high school	instituto
income tax	impuesto sobre la renta
interview	entrevista
job	trabajo
job advertisement	anuncio de trabajo

job centre	INEM
job description	descripción del trabajo
qualification	cualificaciones
rate of pay	salario
reference	referencias
resignation	dimisión
resumé	currículum
salary	salario
school	escuela
specialist	especialista
university	universidad
work permit	permiso de trabajo

ON BUSINESS

Here are some key words and phrases for that quick visit or conference. For more, try one of the many phrasebooks available which specialise in business language.

LATE AFTERNOON

Don't confuse **tarde** - late, with **la tarde** - the afternoon or evening.

I'm here on business.	Estoy de viaje de negocios.
We're attending a conference/ trade fair.	Estamos asistiendo a una conferencia/feria de muestras.
Does the hotel have office facilities?	¿Dispone el hotel de servicios de oficinas?
I need to ...	Tengo que ...
send a fax/email	enviar un fax/email
make photocopies	hacer fotocopias
use a computer	usar un ordenador

I need an interpreter.	Necesito una/un intérprete.
I have an appointment with …	Tengo una cita con …
Thank you for seeing me.	Gracias por atenderme.
Let me introduce my colleague.	¿Puedo presentarle a mi colega?
It was a pleasure meeting you.	Encantada/o de conocerla/lo.
We'll be in touch.	Nos mantendremos en conctacto.
Here's my business card.	Aquí tiene mi tarjeta de visita.

ballpark figure	cifra aproximada
branch office	sucursal
client	clienta/e
colleague	colega
contract	contrato
director	director
distributor	distribuidora; distribuidor
figures	cifras
head office	oficina central
loss	pérdida
manager	encargada/o
mobile phone	teléfono móbil
modem	modem
overhead projector	aparato de transparencias
operations	operaciones
presentation	presentación
profit	beneficio
profitability	rentabilidad
projector	proyector
proposal	propuesta
sales	ventas
sales department	departamento de ventas
secretary	la/el secretaria/o
turnover	facturación

ON TOUR

We're travelling in a group.	Somos parte de un grupo.
I'm with a band/team.	Vengo con un grupo de música/equipo deportivo.
We're here for (three nights).	Nos quedaremos (tres noches).
Please talk to the ...	Por favor, hable con la/el ...
group leader	responsable del grupo
guide	guía
manager	mánager
We've lost our equipment.	Hemos perdido nuestras cosas.
We sent our gear in this ...	Hemos enviado nuestras cosas en este ...
plane	vuelo
train	tren
bus	bus
We're playing on (Saturday night).	Tocamos el (sábado por la noche).
Would you like some tickets?	¿Quieres entradas para nuestro concierto?
I'm still a groupie after all these years.	Todavía soy una/un fan después de tantos años.

band	grupo
coach	entrenadora/entrenador
equipment	equipo
manager	mánager
member	miembro
player	música/o
roadie	transportista
team	equipo
van	furgoneta

FILM & TV

We're on location.	Estamos rodando los exteriores.
We're filming here for (six) days.	Vamos a rodar aquí durante (seis) días.
Who should we ask for permission to film here?	¿A quién tenemos que pedirle permiso para rodar aquí?
May we film here?	¿Podemos rodar aquí?

We're making a …	Estamos haciendo …
documentary	un documental
film	una película
series	una serie de televisión

actor	la actriz/el actor
camera operator	la operadora/el operador
continuity	la secretaria/el secretario
director	la directora/el director
editor	la editora/el editor
presenter	la presentadora/el presentador
producer	la productora/el productor
scriptwriter	la/el guionista

camera	la cámara
editing suite	control de edición
lights	las luces
make-up	el maquillaje
prop	el decorado
rushes	las primeras pruebas
script	el guión
sound	el sonido
stunt	la escena peligrosa
van	la caravana
wardrobe	el vestuario

SPECIFIC NEEDS

THEY MAY SAY …

¡Acción!
 Action!

¡Estamos rodando!
 We're filming!

¡Rodando!
 Rolling!

¡Toma uno!
 Take One!

¡Corten!
 Cut!

PILGRIMAGE & RELIGION

For a list of religions, see page 49.

Is there a church nearby?	¿Hay alguna iglesia aquí cerca?
Where can I pray/worship?	¿Dónde puedo rezar?
Can I receive communion here?	¿Puedo recibir la comunión aquí?
When are services held?	¿Cuándo se celebran los oficios?
When is the church/cathedral open?	¿A qué hora abre la iglesia/catedral?
Can I attend this service?	¿Puedo asistir a este oficio?
I'm walking the Camino de Santiago.	Estoy haciendo el Camino de Santiago.

baptism	bautizo	synagogue	sinagoga
bible	la Biblia	temple	templo
candle	vela	wedding	boda
church	iglesia	worship	adoración
communion	comunión		
confession	confesión		
convent	convento		
funeral	funeral		
God	Dios		
grave	tumba		
mass	misa		
monastery	monasterio		
monk	monje		
mosque	mezquita		
nun	monja		
Pope	Papa		
prayer	oración		
prayer book	devocionario		
priest	sacerdote		
service	oficio		
shrine	capilla (in a church); altar		

SPECIFIC NEEDS

---

monday

Unlike English, Spanish does not use capital letters for languages, months or days of the week.

lunes el 5 de abril
Monday the 5th of April

So Italian, the language, is **italiano** but note, an Italian is **una/un Italiana/o.**

Tracing Roots & History

My family/ancestors came from this area.	Mi familia/mis antepasados viene/n de esta zona.
Is there anyone here by the name of ...?	¿Hay alguien aquí que se llama ...?
I have a relative who was in the International Brigade.	Tengo un pariente que estuvo en las brigadas Internacionales
I think s/he fought/died near here.	Creo que luchó/murió cerca de aquí.
Where is the cemetery?	¿Dónde está el cementerio?
In which cemetery can I find ...?	¿En qué cementerio puedo encontrar ...?

SPECIFIC NEEDS

TALK THROUGH YOUR ELBOWS

goose pimples	**carne de gallina** - *hen's flesh*
to rain cats and dogs	**llover a cántaros** *- to rain jugs/pitchers*
he's no oil painting	**no es ningún Adonis** *- He's no Adonis*
to put one's foot in it	**meter la pata** - *- to put the paw in*
to eat like a horse	**comer como un sabañón** *- to eat like a chilblain!*
you can't teach an old dog new tricks	**loro viejo no aprende a hablar** *- an old parrot doesn't learn to talk*
dirty old man	**viejo verde** - *green old man*
to blow one's own trumpet	**echarse flores** *- throw flowers to oneself*
it cost an arm and a leg	**costó un ojo de la cara** *- it cost an eye from my face*
never mind the quality, feel the width	**burro grande, ande o no ande** *- it's a big donkey, whether it can walk or not is another question*
to pull someone's leg	**tomarle el pelo a alguien** *- to pull someone's hair*
she can talk the hind legs off a donkey	**habla por los codos** *- she talks through her elbows*
I can't stand her	**¡No la puedo ver ni en pintura!** *- I can't even look at a painting of her!*
He walks around like he owns the place	**anda como Pedro por su casa** *- he walks around like Peter in his house*

TIME & DATES

It may take travellers some time to adjust to the Spanish timetable. Work starts in the morning around 9 am and goes through until about 2 pm. After a long lunch break, work resumes about 5 pm and finishes around 8. Between 8 and 10 people tend to spend time with their family and friends before their evening meal. People go out after 10 more than in most other countries, especially at weekends.

TELLING THE TIME

What time is it?	¿Qué hora es?
It's one o'clock.	Es la una.
It's (two o'clock).	Son las (dos).
It's five past six.	Son las seis y cinco.
It's quarter to four.	Son las cuatro menos cuarto.
It's half past eight.	Son las ocho y media.
It's about eleven.	Son las once.

in the early morning (1–6am)	de la madrugada
in the morning (6am–1pm)	de la mañana
at midday (12–3pm)	del mediodía
in the afternoon (3–8pm)	de la tarde
in the evening (9pm–1am)	de la noche

DAYS

Monday	lunes	Friday	viernes
Tuesday	martes	Saturday	sábado
Wednesday	miércoles	Sunday	domingo
Thursday	jueves		

MONTHS

January	enero
February	febrero
March	marzo
April	abril
May	mayo
June	junio
July	julio
August	agosto
September	setiembre; septiembre
October	octubre
November	noviembre
December	diciembre

MORE ABBREVIATIONS

A.C or a.de J.C.	BC
AVE	high-speed railway line
Ayto	Town Hall
C/Av., Avda./Pza.	St, Rd/Ave/Square
UE	EU
D.C. or d.de J.C.	AD
EE.UU.	USA
FEVE	north-coast railway company
h.	o'clock
NN.UU.	UN
N./S.	Nth/Sth
RENFE	Spanish national railway
G.B./R.U.	UK
SIDA	AIDS
Talgo	inter-city train
TIVE	youth travel organisation

TIME & DATES

DATES

Dates are expressed by cardinal numbers (two of May', '23 July', etc), except for the first day of the month which uses the ordinal number: '1st of April'.

What's the date today?	¿Qué día es hoy?
It's 26 April.	Es el veintiséis de abril.
It's 3 August.	Es el tres de agosto.
It's the 1st of October.	Es el primero de octubre.

PRESENT

today	hoy
this morning	esta mañana; madrugada
this afternoon	esta tarde
tonight	esta noche
this week	esta semana
this month	este mes
this year	este año
now	ahora
right now	en este momento

ADVERBS

The equivalent of -*ly* (to create an adverb) is -**mente**:

alegre (happy)

becomes

alegremente (happily)

PAST

yesterday	ayer
day before yesterday	anteayer
yesterday morning	ayer por la mañana/madrugada
yesterday afternoon/night	ayer por la tarde/noche
last night	anoche
last week	la semana pasada
last month	el mes pasado
last year	el año pasado
(half an hour) ago	hace media hora
(three) days ago	hace (tres) días
(five) years ago	hace (cinco) años
a while ago	hace un rato
since (May)	desde (mayo)

FUTURE

tomorrow	mañana
day after tomorrow	pasado mañana
tomorrow morning	mañana por la mañana
tomorrow afternoon/ evening	mañana por la tarde/ noche
next week	la semana que viene
next month	el mes que viene
next year	el año que viene
in (five) minutes	dentro de (cinco) minutos
in (six) days	dentro de (seis) días
within an hour/month	dentro de una hora/un mes
until (June)	hasta (junio)

DURING THE DAY

It's early.	Es temprano.
It's late.	Es tarde.
afternoon (3–8 pm)	de la tarde
evening (9 pm–1 am)	de la noche
lunchtime	hora de comer
midnight	medianoche
morning (6 am–1 pm)	de la mañana
noon	mediodía
sunset	puesta del sol; atardecer
sunrise	amanecer

NUMBERS & AMOUNTS

CARDINAL NUMBERS

0	cero	30	treinta
1	una; uno	31	treinta y uno
2	dos	32	treinta y dos
3	tres	40	cuarenta
4	cuatro	41	cuarenta y uno
5	cinco	50	cincuenta
6	seis	51	cincuenta y uno
7	siete	60	sesenta
8	ocho	70	setenta
9	nueve	80	ochenta
10	diez	90	noventa
11	once	100	cien/ciento
12	doce	110	ciento diez
13	trece	200	doscientos
14	catorce	300	trescientos
15	quince	400	cuatrocientos
16	dieciséis	500	quinientos
17	diecisiete	600	seiscientos
18	dieciocho	700	setecientos
19	diecinueve	800	ochocientos
20	veinte	900	novecientos
21	veintiuno	1000	mil
22	veintidós	2000	dos mil
23	veintitrés	5000	cinco mil
24	veinticuatro	2200	dos mil doscientos

one million	un millón
48	cuarenta y ocho
157	ciento cincuenta y siete
1240	mil doscientos cuarenta
1999	mil novecientos noventa y nueve
14800	catorce mil ochocientos

NUMBERS & AMOUNTS

ORDINAL NUMBERS

1st	primera/o (1r)	6th	sexta/o
2nd	segunda/o	7th	séptima/o
3rd	tercera/o	8th	octava/o
4th	cuarta/o	9th	novena/o
5th	quinta/o	10th	décima/o

FRACTIONS

a quarter	un cuarto	three-quarters	tres cuartos
a third	un tercio	all	todo
half	media/o	none	nada

USEFUL WORDS

a little (amount)	un poquito
double	(el) doble
a dozen	una docena
Enough!	¡Basta!
few	(unas) pocas/(unos) pocos
less	menos
many	muchas/os
more	más
once	una vez
a pair	un par
percent	por ciento
some	algunas/os
too much	demasiado
twice	dos veces

BASQUE

INTRODUCTION

No one quite knows the origin of Basque but that has not stopped some eccentrics from declaring that it is related to the Sioux language, to Japanese, even to the language of the Atlanteans. The most interesting, and plausible, theory is that Basque is the lone survivor of a family of languages which extended across Europe but which were ultimately wiped out and supplanted by such Indo-European invaders as the Celts, Germanic tribes and the Romans. There are those who try to link extinct languages such as those of the Etruscans and Picts to this supposedly defunct language family. Even in recent times, there have been linguists who have called this ancient family of languages 'Basque-Caucasian' implying that Basque may be ultimately related, albeit distantly so, to such languages as Georgian or Chechen. Nevertheless, the ultimate answer to the enigma of where the Basque language actually came from remains lost in the distant hazes of Europe's prehistoric past.

Over the past millennia, Basque has intermingled with the languages of its invaders and neighbours and this is amply reflected in its vocabulary. The Basque number system, like that of the Celts, is based on scores and even the name for 20, **hogei**, is similar to the Welsh word for 20, *ugain*. Basque borrowed words directly from Latin and, unlike the Romance languages, it has kept these words more or less as they were. In more recent times Basque has borrowed heavily from the Gascon dialect of Provençal, Spanish, French, and now even English.

Basque is spoken by about 800,000 people throughout the seven provinces which are divided into three basic political entities: The Basque Autonomous Community (BAC), Navarre, and Iparralde (aka the French Basque Country). Though the only communities where Basque is primarily spoken are smaller towns, it is on the increase in the larger cities, especially among the young people.

BASQUE

Centuries of neglect, marginalization, combined with two centuries of French republicanism and 40 years of Spanish fascism pushed Basque to the brink of extinction. Nevertheless, the situation has improved greatly since it was declared co-official with Spanish in 1979 in the BAC and Navarre (Basque still lacks official recognition of any kind in France). Today, most of the children in the BAC are now being taught in Basque, there is a Basque TV channel, and there are dozens of local municipal channels which feature it prominently or exclusively. There are Basque-language rock bands, rap singers, and even some popular software packages have Basque versions. Basque is going from strength to strength and the fruits of a generation educated in Basque, the first in history, will be readily apparent in 20 years.

Those foreigners who at least make an attempt to try to speak it are lionized and even sometimes invited for a drink. Speaking Spanish in the Basque-speaking towns might be expected from a foreigner but is not as warmly received as someone struggling to communicate something in one of the most ancient languages of Europe. Should you wish to go beyond this phrasebook there is the *Morris Pocket English-Basque Basque-English* dictionary and the *Morris Advanced English-Basque Basque-English* dictionary published by the Klaudio Harluxet Fundazioa. To learn the grammar, *Colloquial Basque* by Alan King, published by Routledge would be an excellent start.

PRONUNCIATION

Basque pronunciation doesn't pose many problems for the English speaker if she/he can roll their 'r's fairly well. The stress in Basque is generally on the second-last syllable. Vowels are pronounced as in Spanish (see page 13). Below are letters which, from the English-speaker's point of view, may often be pronounced differently in Basque.

g   always hard like the 'g' in 'get' or 'Gary'
h   silent in the Spanish Basque Country and pronounced in the French Basque Country

j	generally pronounced as 'y'. This pronunciation is recommended by the Royal Academy of the Basque Language but there are ample stretches of the Basque Country, centered around Donostia-San Sebastian, where it is pronounced as in Spanish, ie a guttural sound similar to 'ch' in Scottish 'loch' or German 'nacht'.
r	almost like 'd'; as in the American pronunciation of words as 'ghetto' or 'butter'
rr	a rolled 'r' as in Spanish or Scottish
x	mostly pronounced as 'sh' as in 'ship'
tx	pronounced as 'ch' as in 'church'.
ts	pronounced more or less like a soft 'ch', rendered 'chy' in this phrasebook. Even Basque-speakers on the coast mix it up with 'tx'.
tz	as in 'tz' in 'Blitz' or 'Ritz'
z	as in the 'ss' in 'Mississippi'

BASQUE

GRAMMATICAL FEATURES

Even if your knowledge of Spanish grammar is sketchy at best, it doesn't take a PhD in linguistics to notice that Basque grammar is radically different from the other languages spoken in Spain. It's impossible to cover Basque grammar completely in only a few pages so only its more important characteristics will be dealt with in the following pages.

Nouns

Basque has no gender. One of the essential aspects of Basque is its use of suffixes. 'The' may be written as -a or in the plural, -ak. Bear in mind, however, that -a or -ak don't always mean 'the'. 'A(n)' is shown by placing bat after the noun.

bide	bidea	bideak	bide bat
road	the road	the roads	a road

ending	singular	plural	personal
the	-a	-ak	
doer (ergative)	-ak	-ek	-(e)k*
possessive	-aren	-en	-(r)en**
to	-ari	-ei	-(r)i
because of	-arengatik	-engatik	-(r)engatik
with	-arekin	-ekin	-(r)ekin
for	-arentzat	-entzat	-(r)entzat
by, with	-az	-ez	-(e)z*

* if the name of the person ends in a vowel, use just k or z
** if the name of the person ends in a vowel, use the r. If it ends with a consonant, leave the r out.

BASQUE

singular	plural
gizon	gizonak
man	men
gizonaren kasetea	gizonen kasetea
the man's cassette	the men's cassette
gizonari	gizonei
to the man	to the men
gizonarengatik	gizonengatik
because of the man	because of the men
gizonarekin	gizonekin
with the man	with the men

The ergative case is unique among Western European languages. Essentially, the subject of a transitive verb takes the ergative case. In simple terms, that means that the doer gets a -( ) stuck on it.

Frank Sinatrak / Supermanek kantatzen du
Frank Sinatra / Superman sings

King Kongek Bambi jan zuen
King Kong ate Bambi

ending	singular	plural	place (proper nouns)
in, on, at	-(e)an*	-etan	-(e)n*
from	-tik	-etatik	-(e)tik*
to	-(e)ra*	-etara	-(e)ra*
towards	-(e)rantz*	-etarantz	-(e)rantz*
up to	-(e)raino*	-etaraino	-(e)raino*
of	-ko	-etako	-(e)ko*
any	-(r)ik*		

* If a noun ends in a consonant, use the e. Otherwise, leave it out.
** If a noun ends in a vowel, use the r. Otherwise, leave it out.

BASQUE

	singular	plural
herri town	herrian in the town	herrietan in the towns
	herritik from the town	herrietatik from the towns
haran valley	haranean in the valley	haranetan in the valleys
	haranera to the valley	haranetara to the valleys

Australiako jendea	New Yorken	whiskyrik ez
people of Australia	in New York	not any whisky

Adjectives

The adjective usually follows the noun. The most important exceptions are beste 'other' and azken 'last'.

bide	bide luze	bide luzea	bide luzeak
road	long road	the long road	the long roads

The comparative of an adjective is formed by adding the ending -ago. Notice below that word order is quite different in Basque.

elurra baino zuriago   'whiter than snow'
(lit. 'snow than whiter')

The superlative is formed by adding the ending -en.

hotz   'cold'   hotzen(a)   '(the) coldest'

BASQUE

Personal Pronouns

	absolutive	ergative	possessive		dative (to)	
I/me	ni	nik	my	nire	to me	niri
you (sg,inf)	hi	hik	your	hire	to you	hiri
you (sg,pol)	zu	zuk	your	zure	to you	zuri
s/he,her him, it	bera	berak	her/his its	haren	to her/ him/it	hari
we, us	gu	guk	our	gure	to us	guri
you (pl)	zuek	zuek	your	zuen	to you	zuei
they/them	beraiek	beraiek	their	haien	to them	haiei

Demonstratives

this	hau
these	hauek
that	hori
those	horiek
that (yonder/further away)	hura
those (yonder/further away)	haiek

These are placed after the noun!

kasete hau	this cassette
kasete eder hau	this beautiful cassette
kasete hauek	these cassettes
kasete eder hauek	these beautiful cassettes

Verbs

As Basque verbs are quite complex, the formation of only the most common verb tenses is shown. All Basque verbs are divided into two categories:

1. intransitive verbs (those that don't take objects) eg 'to come' is intransitive because you can't 'come' someone or something.

2. transitive verbs (those that take objects) eg 'to eat' is transitive because you can 'eat' something.

Below are the forms for izan, 'to be'. We will later see why these are so important if one wishes to learn the fundamentals of Basque quickly.

To Be (present)

Ni naiz	I am	Gu gara	we are
Hi haiz (inf)	you are	Zuek zarete (pl)	you are
Zu zara (pol)	you are		
Bera da	s/he is	Haiek dira	they are

To Be (past)

Ni nintzen	I was	Gu ginen	we were
Hi hintzen (inf)	you were	Zuek zineten (pl)	you were
Zu zinen (pol)	you were		
Bera zen	s/he was	Haiek ziren	they were

Below are some basic sentences. Notice that the verb appears at the end and pronouns may be dropped.

Ni Jon naiz.	I am Jon.
Zu Jane zara.	You are Jane.
Irakaslea nintzen.	I was a teacher.
Irakaslea zinen.	You were a teacher.

Below is the conjugation of ukan, the verb for 'have'. Notice that all the subjects have -k stuck on to them.

To Have (present)

Nik dut	I have	Guk dugu	we have
Hik duk (m)	you have*	Zuek duzue (pl)	you have**
Hik dun (f)	you have		
Zuk duzu (pol)	you have		
Berak du	s/he has, it has	Beraiek dute	they have

To Have (past)

Nik nuen	I had	Guk genuen	we had
Hik huen (inf)	you had	Zuek zenuten (pl)	you had
Zuk zenuen (pol)	you had		
Berak zuen	s/he had, it had	Beraiek zuten	they had

Note: in the present, hik duk is used by men, hik dun by women
*Hi (ee) can be used with friends
**Zuek is the plural you. It is like the American 'you guys'

Zuk liburu bat duzu.	You have a book.
Zuk liburu bat zenuen.	You had a book.

The present tense is formed by adding -tzen or -ten to the basic form of the verb, depending on the class of verb, given below. Then it is combined with izan (used as an auxiliary with intransitive verbs) or ukan (used as an auxiliary with intransitive verbs). This makes conjugation of Basque a breeze because 99% of all the verbs are conjugated in this way.

ateratzen naiz	I go out
ateratzen dira	they go out
ateratzen gara	we go out
beti ateratzen zara	you always go out

ateratzen dut	I take it out
ateratzen dute	they take it out
ateratzen dugu	we take it out

Some of the very basic rules for the present tense are:

- If the verb ends in a vowel or -l, add -tzen

hil	hiltzen	to die
atera	ateratzen	to take out

- If the verb ends in -tu/-du, replace them with -tzen

bukatu	finish
nik hori bukatzen dut	I finish that (I that finish-ing have)

- If the verb ends in -si or -zi, replace the -i with -ten

ikusi	see
nik hori ikusten dut	I see that (I that see-ing have)

- If the verb ends in -n, replace it with -ten

egin	egin
nik hori egiten dut	I see that (I that do-ing have)

The future is made by adding -ko or, after verbs ending in 'n', -go.

atera	go out
aterako naiz	I will go out
aterako dira	they will go out
egin	do
egingo dut	I will do
egingo dute	they will do

The perfect tense (eg I have done, I have spoken) is made by using the basic form of the verb.

atera naiz	I have gone out
atera dira	They have gone out
atera dut	I have taken out
atera dute	They have taken out

BASQUE

Below you can see how many possibilities there are by combining izan and ukan.

Ni atera naiz	I have gone out
Ni ateratzen naiz	I go out
Ni aterako naiz	I will go out
Nik atera dut	I have taken it out
Nik ateratzen dut	I take it out
Nik aterako dut	I will take it out
Ni atera nintzen	I went out
Ni ateratzen nintzen	I was going out
Ni aterako nintzen	I would have gone out
Nik atera nuen	I took it out
Nik ateratzen nuen	I was taking it out
Nik aterako nuen	I would have taken it out

Negation

The negative word ez is placed after the subject. That ez acts as a magnet and pulls the auxiliary verb, ie the form of ukan or izan, up to the front.

Ni Johnny naiz.	I am Johnny.
Ni ez naiz Johnny.	I am not Johnny.
Txokolatea jaten dut.	I eat chocolate.
Ez dut txokolaterik jaten.	I don't eat chocolate.

BASQUE

DID YOU KNOW ...	Thursday - **osteguna** – is named after Ortzi or Urtzi who was the Basque god of the heavens.

GREETINGS & CIVILITIES

Hi!	Kaixo!
Good morning.	Egun on.
Good afternoon.	Arratsalde on.
Good evening.	Arratsalde on.
Good night.	Gabon.
How are you?	Zer moduz?
What's up?	Zer berri?
Fine and you?	Ongi, eta zu?
Fine, thank you.	Ongi, eskerrik asko.
Excuse me.	Barkatu.
Please.	Mesedez.
Thank you.	Eskerrik asko.
You're welcome.	Ez horregatik.

Goodbyes

Goodbye.	Agur.
See you later.	Gero arte.
Take care.	Ondo ibili.

Forms of Address

Mr Agirre	Agirre jauna
Mrs Agirre	Agirre andrea
Hey!	Aizu!

BASQUE

NO GENDER

Remember that Basque has no grammatical gender, unlike Spanish, Catalan and Galician.

Language Difficulties

Do you speak English?	Ingelesez ba al dakizu?
I know a little Basque.	Euskara apur bat badakit.
I don't understand.	Ez dut ulertzen.
Could you speak more slowly please?	Polikiago hitz egingo al duzu?
Could you write that down please?	Idatziko al didazu hori, mesedez?
Could you speak in Castillian please?	Erdaraz egingo al didazu, mesedez?

How do you say ... ? Nola esaten da ... ?
How do you say that in Basque? Nola esaten da hori euskaraz?

UNIQUE BASQUE EXPRESSIONS

Gora gu 'ta gutarrak!	Hurray for us!
Euskal Herrian beti jai	The Basque Country's always partying
Gero arte Bonaparte	See you later alligator
Agur Ben Hur	In a while, crocodile

BASQUE

SMALL TALK
Meeting People

What's your name?	Zer izen duzu?
My name's John.	John dut izena.
I'd like to introduce you to ...	... aurkeztu nahi nizuke
I'm pleased to meet you.	Pozgarria zait zu ezagutzea.
I'm here on holidays; business; studying.	Oporretan; negozietan; ikasten; nago hemen.
How long have you been here?	Noiztik zaude hemen?
I've been here (three days).	(Hiru egun) dira hemen nagoela.
How long are you here for?	Noiz arte egon behar duzu hemen?
We're here for (two weeks).	(Bi aste) egongo gara hemen.
Where are you from?	Nongoa zara?
I'm from ...	... naiz.
Australia	Australiakoa
England	Ingalaterrakoa
Ireland	Irlandakoa

New Zealand	Zeelanda Berrikoa
Canada	Kanadakoa
Scotland	Eskoziakoa
the USA	Estatu Batuetakoa
Wales	Galeskoa

Where do you live?	Non bizi zara?
I live in Darwin.	Darwin-en bizi naiz.

Occupations

What do you do?	Zertan aritzen zara?

I'm a(n) ...	... naiz.
artist	artista
business person	enpresaria
doctor	medikua
engineer	injinerua
journalist	kazetaria
lawyer	abokatua
musician	musikaria
nurse	erizaina
office worker	bulegaria
secretary	idazkaria
student	ikaslea
waiter	kamareroa
retired	erretiratua
unemployed	langabea

Family

Are you married?	Ezkondua al zara?
I'm single	Ezkongabea naiz.

I'm ...	... naiz.
married	ezkondua
separated	banatua
a widow/widower	alarguna

BASQUE

BASQUE

I have a partner.	Badut laguna.
Do you have a girlfriend/ boyfriend?	Andregairik/senargairik ba al duzu?
How many children do you have?	Zenbat seme-alaba dituzu?

Interests

What do you like doing?	Zer egitea gustatzen zaizu?
What do you do in your spare time?	Zer egiten duzu libre zaudenean?
I like swimming and going to the cinema.	Igerian egitea eta zinemera joatea gustatzen zait.
I don't like cooking.	Ez zait sukaldean aritzea atsegin.
I don't like working.	Ez naiz lanzalea.

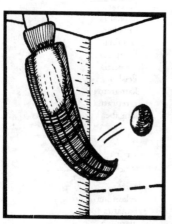

SPORT

Besides cooking, Basques also excel in sport. Of course, soccer is king, and other sports such as basketball and rugby are also widely played. Basque handball, aka pilota or pelota, is quite famous around the world. A variant of it, jai-alai is well known in the United States. Basques also take to folk sports such as wood chopping, stone lifting, and ox-drawn stone dragging. These sports all involve heavy betting.

Do you like sport?	Kirolak atsegin dituzu?
Yes, very much.	Bai, oso.
Not, not at all.	Ez, batere ez.

Do you feel like going for a swim?	Igerian egin nahi al duzu?
Do you want to go hiking this weekend?	Mendira joan nahi al duzu asteburu honetan?
Would you like to go to a football match?	Futbol-partidu batera joan nahi al duzu?
Would you like to see a wood-chopping contest?	Aizkol-apustu bat ikusi nahi al duzu?

Yes, that'd be great!	Bai horixe!
Not at the moment, thanks.	Orain ez, eskerrik asko.
I'm sorry, I can't.	Barkatu, baina ezin dut.
Hurray for Real!	Aupa Erreala!
Hurray for Athletic!	Aupa Athletic!

BASQUE

GETTING AROUND
Finding Your Way

Excuse me, can you help me please?	Barkatu, lagunduko al didazu, mesedez?
How do I get to ...?	Nondik joaten da ...-ra?

Where is the ...?	Non dago ...?
bus station	autobus-geltokia
city centre	hiri-erdia
old part of town	alde zaharra
tourist information office	turismo-bulegoa
train station	tren-geltokia

avenue	etorbidea
street	kalea
square	plaza; enparantza

Directions

Where's the toilet, please?	Komuna non dago?
I don't know.	Ez dakit.

at the end	korridorearen muturrean
on the left	ezkerrean
on the right	eskubian
straight on	zuzen/zuzenean

Bus

Does this bus go to the ...?	Autobus hau ba al doa ...?
beach	hondartzara
city centre	hiri-erdira
station	geltokira

SIGNS	
IRTEERA	EXIT
NORAKOA	DESTINATION
LINEA	LINE

Do you stop at ...?	... (e)n gelditzen al zara?
Where do I change for ...?	Non aldatu behar dut ... ra joateko?
Could you let me know when we get to ...?	Abisatuko al didazu ... ...(e)ra iritsitakoan?

Taxi

Are you free?	Libre al zaude?
Could you take me to ...?	... eramango al nauzu?
this address	helbide honetara
the airport	aireportura
the city centre	hiri-erdira
the railway station	tren-geltokira

BASQUE

How much does it cost to get to ...?	Zenbat kostatzen da .... ra joatea?
Here is fine, thank you.	Hemen ondo da, eskerrik asko.
How much do I owe you?	Zenbat zor dizut?

Telephoning

Hello. (making a call)	Aizu?
Hello. (answering a call)	Bai, esan?
Could I speak to Jon?	Jon hor al dago?
Who's calling?	Noren partez?
It's ...	... naiz.
Just a minute, I'll put (him) on.	Itxaron, oraintxe jarriko da.
I'm sorry (he's) not here just now.	Barkatu, baina une honetan ez dago.
What time will he be back	Zer ordutan itzuliko da?
Can I take a message?	Abisuren bat utzi nahi al diozu?
Yes, please tell (him) I called.	Bai, esaiozu nik deitu diodala.
No, thanks, I'll call back later.	Ez, eskerrik asko, gero deituko diot.

BASQUE

ACCOMMODATION

| Is there a campsite/hotel near here? | Ba al da kanpinik/hotelik hemen inguruan? |

SIGNS	
KANPINA	CAMPING GROUND
GAZTEEN OSTATUA	YOUTH HOSTEL
PENTSIOA	GUESTHOUSE
HOSTALA	BUDGET HOTEL
HOTELA	HOTEL

BASQUE

Do you have any rooms available?	Ba al duzu gela librerik?
Sorry, we're full.	Barkatu, baina dena beteta dugu.

I'd like ...	... nahi dut.
a single room	batentzako gela
a double room	birentzako gela

I want a room with ...	... duen gela nahi dut.
a bathroom	bainugela bat
a double bed	ohe bikoitza
a shower	dutxa

How much is it per night; per person?	Zenbat da gau; pertsona bakoitzeko?
Does it include breakfast?	Gosaria barne al da?
Are there any cheaper rooms?	Ba al dago gela merkeagorik?
It's fine, I'll take it.	Ederki, hartu egingo dut.
How many nights will you be staying for?	Zenbat gau egongo zara?
I'm going to stay for one week.	Astebete egongo naiz.
The key for room (35) please.	(35) garren gelako giltza, mesedez.
I don't like this room.	Gela hau ez dut atsegin.

It's ...	... da.
too small	txikiegia
noisy	zaratatsuegia
too dark	ilunegia
cold	hotzegia

I am/We are leaving now.	Banoa/Bagoaz.
I'd like to pay the bill.	Kontua ordaindu nahi dut.
Can I leave my backpack at reception until tonight?	Motxila harreran uzterik ba al dago gaur gauera arte?
Please, call a taxi for me.	Mesedez, dei egiozu taxi bati.

IN THE COUNTRY
Camping

SIGN	
KANPATZEA DEBEKATUTA	NO CAMPING

Can I camp here?	Ba al daukat hemen kanpatzerik?
Is there a campsite nearby?	Ba al dago kanpinik hemen inguruan?

At the Beach
Is it safe to swim?	Ba al dago igerian egiterik?

coast	kostaldea	sunglasses	eguzkitako
rock	harkaitza		betaurrekoak
sea	itsasoa	surfboard	surf-taula
seaside	itsasaldea	surfer	surflaria
sunblock	eguzkitara ko krema	wave	olatua

BASQUE

GRAFFITI ON THE WALLS	
Presoak kaleral	Free the prisoners!
... askatul	Free ....!
Askatasunal	Freedom!
Gora ...I	Long Live (the) ...!
... herria zurekinl	..., the people are with you!
Herriak ez du barkatuko	The people shall never forgive
Amnistia Osoal	Total Amnesty!
Intsumisioal	No Military Service!
... kanporal	... go home!
Nuklearrik ezl	No nukes!

FOOD

The Basque Country has a reputation for having some of the best food in the world. There are high-class restaurants, smaller restaurants, bars that serve food and cider houses (**sagardotegi**). The coast, of course, is best known for its seafood. Even English-speakers who detest fish in their own countries love the way the Basques cook fish.

In the Restaurant

Waiter!	Aizu!
A little bread, please.	Ogi pixka bat, mesedez.
A bottle of wine.	Botila bat ardoa.

Snacks

barazkiak	vegetables
entsalada	salad
errusiar entsalada	potato and mayonnaise salad
esparragoak	asparagus
frijituak	fritters
patata frijituak	chips (French fries)
piper muturtxodunak bakailuz beteak	fine red pimento peppers stuffed with cod

Fish

Below are some of the best fish you've ever had. Enjoy!

bakailaoa	cod	xipiroiak	squid
legatza	hake	xapoa	angler
txirlak	clams		
kakotxak	area around the neck of the fish, considered to be the best part of the fish		

Meat

eskalopea	breaded fillet	txuleta	steak
saiheskiak	ribs	xerra	chop

Desserts

flana	crème caramel
etxeko kopa	ice cream dessert
gazta	cheese
izozkia	ice cream
mamia	sheep's milk curd (don't be put off by the name, it's great)
menbriluaka	quince jelly
natilak	custard
trufa tarta	chocolate truffles cake
whisky tarta	whiskey-flavoured ice cream cake

At the Bar

I'd like a ...	... nahi nuke.
beer	garagardoa
beer (draught)	kaina bat
red wine	ardo beltza
rosé wine	ardo gorria
plain coffee	kafe hutsa
coffee with a dash of milk	kafe ebakia
coffee and milk	kafesnea
water	ura

SHOPPING

Where can I buy ...?	Non eros nezake ...?
Where is the nearest ...?	Non dago ... hurbilena?
bookshop	liburutegirik
camera shop	argazki-dendarik
department store	erostetxerik
drycleaner's	tindategirik
greengrocer's	frutadendarik
market	merkaturik
newsagency	kioskorik
supermarket	supermerkaturik
tobacconist	estankorik
travel agency	bidai-agentziarik

BASQUE

BASQUE

Making a Purchase

I'd like to buy ...	... erosi nahi nuke.
How much is this?	Hau zenbat da?
Could you write the price down?	Apuntatuko al didazu prezioa?
Can I look at it?	Begiratuko al diot?
I don't like it.	Ez zait gustatzen.
Do you have anything cheaper?	Ezer merkeagorik al duzu?
I'll buy it.	Hartuko dut.
Do you accept credit cards?	Kreditu-txartelik onartzen al duzu?
Can I have a receipt?	Errezibua emango al didazu?
I'm just looking.	Begira nago bakarrik.

Toiletries

comb	orrazia
condoms	kondoiak
deodorant	desodorantea
laxative	libragarria
razor	labaina
sanitary napkins	konpresak
shampoo	xanpua
shaving cream	bizar-krema
soap	xaboia
sunblock	eguzkitarako krema
talcum	talko
tampons	tanpoiak
tissues	musuzapiak
toilet paper	komunerako papera
toothbrush	hortzetako zepilua
toothpaste	hortzak garbitzeko pasta

THEY MAY SAY ..

Zer nahi duzu?
Can I help you?

Besterik?
Will that be all?

Zenbat nahi duzu?
How much/many do you want?

Stationery & Publications

Do you sell any ...?   ... saltzen al duzu?
  envelopes   sobrerik
  magazines   aldizkaririk
  maps   maparik
  newspapers   egunkaririk
  newspapers in English   ingelesezko egunkaririk
  pens (ballpoint)   boligraforik
  postcards   postalik

BASQUE SIGNS

EDARITEGIA	BAR
EMAN BIDEA	YIELD (GIVE WAY)
ERTZAINTZA	BASQUE POLICE
IRTEERA	EXIT
KONTUZI	CAUTION!
LURSAIL JABEDUNA	PRIVATE PROPERTY
SARRERA	ENTRANCE
SARTZEA DEBEKATURIK	NO ENTRY
UDALTZAINGOA	MUNICIPAL POLICE

Looking for that town on the map and can't find it?
Maybe the Spanish was painted out or perhaps
you have an old map with the old, now unofficial
Spanish name. Here's some help.

Arrasate	Mondragon
Bilbo	Bilbao
Donestebe	Santesban
Donostia	San Sebastian
Hondarribia	Fuenterrabia
Iruñea (or Iruña)	Pamplona
Lizarra	Estella
Soraluze	Placencia de las Armas

BASQUE

TIME, DATES & NUMBERS
Telling the Time

What time is it?	Zer ordu da?
It's one o'clock.	Ordu bata da.
It's two o'clock.	Ordu biak dira.
It's three o'clock.	Hirurak dira.
It's four o'clock.	Laurak dira.

It's ...	... dira.
half past three.	Hiru t'erdiak
a quarter to four.	Laurak laurden gutxi
a quarter past five.	Bostak eta laurden

BASQUE

FOLKLORE & FESTIVALS

Aberri Eguna (Day of the Basque Homeland) coincides with Easter & has heavy political overtones. The **San Fermin** festival in Pamplona, July 7, is world famous.

Other important dates in the Basque calendar are:

San Sebastian Eguna (St. Sebastian Day, January 20 in Donostia-San Sebastian)

Ihauteriak (Carnaval – February). The most famous are in Tolosa, Azpeitia, and Lantz

San Fermin (July 7, in Pamplona)

Amabirjina Zuria (Vitoria-Gasteiz (August 4-9)

Aste Nagusia (in Donostia-San Sebastian, during the week which includes August 15)

Aste Nagusia (in Bilbao, following the Aste Nagusia in Donostia)

today	gaur
yesterday	atzo
the day before yesterday	herenegun
tomorrow	bihar
the day after tomorrow	etzi

Days of the Week

Monday	astelehena (lit. week first)
Tuesday	asteartea (lit. week middle)
Wednesday	asteazkena (lit. week-end)
Thursday	osteguna (lit. Ortzi's day - see pg 222)
Friday	ostirala
Saturday	larunbata
Sunday	igandea (lit. resurrection)

BASQUE

FOLKLORE & FESTIVALS

Every town & village also has its own patron saint's day celebrated with festivities, fairs, or in the case of the very smallest places, town picnics or **erromeriak**. The better known festivals include **San Roke** festival in Gernika (August 16), **San Antolin Festival** in Lekeitio (Sept. 2), **San Inazio** in Azpeitia (July 31), **Our Lady of Guadalupe** in Hondarribia (Sept. 9), and the very folk-loric **Basque Festival** in Zarautz (Sept. 9).

The Basque Country is well-known for its **txistu** flutes which are as sweet sounding as they are austere. Basque music is also characterized by **trikitixa** accordion music, played at every festival and accompanied by vigorous dances such as the **zortziko** and the **arin-arin**.

Even though you will understand very little, if anything, it is interesting to see a **bertsolari** in action. A **bertsolari** ad-libs poetry, complete with rhyme and meter, to a particular tune.

In Biscay, the names of the week are different: astelehena, martitzena (Mars' day), eguastena, eguena, barikoa (lit: without day, meatless), zapatua, domeka (lit. Lord's day).

Months

January	urtarrila (year month)
February	otsaila (wolf month)
March	martxoa
April	apirila
May	maiatza
June	ekaina (storm month)
July	uztaila (crop month)
August	abuztua
September	iraila (fern month)
October	urria (scarcity)
November	azaroa (sowing time)
December	abendua (advent)

Numbers

Basques count in scores, a habit some believe came from contact with Celtic peoples. Thus, all the numbers you really need to know are one to twenty. For example, 99 is quite literally four-twenty and nineteen. Those who know some French will be familiar with the system. Basques also tend to count money in duros or hogerlekos rather than in pesetas: 1 duro = 5 pts; 20 duro = 100 pts.

1	bat		6	sei
2	bi		7	zazpi
3	hiru		8	zortzi
4	lau		9	bederatzi
5	bost		10	hamar

11	hamaika	50	berrogeita hamar
12	hamabi	60	hirurogei
13	hamairu		(lit. 3 twenty)
14	hamalau	70	hirurogeita hamar
15	hamabost	80	larogei
16	hamasei		(lit. 4 twenty)
17	hamazazpi	90	larogeita hamar
18	hamazortzi	100	ehun
19	hemeretzi	200	berrehun
20	hogei		(lit. re-hundred)
21	hogeita bat	300	hiru ehun
30	hogeita hamar	400	laurehun
40	berrogei	1000	mila
	(lit. re-twenty)	a million	miloi

BASQUE

FESTIVALS
Festive Sayings & Well-Wishing

Notice how Basques use **zorionak** (lit. good fortunes) for 'many happy returns!'

Happy Birthday!	Zorionak!
Merry Christmas!	Eguberri On; Zorionak!
Happy New Year!	Urte Berri On!
Congratulations!	Zorionak; Bejondeizula
Cheers!	Topa!
Bon appetit!	On egin!
Get well soon!	Sendatu agudo!
Bless you! (when sneezing)	Jexux!
What a shame!	Lastima!
Good luck.	Zorte on!

CROSSWORD – BASQUE

BASQUE

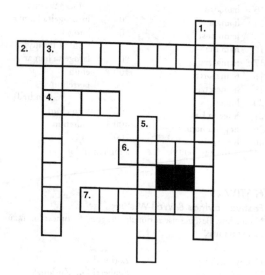

Across:
2. Municipal Police
4. I am (second word)
6. In English, a word spoken a second before a photo is taken
7. Around the world in ... days

Down:
1. Usually in tabloid size or bigger
3. Basque name for their biggest port
5. Cleansing agent, fiendishly difficult to grasp when wet

Answers: page 366

INTRODUCTION

Catalan is one of the nine Romance languages. It is spoken by up to 10 million people in the north-east of Spain, a territory that comprises Catalonia proper, coastal Valencia and the Balearic Islands (Majorca, Minorca and Ibiza). Outside Spain, Catalan is also spoken in Andorra, the south of France and the town of Alguer (Alghero) in Sardinia. In the Spanish areas mentioned above, Catalan is an official language alongside Castilian Spanish, taught in schools and widely spoken. Despite the fact that almost all Catalan speakers from Spain are bilingual, they usually appreciate it when visitors attempt to communicate, if even in rudimentary fashion, in Catalan. Catalan's rich cultural heritage has produced painters like Dalí, architects like Gaudí and great writers like Mercè Rodoreda.

PRONUNCIATION

Catalan sounds are not hard for an English-speaker to pronounce. You should, however, note that vowels will vary according to whether they occur in stressed or unstressed syllables.

Vowels

a   stressed, as the 'a' in 'father'. Unstressed, as in 'about'
e   stressed, as in 'pet'. Unstressed, like the 'e' in 'open'
i   like the 'i' in 'machine'
o   stressed, as in 'pot'. Unstressed, like the 'oo' in 'zoo'.
u   like the 'u' in 'humid'

Consonants

b   pronounced 'p' at the end of a word
c   hard before 'a', 'o', and 'u'. Soft before 'e' and 'i'.

ç	like 'ss'
d	pronounced 't' at the end of a word
g	hard before 'a', 'o' and 'u'. Before 'e' and 'i', like the 's' in 'measure'
h	silent
j	like the 's' in 'pleasure'
r	as in English in the middle of a word. Silent at the end.
rr	the roll of the tongue 'r', at the beginning of a word, or 'rr' in the middle of a word
s	as in English at the beginning of a word. In the middle as 'z'.
v	as 'b' in Barcelona. Pronounced 'v' in some other areas.
x	mostly as in English but sometimes 'sh'

Other letters are approximately as in English. There are a few odd combinations:

l.l	repeat the 'l'
tx	like 'ch'
qu	like 'k'

GRAMMATICAL FEATURES

Although Catalan belongs to the Romance languages group, with which it has much in common, there are many grammatical features which separate it from the others. We can't list all of these here, but there are two basic differences between Catalan and Castilian Spanish which it is important to understand.

Use of Pronouns

In Catalan, unlike in Castilian, any substitution of a word or phrase must be with a pronoun.

Vas a Mallorca?	Are you going to Mallorca?
Sí, voy. (Castilian)	Yes, I'm going.
Sí, hi vaig. (Catalan)	Yes, I'm going (there).

CATALAN

One of the most striking things about spoken Catalan is the number of pronouns which are used and their many permutations. Here are the most common Catalan pronouns:

- hi – 'there'; a place

Vius a Olot?	Do you live at Olot?
No, no hi visc.	No, I don't live there.

- la/el/les/els – used in replies when the noun in the question is preceded by la/el/les/els

Escrius les cartes?	Are you writing the letters?
Sí, les escric.	Yes, I'm writing them.

- en – used in replies when the noun in the question doesn't begin with the pronouns la/el/les/els

Compres pomes?	Are you buying apples?
Sí, en compro.	Yes, I'm buying them.

- ho – like 'it' in English

Comprarem això?	Shall we buy this?
Sí, ho comprarem.	Yes, let's buy it.

- li/els – 'to her/him' in English

Telefones a en Pere?	Are you phoning Pere?
Sí, li telefono.	Yes, I'm phoning him.

DID YOU KNOW ... Many famous creative people have been Catalan speakers – Pablo Picasso, Antonio Gaudi, Joan Miró and Salvador Dali.

CATALAN

Verbs in the Past Tense

In Spanish, verbs describing completed actions in the past use the simple past tense: canté (I sang), dormiste (you slept), bebió (she drank). The simple past does exist in Catalan but you are much more likely to come across this alternative and very simple way of expressing past actions, which involves the following words being added before the verb (which remains in its infinitive, or dictionary, form):

(I)	**vaig**	(we)	**vam**
(you, inf)	**vas**	(you, pl inf)	**vau** + infinitive
(s/he, it, you polite)	**va**	(they, you, pl polite)	**van**

La Isabel va cantar una cançó.   Isabel sang a song.
Jo vaig beure un got d'aigua.   I drank a glass of water.
Nosaltres vam dormir.   We slept.
On vau néixer?   Where were you (pl, inf) born?

GREETINGS & CIVILITIES
Top Useful Phrases

Hello!	Hola!
Goodbye.	Adéu!; Adéu-siau!
Yes; No.	Sí; No.
Excuse me.	Perdoni.
May I?/Do you mind?	Puc?; Em permet?
Sorry. (excuse me, forgive me).	Ho sento. Perdoni.
Please.	Sisplau; Si us plau.
Thank you.	Gràcies.
Many thanks.	Moltes gràcies.
That's fine. You're welcome.	De res.

Greetings

Good morning.	Bon dia.
Good afternoon.	Bona tarda.
Good evening.	Bon vespre.
Goodnight.	Bona nit.
See you later.	Fins ara.
See you.	A reveure.
How are you?	Com estàs?
(Very) well.	(Molt) bé.
Not too bad.	Anar fent.
Awful.	Malament.

Forms of Address

Madam/Mrs	Senyora
Sir/Mr	Senyor
Mate	Col.lega

LANGUAGE DIFFICULTIES

Do you speak English?	Parla anglès?
Could you speak in Castilian please?	Pot parlar castellà sisplau?
I speak a little Catalan.	Parlo una mica de català.
I understand some Catalan but I don't speak it.	Entenc una mica de català però no el parlo.
I (don't) understand.	(No) ho entenc.
Could you speak more slowly please?	Pot parlar més a poc a poc sisplau?
Could you repeat that?	Pot repetir-ho?
Could you write that down please?	Pot escriure-ho, sisplau?
How do you say ...?	Com es diu ...?
What is this called in Catalan?	Com es diu això en català?

SMALL TALK
Meeting People

What is your name?	Com et dius?
	Com es diu?
My name's ...	Em dic ...
I'd like to introduce you to ...	Voldria presentar-te á ...
I'm pleased to meet you.	Molt de gust.
	Encantada/Encantat.
How long have you been here?	Quant de temps fa que ets aquí?
I've been here (three days).	Fa (tres dies).
How long are you here for?	Quant de temps et penses quedar?
We're here for (two weeks).	Ens quedarem (dues setmanes).
Where are you from?	D'on ets?
I'm (Irish).	Sóc (irlandesa/irlandès).
Where do you live?	On vius?
I live in (Darwin).	Visc a (Darwin).
I'm here ...	Sóc aquí ...
holiday	de vacances
business	de viatge de negocis
studying	estudiant

Age

How old are you?	Quants anys tens?
I am ... years old	Tinc ... anys.

Occupations

What do you do?	A què et dediques?
I'm (a/an ...)	Sóc ...
artist	artista
business person	comerciant
doctor	metgessa/metge
engineer	enginyera/enginyer

journalist	periodista
lawyer	advocada/advocat
musician	música/músic
nurse	infermera/infermer
office worker	oficinista
scientist	científica/científic
secretary	secretària/secretari
student	estudiant
teacher	professora/professor
waiter	cambrera/cambrer

I'm ...	Estic ...
retired	jubilada/jubilat
unemployed	a l'atur

Family

Are you married?	Ets casada/casat?
I have a partner.	Tinc parella.
Do you have a girlfriend/boyfriend?	Tens xicota/xicot?
How many children do you have?	Quants fills tens?

I'm ...	
single	Sóc soltera/solter.
married	Sóc casada/casat.
separated	Estic separada.
a widow/widower	Sóc vídua/vidu.

GETTING AROUND
Finding Your Way

How do I get to ...?	Com puc arribar a ...?
Where is ...?	On és ...?
the bus station	l'estació d'autobús/ autocar
the city centre	el centre de la ciutat
the train station	l'estació de tren
the tourist office	l'oficina de turisme
the subway station	la parada de metro

avenue	avinguda/rambla
square	plaça
street	carrer/passeig

Buying Tickets

Excuse me, where is the ticket office?	Perdoni, on és la taquilla?
How long does the flight take?	Quant de temps dura el vol?
Do I have to change trains?	He de canviar de tren?
What is the cheapest fare to (Tarragona)?	Quin és el preu més barat cap a (Tarragona)?
Do I need to book?	He de fer una reserva?
I want to go to ...	Vull anar a ...
I'd like to book a seat to ...	Voldria reservar un seient per a ...
When is the next ... to ...?	Quan surt el proper ... cap a ...?
Is there a ... to ...?	Hi ha un ... cap a ...?
What time does ... leave?	A quina hora surt ...?
flight	vol
train	tren
bus	autobús
I'd like ...	Voldria...
a one-way ticket	un bitllet d'anada
a return ticket	un bitllet d'anar i tornar
two tickets	dos bitllets
It's full.	És ple.
Is there a discount for ...?	Hi ha algun descompte per a ...?
childen	nens
students	estudiants
pensioners	pensionistes
arrivals	arribades
baggage claim	recollida d'equipatges
check-in	facturació d'equipatges

CATALAN

customs	duana
departures	sortides
domestic	vols domèstics
exchange	canvi
platform	andana

Bus & Metro

Does this bus go to ...?	Aquest autobús va a ...?
the beach	la platja
the city centre	el centre de la ciutat
the station	l'estació
Do you stop at...?	Para a ...?
Which line takes me to ...?	Quina línia agafo per a ...?
Where do I change for...?	On he de fer transbord per a ...?
Could you let me know when we get to ...?	Pot avisar-me quan arribem a ...?

SIGN	
SORTIDA	EXIT

destination	destinació
line	línia

Taxi

Are you free?	Està lliure?
Please take me ...	Sisplau, dugui'm ...
to this address	a aquesta adreça
to the airport	a l'aeroport
to the railway station	a l'estació de trens
How much is it to go to ...?	Quant val anar a ...?
Here is fine, thank you.	Aquí ja va bé, gràcies.
How much do I owe you?	Quant és?

CATALAN

ACCOMMODATION

SIGNS

SORTIDA	WAY OUT
CAMPING	CAMPING GROUND
ALBERG JUVENIL	YOUTH HOSTEL
REFUGI DE MUNTANYA	MOUNTAIN LODGE
PENSIÓ (P)	GUESTHOUSE
HOSTAL (Hs)	BUDGET HOTEL
HOTEL (H)	HOTEL
PROHIBIT ACAMPAR	NO CAMPING

CATALAN

Is there a campsite/hotel near here?
Hi ha algun càmping/hotel a prop d'aquí?

Can I camp here?
Es pot acampar aquí?

Do you have any rooms available?
Hi ha habitacions lliures?

Sorry, we're full.
Ho sento, però no en tenim cap.

I'd like ...
Voldria ...
    a single room — una habitació individual
    a double room — una habitació doble
    to share a dorm — compartir un dormitori

I want a room with a ...
Vull una habitació amb ...
    bathroom — cambra de bany
    double bed — llit de matrimoni
    shower — dutxa

How much is it per night/ per person?
Quant val per nit/persona?

Does it include breakfast?
Inclou l'esmorzar?

Are there any cheaper rooms?

It's fine, I'll take it.

How many nights will you be staying?

I'm going to stay for (one week).

The key for room (311) please.

I don't like this room.

Hi ha habitacions més barates?

D'acord, me la quedo.

Quantes nits es pensa quedar?

Em quedaré (una setmana).

La clau per a l'habitació (311), sisplau.

No m'agrada aquesta habitació.

It's …
  too small
  noisy
  too dark

És …
  massa petita
  sorollosa
  massa fosca

Can I change to another dormitory?

I am/We are leaving now.

I'd like to pay the bill.

Can I leave my backpack at reception until tonight?

Please call a taxi for me.

Pot canviar-me d'habitació?

Me'n vaig/Marxem ara.

Voldria pagar el compte.

Puc deixar la meva motxilla a la recepció fins aquesta nit?

Pot trucar un taxi per mi, sisplau?

AROUND TOWN

I'm looking for …
  a bank
  the city centre
  the police
  the post office
  a public toilet
  a restaurant
  the telephone centre
  the tourist information office

Estic buscant …
  un banc
  el centre de la ciutat
  la policia
  correus
  els lavabos públics
  un restaurant
  la central telefònica
  l'oficina de turisme

CATALAN

CATALAN

What time does it open?	A quina hora obren?
What time does it close?	A quina hora tanquen?

At the Bank

I want to exchange some money/travellers' cheques.	Voldria canviar diners/txecs de viatge.
I want to change (dollars) into pessetes.	Vull canviar (dòlars) en pessetes.
What is the exchange rate?	A com està el canvi?
Please write it down.	M'ho pot escriure sisplau?
What is your commission?	Quant cobren de comissió?
Can I have smaller notes?	M'ho pot donar en bitllets més petits?

At the Post Office

I'd like to send a letter/parcel.	Voldria enviar una carta/un paquet.
I'd like some stamps.	Voldria segells.
How much is it to send this to ...?	Quant val enviar això a ...?
Where is the poste restante section?	On és la llista de correus?
Is there any mail for me?	Hi ha correu per a mi?

Telephone

I want to ring (Australia).	Vull trucar a (Austràlia).
Is there a cheap rate for evenings and weekends?	Hi ha algun preu especial per a les trucades nocturnes o de cap de setmana?
The number is ...	El número és ...
I want to make a reverse-charges phone call.	Voldria fer una trucada de cobrament a destinació.
Hello! (making a call)	Hola!

Hello! (answering a call)	Digui?
Can I speak to (Roger)?	Que hi ha (en Roger)?
Who's calling?	De part de qui?
It's (Núria).	De (la Núria).
Just a minute, I'll put her on.	Un moment, ara s'hi posa.
I'm sorry he's not here just now.	Ho sento però ara no hi és.
What time will (she) be back?	A quina hora tornarà?
Can I take a message?	Vols deixar un missatge?
Yes, please tell him I called.	Sí, sisplau, digues-li que li he trucat.
No, thanks, I'll call back later.	No gràcies, ja trucaré més tard.

SIGNS

OBERT/TANCAT	OPEN/CLOSED
DUANA	CUSTOMS
ENTRADA	ENTRANCE
INFORMACIO	INFORMATION
NO TOCAR	DO NOT TOUCH
PROHIBIT	PROHIBITED
PROHIBIT ENTRAR	NO ENTRY
PROHIBIT FUMAR	NO SMOKING
PROHIBIT FER FOTOS	NO PHOTOGRAPHY
RESERVAT	RESERVED
SORTIDA	EXIT
SERVEIS	TOILETS
TELÉFON	TELEPHONE

CATALAN

CATALAN

INTERESTS

The following phrases are examples of how to say what you like, don't like, like to do, and so on. Use your imagination, add whichever words you like (even if you have to use Castilian words, at least you'll have the backbone of the phrase correct).

What do you like doing?	Què t'agrada fer?
I like swimming and going to the cinema.	M'agrada nedar i anar al cine.
I don't like cooking.	No m'agrada gens cuinar.
I don't like working.	No m'agrada treballar gens ni mica.
What do you do in your spare time?	Què fas en el teu temps lliure?
I play chess.	Jugo a escacs.
Do you like sport?	T'agraden els esports?
Yes, very much.	M'encanten.
No, not at all.	No m'agraden gens.
Do you feel like (going for a swim)?	Et ve de gust (nedar)?
Yes, that'd be great.	Em ve molt de gust.
Not at the moment, thanks.	No gràcies, ara no.
I'm sorry, I can't.	Ho sento però no puc.

Arranging to Go Out

What are you doing this evening?	Què fas aquesta nit?
What are you doing this weekend?	Què fas aquest cap de setmana?
Would you like to go out somewhere?	Vols sortir amb mi?
Yes, let's. Where shall we go?	D'acord, on anem?
No, I'm afraid I can't. What about tomorrow?	Ho sento però no puc, i demà?

Would you like to go for a drink/meal? I'll buy.
I feel like going to …

Vols venir a fer una copa/a sopar? Et convido.
Tinc ganes d'anar …

Arranging to Meet

What time shall we meet?
Where shall we meet?
Let's meet at (eight o'clock) in the Rambles.
OK. I'll see you then.

A quina hora quedem?
On quedem?
Quedem a les (vuit) a les Rambles.
D'acord. Fins llavors!

Afterwards

It was nice talking to you.
I have to get going now.
I had a great day/evening.
Hope to see you again soon.
I'll give you a call.

M'ha encantat xerrar amb tu.
Ara he de marxar.
M'ho he passat pipa.
Espero veure't aviat.
Ja et trucaré.

Cinema & Theatre

What's on at the cinema/theatre tonight?
Are there any tickets for …?
Sorry, we are sold out.

Quina pel.lícula fan al cine aquesta nit?
Hi ha entrades per …?
Ho sento, però s'han esgotat les entrades.

How much are the tickets?
Are there any cheaper seats?
Is it in English?

Què valen les entrades?
Hi ha entrades més barates?
És en anglès?

CATALAN

DID YOU KNOW … Catalan is recognised as an official language by the UN because it is the principal language of Andorra.

FOOD

breakfast	esmorzar
lunch	dinar
dinner	sopar

Eating Out

Table for ..., please.	Una taula per ..., sisplau.
Can I see the menu please?	Puc veure el menú, sisplau?
I would like the set lunch, please.	Voldria el menú del dia, sisplau
What does it include?	Què inclou?
The bill, please.	El compte, sisplau.

first course/entrée	primer plat
second/main course	segon plat
dessert	postres
a drink	una beguda

Bon appétit.	Salut!
Cheers!	Bon profit!

Some Popular Catalan Dishes

allioli	garlic sauce
calçots	shallots, usually served braised with an almond dipping sauce. A seasonal delicacy.
coca	a dense cake, especially popular during St Joan (John) celebrations, when it is decorated with candied peel or pine nuts
crema catalana	a light crème caramel with a burnt toffee sauce
ensaïmada mallorquina	a sweet Mallorcan pastry
escalivada	roasted red peppers and eggplant in olive oil
escudella i carn d'olla	a Christmas dish of soup and meatballs

fuet	a thin pork sausage, native to Catalunya
mel i mató	a dessert of curd cheese with honey
mongetes seques i butifarra	haricot beans with thick pork sausage
pa amb tomàquet (i pernil)	crusty bread rubbed with ripe tomatoes, garlic and olive oil, often topped with cured ham
paella	remember, paella is Valencian in origin – if you only have it once, try to have it in Valencia.
sobrassada	a spreadable red sausage, speciality of Majorca

Drinks
Soft Drinks

almond drink	orxata
fruit juice	suc
mineral water	aigua mineral
plain (no gas)	sense gas
tap water	aigua de l'aixeta
soft drinks	refrescs

Tea & Coffee

black coffee	cafè sol
long black	doble
coffee…	cafè…
with liquer	carajillo (cigaló in north Catalunya)
with a little milk	tallat
with milk	amb llet
with milk and liquer	trifàsic
iced coffee	cafè gelat
decaffeinated coffee	cafè descafeinat
tea	te

Alcoholic Drinks

Catalunya is famous for its champagne (cava).

beer	una cervesa
champagne	un cava
rum	un rom
whisky	un whisky
glass of …wine	un vi…
red	negre
white	blanc
rosé	rosat
sparkling	d'agulla
muscatel	moscatell
ratafia (liquer)	ratafia

What will you have?	Què volen prendre?
I'll have a/an …	Em ve de gust …
	Jo prendré …
I don't drink [alcohol].	No bec.
It's on me.	Pago jo.

CATALAN

FOLKLORE & FESTIVALS

There are numerous festivals held in Catalunya through the year to mark special days on the calendar, like Saint Jordi (George) day on 23 April, when the nation's patron saint is honoured through the tradition of giving a rose or a book as a gift and La Diada, Catalan Independence Day, on 11 September. In addition, every village, town or neighborhood goes into festival mode at least one day a year to celebrate its local saint with a **festa major** (main festival). The emphasis is on local customs, music and dancing and you'll probably encounter some of the following traditions:

FOLKLORE & FESTIVALS

Sardanes	Catalan national dance
Castellers	Human towers. Neighborhoods or villages compete for the honour of building the most impressive tower.
Nans i gegants	A procession of people wearing huge papier mâché painted heads or riding inside painted wooden giants.
Correfoc	A popular event at which dracs and dimonis (people dressed as giant dragons and devils) chase spectators along the street breathing fireworks.
Cercavila	Groups of local residents go around the neighbourhood dressed up on a festival day.

Festive Sayings & Well-Wishing

Happy birthday!	Per molts anys!
Happy saint's day!	Per molts anys!
Happy Christmas!	Bon nadal!
Happy New Year!	Bon any nou!
Congratulations!	Felicitats!
To the bride and groom!	Visca els nuvis!
Good health!/Cheers!	Salut!; Salut i força al canut!
Bon apetit!	Bon profit!
Get well soon!	Que et milloris!
Bless you! (when sneezing)	Jesús!; Salut!
My deepest sympathy.	T'acompanyo en el sentiment.
Bon voyage!	Bon viatge!
Good luck!	Bona sort!
Hope it goes well!	Que vagi bé!

CATALAN

SHOPPING

Where can I buy…?	On puc comprar … ?

Where is the nearest…?	On és la/el … més propera/proper?
bookshop	llibreria
camera shop	botiga de fotos
department store	grans magatzems
greengrocer	botiga de verdures; fruiteria
launderette	bugaderia
market	mercat
newsagency	quiosc
pharmacy	farmàcia
supermarket	supermercat
travel agency	agència de viatges

Making a Purchase

I'd like to buy …	Voldria comprar …
How much is this?	Quant val això?
Can you write down the price?	Pot escriure'm el preu?
Can I look at it?	Puc veure-la/veure'l?
I don't like it.	No m'agrada.
Do you have anything cheaper?	Té alguna cosa més barata?
I'll buy it.	La/el compro.
Do you accept credit cards?	Accepten targetes de crèdit?
Can I have a receipt?	Podria donar-me un rebut?
I'm just looking.	Només estic mirant.

Toiletries

condoms	preservatius; condons
deodorant	desodorant
razor blades	fulles d'afaitar
sanitary napkins	compreses
shampoo	xampú

CATALAN

shaving cream	crema d'afaitar
soap	sabó
sunblock cream	crema solar
tampons	tampons
tissues	mocadors de paper
toilet paper	paper higiènic
toothbrush	raspall de dents
toothpaste	pasta de dents

Stationery & Publications

Do you sell…?	Venen …?
magazines	revistes
newspapers	diaris
postcards	postals

envelope	sobre
magazine	revista
map	mapa
newspaper	diari
newspaper in paper	diari en paper
pen (ballpoint)	bolígraf
stamp	segell

> **THEY MAY SAY …**
>
> **Què desitja?**
>   Can I help you?
>
> **Alguna altra cosa?**
>   Will that be all?
>
> **Quant/s en vol?**
>   How much/many
>   do you want?

CATALAN

PAPERWORK

nom i cognom	name & surname
adreça	address
data de naixement	date of birth
lloc de naixement	place of birth
edat	age
sexe	sex
nacionalitat	nationality
estat civil	marital status

passaport	passport
visat	visa
carnet d'identitat	identification
carnet de conduir	driver's licence

TIME, DATES & NUMBERS
Telling the Time

One thing to remember when asking about times in Catalan: minutes past the hour (eg quarter past, twenty-five past) are referred to as being before the next hour. Thus 'half past two' becomes **dos quarts de tres** (two quarters to three) and 'twenty past nine' becomes **un quart i cinc de deu** (one quarter and five minutes to ten). This is repeated in minutes to the hour, where 'ten to five' becomes **tres quarts i cinc de cinc** (three quarters and five minutes to five).

What time is it?	**Quina hora és?**
It's one o'clock.	**És la una**
It's two o'clock.	**Són les dues.**
It's quarter past six.	**És un quart de set.**
It's quarter to four.	**Són tres quarts de quatre.**
It's half past eight.	**Són dos quarts de nou.**

CATALAN

Days of the Week

Monday	dilluns	Friday	divendres
Tuesday	dimarts	Saturday	dissabte
Wednesday	dimecres	Sunday	diumenge
Thursday	dijous		

Months

January	gener	July	juliol
February	febrer	August	agost
March	març	September	setembre
April	abril	October	octubre
May	maig	November	novembre
June	juny	December	desembre

NUMBERS

0	zero	6	sis
1	un, una	7	set
2	dos, dues	8	vuit
3	tres	9	nou
4	quatre	10	deu
5	cinc	11	onze

CATALAN

SOME EXPRESSIONS UNIQUE TO CATALUNYA

rauxa	impulse
Quina rauxa en Joan!	*How impulsive Joan is!*
seny	intuitive common sense
L'Ana té molt de seny.	*Ana is really savvy*
déu n'hi do	a fair amount
això rai	no problem!
Quin tip de riure!	What a laugh!
força Barça	Go Barça
(Barcelona Football Club)!	
guaita!	Look out!

12	dotze	30	trenta
13	tretze	40	quaranta
14	catorze	50	cinquanta
15	quinze	60	seixanta
16	setze	70	setanta
17	disset	80	vuitanta
18	divuit	90	noranta
19	dinou	100	cent
20	vint	1000	mil

1st	primera/primer
2nd	segona/segon
3rd	tercera/tercer

CROSSWORD – CATALAN

CATALAN

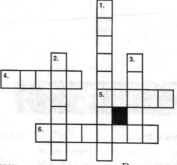

Across:
4. A wife bereaved
5. Bond film character: ... No
6. First meal of the day

Down:
1. Hospital patient care specialist
2. Shop that sells newspapers
3. Alternative to a bath

Answers: page 366

GALICIAN

INTRODUCTION

Galician, or 'Galego', is, with Castilian Spanish, one of the two official languages of the Autonomous Community of Galicia. It is also spoken in parts of the neighbouring Communities of Asturias and Castilla-León (part of the Province of Zamora). The majority of these populations can speak Galician and everyone understands it.

There are still rural areas where the visitor may come across people talking in Galician among themselves, although they will most likely revert to Spanish when addressing a stranger, especially a foreigner. Galician is very similar to Portuguese. In fact, up until the 13th century they were pretty much identical, both having descended from the Vulgar Latin that was spoken in the west of the Peninsula. But with the independence of Portugal in the 12th century and the Castilian rule of Galicia around the same time, the two languages began to diverge and develop into their modern forms. The debate over the status of Galician as a dialect of Portuguese or a separate language still rages today.

PRONUNCIATION
Vowels

a	as in 'hat'
e	as in 'bed'
i	as the 'ea' in 'easy', never as in 'bit'
o	as in the British 'hot'; also as in 'hole'
u	as in 'through'
ou	as in 'low'

Consonants

Some consonants are the same as their English counterparts. The following need to be remembered:

g	as in 'good'
h	silent
ñ	as in 'onion'
r	rolled, like the Spanish 'r'. When a word begins with 'r', or if there is a double 'r', they should be pronounced with extra force.
b & v	like the 'b' in 'book'
x	as in 'ship'. In some words such as 'exterior' it is pronounced 's' or 'x'.
ll	may be pronounced as in 'million', but is usually closer to 'j' as in 'jam'
nh	like the 'ng' sound in 'finger'. When 'n' is at the end of a word it is also pronounced 'ng'.
ch	as in 'chips'
c	like 'th' in 'thing' or 's' in 'sing' before i and e; like the 'k' in 'king' elsewhere
z	either as 'th' in 'third' or 's' in 'soup'

One dialectal feature which might confuse would-be Galician-speakers is something called gheada, whereby a 'g' before a, o or u may be pronounced like the 'h' in 'hat'. For example the word for cat may be gato or hato. This phenomenon is very wide-spread in the touristic coastal areas of southern Galicia.

GRAMMATICAL FEATURES

Although Galician belongs to the Romance languages group, with which it has much in common, there are many grammatical features which separate it from the others. We can't list all of these here, but there are several basic differences between Galician and Castilian Spanish which are important to understand.

Definite Articles ('the')

a (f, sg)	a muller	the woman
as (f, pl)	as mulleres	the women
o (m, sg)	o home	the man
os (m, pl)	os homes	the men

GALICIAN

Indefinite Articles ('a/an')

unha	unha muller	a woman
unhas (f, pl)	unhas mulleres	some women
un (m, sg)	un home	a man
uns (m, pl)	uns homes	some men

Prepositions

with	con
without	sen
to	a
by	por
for	para
from; of	de
in	en

Note that prepositions tend to combine with the article, creating a different word:

con + as = coas	'with them' (f)
por + o = polo	'by him/it'
en + o = no	'in it'
a + a = á	'to her/it'
de + as = das	'from them' (f)

Tip: Don't confuse **no** (in the) and **non** (no/not)!

Verbs

A neat way of avoiding having to conjugate verbs is to use the structure **estar + a +** the infinitive. For instance **Estou a comer** ('I am eating').

A good way of getting around verbs in the future tense is to use the structure meaning 'have to', **haver + (de) +** the infinitive. For example **Hei (de) ir mañán** ('I have to go [ie will go] tomorrow').

GREETINGS & CIVILITIES
Top Useful Phrases

Hello!	Ola!
Goodbye.	Adeus; Até logo.
Yes./No.	Si./Non.
Excuse me.	Perdón.
May I? Do you mind?	Importa-che?
Sorry (excuse me, forgive me).	Desculpa.
Please.	Por favor.
Thank you.	Grácias; Graciñas.
Many thanks.	Moitas grácias.
That's fine. You're welcome.	De nada.

Greetings

Good day.	Bon dia; Bo dia.
Good afternoon/evening.	Boa tarde.
Goodnight.	Boa noite.
See you later.	Vemo-nos.
See you.	Até logiño.
How are you?	Comos está? (pol)
	Como che vai? (inf)
(Very) well.	(Moi) ben.
Not too bad.	Regular.
Awful.	Fatal.

Forms of Address

Mrs	Señora
Sir/Mr	Señor
mate; friend; buddy	nacho; meu (very informal)

GALICIAN

DID YOU KNOW ...	Yet another language of Spain is Romany, spoken exclusively by Gypsies.

LANGUAGE DIFFICULTIES

Do you speak English?	Fala inglés?
Could you speak in Castilian please?	Pode falar en español, por favor?
I speak a little Galician.	Só falo un pouco de galego.
I understand some Galician but I don't speak it.	Entendo o galego, mais non o falo.
I (don't) understand.	(Non) entendo.
Could you speak more slowly please?	Fale máis a modiño, por favor.
Could you write that down please?	Escreva-o, por favor.
How do you say ...?	Como se di ...?
What is this called in Galician?	Como se chama iso en galego?

SMALL TALK

Meeting People

What's your name?	Como se chama?
My name is ...	Chamo-me ...
I'd like to introduce you to ...	Quero apresentar-te a ...
I'm pleased to meet you.	Encantada/o.
How long have you been here?	Canto tempo leva aqui?
I've been here (three days).	Xa levo (tres dias).
How long are you here for?	Canto tempo vai quedar?
We're here for (two weeks).	Quedamos duas semanas.
Where are do from	De onde é?
I'm (Irish).	Son (irlandesa/irlandés).
Where do you live?	Onde vive?
I live in (Darwin).	Vivo en (Darwin).

Age

How old are you?	Cantos anos ten?
I'm ....years old.	Teño ... anos.

GALICIAN

Occupations

What do you do?	En que traballa?

I'm a/an ... | Son ...
business person	empresária/o
engineer	enxeñeira/o
jounalist	xornalista
lawyer	avogada/o
nurse	enfermeira/o
office worker	administrativa/o
scientist	científica/o
waiter	camareira/o

I'm ... | Estou ....
| retired | xubilada/o |
| unemployed | no paro |

Family

Are you married?	Está casada/o ?
I'm single.	Son solteira/o.

I'm ... | Estou
married	casada/o
separated	separada/o
widow/widower	viúva/viúvo

I have a partner.	Teño parella.
Do you have a girlfriend/ boyfriend?	Ten moza/o?
How many children do you have?	Cantos fillos ten?

GETTING AROUND
Finding Your Way

Excuse me, can you help me please?	Desculpe, pode axudar-me?

How do I get to ...?	Como se vai a ...?

Where is the ...?	Onde está ...?
bus station	a estación de autobuses
city centre	o centro da cidade
old part of town	a parte vella; o casco vello
tourist information centre	a oficina de turismo
train station	a estación de trens

avenue	avenida
road/street	rua
road (highway)	estrada
square	praza

Buying Tickets

Excuse me, where is the ticket office?	Onde está a ventanilla, por favor?
I want to go to ...	Quero ir a ...
Is there a train/bus to ...?	Hai un tren/autobus para ...?
How long does the journey take?	Canto tempo tarda a viaxe?
What time does it leave?	A que hora sae?
Do I have to change?	Teño que cambiar?
What is the cheapest fare to (A Coruña)?	Cal é o billete máis barato para (A Coruña)?
Do I need to book?	Teño que reservar?
I'd like to book a seat to ...	Quero reservar un billete para ...
It's full.	Está completo.
	Xa non hai sítio.

I'd like ...	Quero ...
a one-way ticket	un billete de ida e volta
a return ticket	un billete de ida
two tickets	dous billetes

arrivals	chegadas
baggage claim	recollida de equipaxes
check-in	facturación (de equipaxes)
customs	alfándega
departures	saídas
domestic flights	vós internos/vós nacionais
platform	plataforma

Bus

Does this bus go to ...?	Este autobus vai para ....?
the beach	a praia
the city centre	o centro da cidade
the station	a estación

Do you stop at ...?	Pára en ...?
Where do I change for ...?	Onde teño que cambiar para ir a ...?
Could you let me know when we get to ...?	Pode dicer-me cando cheguemos a ...?

SIGNS

SAÍDA	EXIT
DESTINO	DESTINATION
LIÑA	LINE

GALICIAN

Taxi

| Are you free? | Está livre? |

Please take me ...?	Pode levar-me ....?
to this address	a este enderezo
to the airport	ao aeroporto
to the city centre	ao centro da cidade
to the railway station	á estación de trens

How much is it to get to ...?	Canto custa ir a ....?
Here is fine, thankyou.	Pode deixar-me aqui, por favor.
How much do I owe you?	Canto é?

ACCOMMODATION

Can I camp here?	Podo acampar aqui?
Is there a campsite/hotel near here?	Hai algun cámping/hotel aqui perto?
Do you have any rooms available?	Hai habitacións?
Sorry, we're full.	Sinto-o moito, está cheo/completo.

I'd like ...	Quero ...
a single room	unha habitación individual
a double room	unha habitación doble
to share a dorm	compartir un dormitório

I want a room with ...	Quero unha habitación con ...
a bathroom	cuarto de baño
a double bed	cama de matrimónio
a shower	ducha

SIGNS	
UN CÁMPING	CAMPING GROUND
ALBERGUE DA XUVENTUDE	YOUTH HOSTEL
ALBERGUE DO PEREGRINO	PILGRIM'S HOSTEL
FONDA (F)	CHEAP LODGINGS
PENSIÓN (P)	GUESTHOUSE
HOSTAL (HS)	BUDGET HOTEL
HOTEL (H)	HOTEL
PROHIBIDO ACAMPAR	NO CAMPING

GALICIAN

How much is it per night/ per person?	Canto custa unha noite por persoa?
Does it include breakfast?	O almorzo vai incluído?
Are there any cheaper rooms?	Hai algunha habitación máis barata?
It's fine, I'll take it.	Dacordo, quedo-me con esta.
How many nights will you be staying for?	Canto tempo vai quedar?
I'm going to stay for one week.	Hei quedar aquí unha semana.
The key for room (35) please.	A chave da habitación (35), por favor.
I don't like this room.	Non me gusta esta habitación.

It's ...	É ...
too small	pequena de máis
noisy	ruidosa de máis
too dark	escura de máis
cold	fria de máis

Can I change to another dormitory?	Seria posíbel cambiar de dormitório?
I am /we are leaving now.	Xa deixo/deixamos a habitación.
I'd like to pay the bill.	Quero pagar a conta.
Can I leave my backpack at reception until tonight?	Pode deixar a mochila aquí até a tarde, por favor?
Please call a taxi for me.	Pode chamar-me un táxi, por favor?

GALICIAN

COMPLAINING

Galicians tend not to complain, or at least not in a direct fashion. It would be considered almost rude to say; **Non me gusta esta habitación** (I don't like this room), preferring instead a more roundabout sentence such as **Case prefiro outra habitación.** (I almost prefer another room). This beating about the bush may well disconcert the uninitiated, but the Galicians know what they really mean.

AROUND TOWN

SIGNS

ABERTO/PECHADO	OPEN/CLOSED
ALFÁNDEGA/ADUANA	CUSTOMS
ENTRADA	ENTRANCE
INFORMACIÓN	INFORMATION
NON TOCAR	DO NOT TOUCH
PROHIBIDO	PROHIBITED
PROHIBIDO O PASO	NO ENTRY
PROHIBIDO FUMAR	NO SMOKING
PROHIBIDO SACAR FOTOS	NO PHOTOGRAPHY
RESERVADO	RESERVED
SAÍDA	EXIT
SAÍDA DE EMERXENCIA	EMERGENCY EXIT
SERVICIOS/ASEOS	TOILETS
TELÉFONO	TELEPHONE

I'm looking for ...	Estou a buscar ...
a bank	un banco
the city centre	o centro da cidade
the old part of town	o casco vello
the police station	a comisaria
a public toilet	o baño público/os aseos
a restaurant	un restaurante
a telephone centre	un locutório telefónico
the tourist information office	a oficina de turismo

What time does it open?	A que hora abre?
What time does it close?	A que hora fecha?

At the Bank

I want to change some money/travellers' cheques.	Quero cambiar diñeiro/cheques de viaxe.

GALICIAN

I want to change (dollars) into pesetas.	Quero cambiar estes dólares por pesetas.
What is the exchange rate?	A como está o cámbio?
Can you write it down please?	Pode escrevé-lo, por favor?
What is your commission?	Canta comisión vai cobrar?
Can I have smaller notes?	Pode dar-me billetes máis pequenos?

At the Post Office

I'd like some stamps please.	Quero selos por favor.
How much is it to send this to ...?	Canto custa mandar iso a ...?
Where is the poste restante section?	Onde está a lista de correios?
Is there any mail for me?	Hai algunha carta para min?

Telephone

I want to ring (Australia).	Quero facer unha chamada a (Austrália).
Is there a cheap rate for evenings and weekends?	A que hora resulta máis barato chamar?
The number is ...	O número é o ...
I want to make a reverse-charges phone call.	Quero chamar a cobro revertido.

Making a Call

Hello (making a call)	Ola?
Hello (answering a call)	Diga?
Can I speak to (Xan)?	Quero falar con (Xan).
Who's calling?	De parte de quen?
It's ...	De parte de ...
Just a minute. I'll put her/him on.	Agarda un momentiño, xa se pon agora mesmo.
I'm sorry s/he's not here just now.	Sinto-o, neste momento non está.

GALICIAN

What time will s/he be back?	A que hora estará de volta?
Can I take a message?	Quere deixar un recado?
Yes, please tell her/him I called.	Si, di-lle que chamei.
No, thanks, I'll call back later.	Non fai falta, xa volverei a chamar.

UNIQUE GALICIAN EXPRESSIONS

e logo?
Galicians are renowned for answering questions with another question. This particular reply is very common and allows the speaker to avoid giving a direct answer. It can mean anything from 'Tell me more', 'How about that!' to 'Mind your own business'

> Question: **Traballas?** (Do you work?),
> Answer: **E logo?** (And you, what do you do?)

Che
Meaning 'to you' is thrown in to give any sentence a more familiar flavour

Non che sei (I don't know), **É-che ben difícil** (It's difficult)

ho/hou
This interjection can be thrown in at the end of suggestions to make them sound less direct

Vamos, ho? (Shall we go?)

carallo!
Galicians swear a lot! This swear-word is particularly popular and can mean 'Well, I'll de damned', 'You don't say!' or worse!

case
To avoid giving a categorical 'yes' or 'no' answer, Galicians will often resort to such expressions as **Case mellor** (It would be better, ie. 'yes'), **Case si** (lit. 'Almost yes') and **Case non** (lit. 'Almost no')

MORE UNIQUE EXPRESSIONS

non é?/non si?
A sort of tag question. 'Yes' and 'No' answers involve repetition of the verb

O teu irmán para Ourense mañán, non si? (Your brother's going to Ourense tomorrow, isn't he?)

Vai (Yes, he is, lit. he goes)

retranca
The name given to the Galician habit of providing evasive, cryptic, humouristic or even biting replies to questions they prefer to avoid giving a straight answer to. The more unfriendly variety is refered to as 'sorna'

morriña/saudade
A particularly strong sense of homesickness felt by Galicians who have emmigrated abroad in search of work

---

INTERESTS & SOCIALISING

What do you like doing?	Que lle gusta facer?
I like (going to the cinema).	Gusta-me (ir ao cine).
I don't like (working).	Non me gusta (traballar).
What do you do in your spare time?	Que fai nos seus momentos livres?
I play (chess).	Xogo ao (xadrez).
Do you like (sport)?	Gusta-lle (o deporte)?
	Gosta (do deporte)?
Yes, very much.	Encanta-me.
No, not at all.	Non, en absoluto.
	semana?

Arranging to Go Out

What are you doing this evening/this weekend?	Que pensa facer esta tarde/este fin de semana?

Would you like to go out somewhere?	Apetece-lle sair comigo?
I feel like going to ...	Apetece-me ir ...
Do you feel like going (to the pool)?	Apetece-lle ir (á piscina)?
Do you want to (go hiking) this weekend?	Apetece-lle (facer un pouco de sendeirismo) este fin de
Would you like to go to a football game?	Gustaria-lle ir ao partido de fútebol?

Accepting & Declining Invites

Yes, let's. Where shall we go?	Dacordo! A onde imos?
Yes, that'd be great.	Encantaria-me.
Not at the moment, thanks.	Noutro momento ao mellor, grácias.
I'm sorry, I can't.	Sinto-o, non podo.
No, I'm afraid I can't. What about tomorrow?	Sinto-o moito, non podo. E mañán?

Goodbyes

It was nice talking to you.	Gustou-me moito charlar contigo.
I have to go now.	Teño que marchar.
I had a great day/evening.	Pasei un dia estupendo/unha tarde maravillosa.
Hope to see you again soon.	Vemo-nos logo.
I'll give you a call.	Xa te chamarei.

Cinema & Theatre

What's on at the cinema/ theatre tonight?	Que botan no cine/no teatro hoxe pola tarde?
Are there any tickets for ...?	Quedan entradas para ...?
Sorry, we're sold out.	Sinto-o, xa non quedan entradas.

| How much are the tickets? | A como están as entradas? |
| Are there any cheaper seats? | Hai entradas máis baratas? |

Is there a discount for ...?	Hai algun desconto para ...?
children	nenos
students	estudantes
pensioners	a terceira idade

| Is it in English? | Está en inglés? |
| Are those seats taken? | Estes asentos están ocupados? |

FOOD

breakfast	almorzo
lunch	xantar
dinner	cea

Table for ...please.	Unha mesa para ...persoas, por favor.
Can I see the menu, please?	Trae-me o menú, por favor.
What does it include?	Que entra no menú?
The bill, please.	A conta, por favor.

first course/entrée	primeiro prato
second/main course	segundo prato
set meal	prato combinado
dessert	sobremesa; postre
a drink	unha bebida
Cheers!/Bon apétit!	Saúde! Que aproveite!

Some Popular Galician Dishes

empanada

a savoury pie filled with spicy minced beef, tuna fish or salt cod with currants

polvo á feira

octopus boiled in a big copper cauldron served on a wooden dish with olive oil and paprika

GALICIAN

lacón con grelos
  shoulder of ham boiled with turnip leaves, served with olive oil and paprika

caldo galego
  broth made with meat, turnips, cabbage and beans. Vegetarians beware! The traditional caldo galego (Galician vegetable broth) may well be made using unto (pig fat). Enquire first.

bacallau
  salt cod, often served with chickpeas

pescada á galega
  hake with a sauce made of garlic and paprika fried in lots of olive oil

mariscada
  seafood platter, usually for two or more people. Don't miss the grusome percebes (goose barnacles).

tarta de Santiago
  cake made of powdered almonds

Soft Drinks

fruit juice	sumo; zume
mineral water	auga mineral
fizzy	con gas
still	sen gas
tap water	auga da billa; auga do grifo
soft drinks	refrescos
a coca cola ...	coca cola
at room temperature	do tempo
straight out of the fridge	fresco/fresca

Tea & Coffee

black coffee	café so
long black	dobre

GALICIAN

coffee...	café...
with a little milk	cortado
with milk	con leite
weak coffee	americano
iced coffee	un café con xelo
decaffeinated coffee	descafeinado
tea	te
lemon tea	te con limón

Alcoholic Drinks

What will you have?	Que tomas?
I'll have a/an ...	Un .../Unha ...para min.
beer	cervexa
cider	
rum	
whisky	whisky /guísgi
long drink	cubata /cacharro
white wine	viño branco
red wine	un viño tinto
house wine	viño da casa

I don't drink alcohol.	Non bebo alcool.
It's on me.	Convido eu.

Galician Drinks

augardente .../caña ...
> Galician strong spirits. Often added to black coffee after a meal (refered to as café con gotas).

> branco
> de ervas

queimada
> Galician speciality made by burning augardente with citrus peel, coffee beans and lots of sugar

licor-café
  strong coffee liqueur made by leaving coffee beans to
  macerate in augardente with sugar

Ribeiro
  Galician white table wine (often served in small bowls
  called tazas).

Albariño
  a fine Galician white wine

Valdeorras
  another fine Galician red wine

SHOPPING

Where can I buy ...?	Onde podo mercar/comprar ...?

Where is the nearest ...?	Onde hai ...?
bookshop	unha livraria
camera shop	unha tenda de fotografia
department store	un grande armacén
greengrocer's	unha frutaria; tenda de verduras
lauderette	unha lavandaria
drycleaner's	unha tintoraria
market	un mercado
newsagency; kiosk	papelaria; quiosco
tabaconists	un estanco; un tabacaria
supermarket	un supermercado
travel agency	unha axéncia de viaxes

Making a Purchase

I'd like to buy ...	Quero mercar/comprar ...
How much is this?	Canto custa?
Can you write down the price.	Pode ecrever o prezo, por favor?
Can I look at it?	Podo vé-lo?
I don't like it.	Non me gusta.

GALICIAN

Do you have anything cheaper?	Ten algo máis barato?
I'll buy it.	Levo este.
Do you accept credit cards?	Podo pagar con tarxeta?
Can I have a receipt?	Quero un recibo (invoice)/ tique (receipt from till).
I'm just looking.	Só estou a mirar.

Toiletries

condoms	preservativos; condóns
deodorant	desodorizante
razor blades	follas de afeitar; coitelas
sanitary napkins	compresas; salva-slips
shampoo	champú
shaving foam/cream	espuma; crema de afeitar
soap	xabón
sunblock cream	crema solar
tampons	tampóns
tissues	pañuelos; lenzos
toilet paper	papel hixiénico
toothbrush	cepillo de dentes
toothpaste	pasta de dentes

GALICIAN

Stationery & Publications

Do you sell ...?	Hai ...?
magazines	revistas
newspapers	xornais
postcards	postais
envelope	sobres; envelope
map	mapa
newspaper	xornal
newspaper in English	xornal en inglés
pen (ballpoint)	bolígrafo

THEY MAY SAY

Necesita axuda?
  Can I help you?

Algo máis?
  Will that be all?

Canto/
Cantos quere?
  How much/many
  do you want?

FOLKLORE & FESTIVALS

Galician National Day (**Dia da Pátria Galega**) coincides with the Feast Day of Saint James the Apostle (Santiago), Patron Saint of Galicia, and falls on 25 July. The big firework display (**a queimada da fachada**) in front of the cathedral in the capital city, Santiago de Compostela, the night before is well worth a visit.

Other important dates in the Galician calendar are:

Magosto (All Saint's Day – 31 October), when people eat chestnuts and light bonfires

a Noite de San Xoán (Midsummer's Eve – 24 June), when people leap bonfires and eat sardines

Entroido (Carnaval – February) which has remained very traditional in many parts of Galicia

Every village also celebrates its own Saint's Day with fares (**romaria popular**), attractions, mass, etc. Local and provincial patron saints are of great importance in Galicia, some of the more notable ones include San Bieito in Pontevedra, San Froilán in Lugo and San Martiño in Ourense.

Galicia is well-known for its **gaitas** (bagpipes) and two of the most well-known dances are the **muiñeira** and the **agorada.**

GALICIAN

GALICIAN

FESTIVE SAYINGS & WELL-WISHING

Happy birthday!	Feliz aniversário!; Feliz cumpreanos!
Happy Saint's Day!	Feliz Santo!
Merry Christmas!	Feliz Nadal!; Felices Páscuas!
Happy New Year!	Feliz Ano Novo!
Congratulations!	Parabéns!; En hora boa!
To the bride and groom!	Que vivan os noivos!
Good health!; Cheers!	Saúde!
Bon appetit	Bon aproveito!; Que aproveite!
Get well soon!	Que mellores!
Bless you! (sneezing)	Saúde!; Xesús!
What a shame!; What a pity!	Mágoa!; Lástima!; Pena!
Good luck!	Boa sorte!
Hope it goes well!	Que che vaia ben!

PAPERWORK

nome e apelido(s)	name & surname(s)
enderezo	address
idade	age
data de nacemento	date of birth
carné de conducir	driver's licence
Carné de Identidade (D.N.I.)	identification
estado civil	marital status
lugar de nacemento	place of birth
sexo (muller/varón)	sex (f/m)

TIME, DATES & NUMBERS
Time

What time is it?	Que hora é?
It's one o'clock.	É a unha.

It's ...	Son as ...
two o'clock	duas
half past three	tres e meia
a quarter to four	catro menos cuarto
a quarter past five	cinco e cuarto

Days

today	hoxe
yesterday	onte
tomorrow	mañán

Monday	luns	Thursday	xoves
Tuesday	martes	Friday	venres
Wednesday	mércores;	Saturday	sábado
	corta-feira	Sunday	domingo

Months

January	xaneiro	July	xullo
February	fevereiro	August	agosto
March	marzo	September	setembro
April	abril	October	outubro
May	maio	November	novembro
June	xuño	December	decembro

GALICIAN

Numbers
Note that Galicians often count money in 'pesos' rather than in pesetas. 1 peso = 5 pts; 20 pesos =100pts; 40 pesos = 200pts; 100 pesos = 500pts.

1	unha; un	16	dezaseis
2	duas; dous	17	dezasete
3	tres	18	dezaoito
4	catro	19	dezanove
5	cinco	20	vinte
6	seis	21	vinteunha; vinteun
7	sete	30	trinta
8	oito	40	corenta
9	nove	50	cinquenta
10	dez	60	sesenta
11	once	70	setenta
12	doce	80	oitenta
13	trece	90	noventa
14	catorce	100	cento; cen (before a noun)
15	quince		

200 pesetas	duas centas pesetas
a thousand	mil

CROSSWORD – GALICIAN

Across:

4. The best part of dinner
5. Form by which the location of a building is described
6. Domestic flights (second word)

Down:

1. Notorious denizens of schools and universities
2. The happiest day of the working week
3. Month before the one named for Julius Caesar

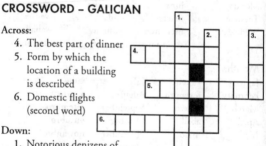

Answers: page 366

GALICIAN

EMERGENCIES

Help!	¡Socorro! ¡Auxilio!
Call the police!	¡Llame a la policía!
Where is the police station?	¿Dónde está la comisaría?
It's an emergency!	¡Es una emergencia!
I need assistance!	¡Necesito ayuda!
Could you help me please?	¿Puede ayudarme, por favor?
Could I please use the telephone?	¿Puedo usar el teléfono, por favor?
I want to report an offence.	Deseo presentar una denuncia.

Look out!	¡Ojo!
Fire!	¡Fuego!

There's been an accident!	¡Ha habido un accidente!
Call a doctor!	¡Llame a un médico!
Call an ambulance!	¡Llame a una ambulancia!
I am ill.	Estoy enferma/o.
My friend is ill.	Mi amiga/o está enferma/o.
I have medical insurance.	Tengo seguro médico.

I've been raped.	He sido violada/o.
I want to see a female police officer.	Deseo hablar con una mujer policía.
Could you please organise an official medical examination?	¿Pueden hacerme un exámen médico oficial?

Go away!	¡Váyase!
I'll call the police!	¡Voy a llamar a la policía!
Thief!	¡Ladrón!
I've been robbed!	¡Me han robado!
This woman/man has been robbed.	¡Han robado a esta/e señora/señor.

My… was stolen.	Me robaron mi(s)…
bags	maletas
backpack	mochila
handbag	bolso
money	dinero
wallet	cartera
papers	todos mis papeles
travellers' cheques	cheques de viaje
passport	pasaporte
My possessions are insured.	Tengo seguro contra robo

I am lost.	Estoy perdida/o
I have lost my friend.	He perdido a mi amiga/o
I've lost…	He perdido…/Perdí…

DEALING WITH THE POLICE

SIGNS	
POLICÍA	POLICE
COMISARÍA DE POLICÍA	POLICE STATION

I'm sorry (I apologise).	Lo siento/Discúlpeme.
I didn't realise I was doing anything wrong.	No sabía que no estabá permitido.
I'm innocent.	Soy inocente.
I didn't do it.	No lo he hecho yo.
I'm a foreigner.	Soy extranjera/o.
I'm a tourist.	Soy turista.
What am I accused of?	¿De qué se me acusa?
Do I have the right to make a call?	¿Tengo derecho a hacer alguna llamada?
Can I call someone?	¿Puedo llamar a alguien?
I wish to contact my embassy/ consulate	Deseo comunicarme con mi embajada/consulado.

EMERGENCIES

Can I call a lawyer?	¿Puedo llamar a una abogada/o?
I'd like to see a duty solicitor.	Quiero ver a una/un abogada/o de oficio.
I will only make a statement in the presence of my lawyer.	Sólo declararé en presencia de mi abogada/o.
I understand.	Entiendo.
I don't understand.	No entiendo.
Is there someone here who speaks English?	¿Hay alguien aquí que hable inglés?
I'm sorry, I don't speak Spanish.	Lo siento, pero no hablo castellano.

police officer	policía/ pasma/ madera
arrested	detenida/o
police station	comisaría
police car	furgón policial
prison	cárcel
cell	celda
lawyer	abogada/o
police court	juzgado de guardia
judge	jueza/juez
Identity papers	DNI

THEY MAY SAY ...

¡Eséñeme su ...!
   Show me your ...

pasaporte
   passport

DNI
   identity papers

carné de conducir
   drivers' licence

¡Identifíquese!	Show me your identification!
¡Muéstreme su permiso de trabajo!	Show me your work permit!
Está usted detenida/o.	You have been arrested.
Vamos a ponerle una multa.	We're giving you a traffic fine.
Acompáñenos a la comisaría.	You must come with us to the police station.

EMERGENCIES

Puede no hacer ninguna declaración hasta que esté en presencia de su abogada/o.

You don't have to say anything until you are in the presence of a lawyer.

¿Cuáles son sus datos personales?

What is your name and address?

Ahora va a pasar usted al juzgado de guardia.

Now you will be taken to the police court.

Le hemos asignado una/un abogada/o de oficio.

We have assigned you a duty solicitor.

In this dictionary we have included the definite (**la** or **el**, corresponding to 'the' in English) or indefinite article (**una** or **un**, corresponding to 'a' or 'one' in English) with each noun. We have chosen either the definite or indefinite article according to the way the word is most likely to be used.

However, note that in most cases the articles are interchangeable. Thus **un abanico**, 'a fan' may also be **el abanico**, 'the fan'. **La abuela**, 'the grandmother', may also be **una abuela**, 'a grandmother'. Just remember, **el** becomes **un**, while **la** becomes **una**.

A

able (to be);		poder;
can		ser capaz de
Can (may) I take your photo?		
¿Puedo sacar un foto?		
Can you show me on the map?		
¿Me puede mostrar en el mapa?		
aboard		a bordo
abortion	el	aborto
above		arriba; sobre; encima de
abroad		en el extranjero; en el exterior
to accept		aceptar
accident	un	accidente
accommodation	el	alojamiento
acid (drug)		LSD; ácidos tripi (slang)
across		a través
action movies	las	películas de acción
activist		una/un activista
actor		una actriz/un actor
addict	un	adicto
addiction	la	drogadicción; dependencia
address	la	dirección
to admire		admirar
admission	la	entrada
to admit		admitir
adult		una/o adulta/o
advantage	una	ventaja
advice	el	consejo
aerogram	una	aerograma
aeroplane	el	avión
to be afraid of		tener miedo de
after		después de
[in the] afternoon (3 – 8pm)		[de la] tarde
this afternoon		esta tarde
again		otra vez
against		contra
age	la	edad
aggressive		agresivos
[a while] ago		hace [un rato]
[half an hour] ago		hace [media hora]
[three days] ago		hace [tres días]
to agree		estar de acuerdo
I don't agree.		
No soy de acuerdo.		
Agreed!		¡Hecho!
agriculture	la	agricultura

ahead		delante; adelante
aid (help)	la	ayuda
AIDS	la	SIDA
air	el	aire
air-conditioned		con aire acondicionado
air mail		por vía aérea
airport	el	aeropuerto
airport tax	la	tasa del aeropuerto
alarm clock	un	despertador
all		todo
an allergy	una	alergia
to allow		permitir
almost		casi
alone		sola/o
already		ya
also		también
altarpiece	el	retablo
altitude	la	altura
always		siempre
amateur	una/o	amateur; aficionada/o
amateur film	el	cine amateur
ambassador	la	embajadora
	el	embajador
among		entre
anaemia	la	anemia
anarchist	una/un	anarquista
ancient		antigua/o
and		y
angry		enojada/o
animals	los	animales
ankle	el	tobillo
annual		anual
answer	una	respuesta
answering machine	el	contestador automático
ant	la	hormiga
antenna	la	antena
anthologies	las	antologías
antibiotics	los	antibióticos
antinuclear group	un	grupo antinuclear
antiques	los	antigüedades
antiseptic		antiséptico
any		algúna/o
appendix	el	apéndice
appointment	una	cita
April		abril
arcades	los	portales
archaeological		arqueológica/o
architect		arquitecta/o
architecture	la	arquitectura
to argue		discutir
arm	el	brazo
aromatherapy	la	aromaterapia
to arrive		llegar
arrivals		llegadas
art	el	arte
art films	el	arte y ensayo
art gallery	el	museo
	la	galería de bellas artes
artist	una/un	artista
artwork	una	obra de arte
as big as		tan grande como
ASA; film speed	la	ASA; sensibilidad
ashtray	el	cenicero
to ask (for something)		pedir
to ask (a question)		preguntar
aspirin		aspirina
asthmatic		asmática/o
astronaut	una/un	astronauta
astronomer	una/un	astrónoma/o
athletics	el	atletismo
atmosphere	la	atmosfera
August		agosto
aunt	la	tía

automatic teller	el	cajero automático
autumn	el	otoño
avenue	el	avenida
awful		horrible

B

baby	un	bebé
baby food	la	comida de bebé potitos
baby powder	el	talco
babysitter	el	servicio de canguros
back (body)	la	espalda
at the back (behind)		detrás de
backpack	la	mochila
bad		mala/o
badger	el	tejón
bag	el	bolso
baggage	el	equipaje
baggage claim	la	recogida de equipajes
bakery	la	panadería
balcony	un	balcón
ball	la	pelota; el balón
ballet	el	ballet
ballpark figure	una	cifra aproximada
ballroom	la	sala de fiestas
band (music)	el	grupo
bandage	el	vendaje
bank	el	banco
banknotes	los	billetes (de banco)
baptism	el	bautizo
a bar; café	un	bar; café
bar with music	un	bar musical; pub
baseball	el	béisbol
basket	la	canasta; cesta

basketball	el	baloncesto
bastard	una/un	cabronaza/o
bat	el	bate
bath; shower gel	el	gel de baño
bathing suit	el	bañador
bathroom	el	baño
battery	la	batería; el acumulador
battery (small)	la	pila
to be		ser; estar
		see page 32
beach	la	playa
beak	el	pico
bear	el	orso
beautiful		bonita/o; hermosa/o
because		porque
bed	la	cama
bedroom (hotel)	una	habitación
bedroom (house)	una	alcobar
bees	las	abejas
before		antes
beggar	una/un	mendiga/o
begin		comenzar
behind		detrás de
below		abajo
beside		al lado de
best	la/el	mejor
a bet	una	apuesta
between		entre
bib	el	babero
the Bible	el	Biblio
bicycle	la	bicicleta
big		grande
bike	un	bici
bill	la	cuenta
billiards	el	billar español
binoculars	los	prismáticos
biodegradable		biodegradable
biography	la	biografía
bird	el	pájaro

D I C T I O N A R Y

birth certificate	la	partida de nacimiento
birthday	los	cumpleaños
birthday cake	el	pastel de cumpleaños
bite (dog)	una	mordedura
bite (insect)	una	picadura
black		negra/o
B&W (film)		blanco y negro
blanket	la	manta
to bleed		sangrar
to bless		bendecir
Bless you! (when someone sneezes)		¡Jesús!; ¡Salud!
blind		ciega/o
a blister	una	ampolla
blood	el	sangre
blood group	el	grupo sanguíneo
blood pressure	la	presión arterial
blood test	un	análisis de sangre
blue		azul
to board (ship, etc)		embarcarse
boarding pass	la	tarjeta de embarque
boat	el	barco
body	el	cuerpo
Bon appétit!		¡Buen provecho!
Bon voyage!		¡Buen viaje!
bone	el	hueso
book	un	libro
to book (make a reservation)		reservar
bookshop	la	librería
boots	las	botas
border	la	frontera
boring; bored		aburrida/o
to borrow		pedir
both		las/los dos

bottle	la	botella
bottle opener	el	destapador
[at the] bottom		[en el] fondo
box	la	caja
boxing	el	boxeo
boy	el	chico
boyfriend	el	novio
bra	el	sujetador
brakes	los	frenos
branch office	el	sucursal
of brass		de latón
brave		brava/o
bread	el	pan
to break		romper
broken (out of order)		rota/o; descompuesta/o
breakfast	el	desayuno
breast	el	pecho
breasts	los	senos
to breathe		respirar
a bribe	un	soborno
to bribe		sobornar
bridge	el	puente
brilliant		cojonuda/o
to bring		traer
broken		estropeado/a
bronchitis	el	bronquitis
brother	el	hermano
brown		marrón
a bruise	un	cardenal
bucket	un	cubo; balde
Buddhist	una	budista
bug	un	bicho
to build		costruir
building	el	edificio
bull	el	toro
a bullfight	una	corrida
bullfighting	los	toros
bullring	la	plaza de toros
bum; ass	el	culo
a burn	una	quemadura

bus (city)	el	autobús
bus (intercity)	el	autocar
business	la	economía;
	los	negocios;
	el	comercio
business person	una/un	comerciante
busker	una/un	artista;
		callejera/o
bus station	la	estación de
		autobús/
		autocares
bus stop	la	parada de
		autobús
busy		ocupada/o
but		pero
butterfly	la	mariposa
buttons	los	botones
to buy		comprar

I'd like to buy ...
Quisiera comprar ...

Where can I buy a ticket?
¿Dónde puedo comprar un boleto?

C

cable car	el	teleférico
cable TV	el	cable
cactus	un	cacto
cake shop	la	pastelería
calendar	el	calendario
calf	el	ternero
camera	la	cámara
		(fotográfica)
camera operator	el	operador
camera shop	la	tienda de
		fotografía
to camp		acampar

Can we camp here?
¿Está permitido acampar aquí?

campsite	el	camping

can (to be able)		poder; ser
		capaz de
We can do it.		Podemos hacerlo.
I can't do it.		No puedo hacerlo.
can (aluminium)	la	lata
can opener	las	abrelatas
canary	un	canario
to cancel		cancelar
candle	la	vela
canter	un	medio galope
canvas	el	lienzo
cape	la	capa
car	el	coche
car owner's title	los	papeles del
		coche
car registration	la	matrícula
to care (about something)		preocuparse por
to care (for someone)		cuidar de
Careful!		¡Cuidado!
cards	las	cartas
Careful!		¡Ojo!
caring		bondadosos
carrier bag	la	bolsa
	el	carro de la
		compra
to carry		llevar
carton	el	cartón
cartoons	los	dibujos
		animados
cash register	la	caja
		registradora
cashier	la	caja
cassette	el	casete
castle	el	castillo; la torre
cat	la/el	gata/o
cathedral	el	catedral
Catholic	la/el	católica/o
caves	las	cuevas
CD	el	compact

to celebrate		
(an event)		celebrar
(in general)		festejar
cemetary	el	cementerio
centimetre	el	centímetro
ceramic	la	cerámica
certificate	el	certificado
chair	la	silla
champagne	la	cava; champán
championships	los	campeonatos
chance	la	oportunidad
to change		cambiar
change (coins)	el	cambio
changing rooms	los	vestuarios
channel	el	canal
charming		encantadores
to chat up		ligar
cheap hotel	un	hotel barato
a cheat	una/un	tramposa/o
Cheat!		¡Tramposa/o!
to check		revisar
check-in (desk)	el	facturación de equipajes
Checkmate!		¡Jaque mate!
checkpoint (police)	un	retén
cheese	el	queso
chemist	la	farmacia
chess	el	ajedrez
chess board	el	tablero de ajedrez
chest	el	pecho
chewing gum	el	chicle
chicken	el	pollo
child	una/un	niña/o
childminding service	la	guardería
children	los	hijos; niños
chocolate	el	chocolate
to choose		escoger
Christian	una/un	cristiana/o
christian name	el	nombre de pila
Christmas Day	la	Navidad
Christmas Eve	la	Nochebuena
church	una	iglesia
a cigarette	un	cigarro
cigarette machine	la	máquina de tabaco
cigarette papers	el	papel de fumar
cigarettes	los	cigarrillos
cinema	el	cine
circus	el	circo
citizenship	la	ciudadanía
city	la	ciudad
city centre	el	centro de la ciudad
city walls	las	murallas
class	la	clase
class system	la	sistema de clases
classical art	el	arte clásico
classical theatre	el	teatro clásico
clean		limpia/o
clean hotel	un	hotel limpio
cleaning		el trabajo de limpieza
client	la/el	clienta/e
cliff	el	acantilado
to climb		subir
cloak	el	capote
cloakroom	la	guardarropía
clock	el	reloj
to close		cerrar
closed		cerrado
clothing	la	ropa
clothing store	la	tienda de ropa
cloud	el	nube
cloudy		Está nublado; Estará nublado.
clown	la/el	payasa/o
clutch (car)	el	embrague
coach (trainer)	la	entrenadora
	el	entrenador

English	Spanish
coast	la costa
coat	el abrigo
cocaine	la cocaína (coca)
cocaine addict	una/un cocainómana/o
cockerel	el gallito
cockroach	una cucaracha
codeine	la codeína
coins	las monedas
a cold	un resfriado; un catarro
cold (adj)	fría/o
It's cold.	
Hace frío; Hará frío.	
to have a cold	
estar constipada/o	
cold turkey	el síndrome de abstinencia mono (slang)
cold water	el agua fría
colleague	una colega
college	la residencia de estudiantes
colour (film)	el (película) en color
comb	un peine
to come	venir
to come; arrive	llegar
comedy	la comedia
comet	la cometa
comfortable	cómoda/o
comics	los comics
communion	la comunión
communist	el comunista
companion	una/un compañera/o
company	la compañía
compass	la brújula
computer games	los juegos de ordenador
a concert	un concierto
concert hall	el teatro;

English	Spanish
condoms	los preservativos; condones
conductor	una cobradora; un cobrador
confession	una confesión
to confirm	confirmar
Congratulations!	¡Felicidades!
conservative	conservador
to be constipated	estar estreñida/o
constipation	el estreñimiento
construction work	la construcción
consulate	el consulado
contact lenses	los lentes de contacto
contemporary	contemporána/o
contraception	el anticonceptivo
contraceptives	los anticonceptivos
contract	el contrato
convent	el convento
to cook	cocinar
cool [colloquial]	guay
cork oak	un alcornoque
corner	
(interior)	el rincón
(exterior)	la esquina
corrupt	corrupta/o
to cost	costar; valer
How much does it cost to go to ...?	
¿Cuánto cuesta/vale ir a ...?	
It costs a lot.	
Cuesta bastante.	
cotton	el algodón
country	un aís
countryside	el campo
a cough	un tos
to count	contar
coupon	uno cupón
court (legal)	el tribunal; el juzgado
court (tennis)	la cancha
cow	la vaca

crafts	la	artesanía
crafty		habilidosa/o; ingeniosa/o
crag; wall of rock	un	peñón
crane (bird)	la	grulla
crazy		loca/o
credit card	una	tarjeta de crédito
creep (slang)	una/un	desgraciada/o
cricket	el	críquet
cross (religious)	el	cruz
cross (angry)	el	enojada/o
cross-country trail	el	camino
a cuddle	un	abrazo
cup	una	copa
cupboard	el	armario
curator	la	conservadora;
	el	conservador
current affairs	un	informativo
customs	la	aduana
to cut		cortar
cyber art	el	arte cibernético
to cycle		andar en bicicleta
cycling	el	ciclismo
cyclist	una/un	ciclista
cystitis	la	cistitis

D

dad		papá
dag; bozo		hortera
daily		diariamente
dairy products	los	productos lácteos
to dance		bailar
dancing	el	bailar
dangerous		peligrosa/o
dark		oscuro
date (appointment)	una	cita

date (time)	la	fecha
to date		citarse
date of birth	la	fecha de nacimiento
daughter	la	hija
dawn	la	madrugada
day	el	día
day after tomorrow		pasado mañana
day before yesterday		anteayer
in (six) days		dentro de [seis] días
dead		muerta/o
deaf		sorda/o
to deal		repartir
death	la	muerte
December		diciembre
to decide		decidir
deck (of cards)	una	baraja
deep		profunda/o
deer	el	ciervo; corzo; gamo
deforestation	la	deforestación
degree	el	título
delay	una	demora
delicatessen	la	charcutería
delirious		delirante
democracy	la	democracia
demonstration	una	manifestación
dental floss	el	hilo dental
dentist	el	dentista
to deny		negar
deodorant	el	desodorante
to depart (leave)		partir; salir de
department stores	los	grandes almacenes
departure	la	salida
descendent	el	descendiente
desert	el	desierto
design	el	diseño
destination	el	destino
to destroy		destruir

English		Spanish
detail	una	detalle
detox	el	desintoxicación
deuce		iguales
diabetic		diabética/o
dial tone	el	tono
diaphragm	la	diafragma
diarrhoea	la	diarrea
diary	la	agenda
dice; die	los	dados
dictionary	el	diccionario
different		diferente
difficult		difícil
dining car	el	vagón restaurante
dinner	la	cena
direct		directo
director	la	directora;
	el	director
dirty		sucia/o
disabled		minusválida/o
disadvantage	una	desventaja
discount	un	descuento;
	una	rebaja
to discover		descubrir
discrimination	el	discriminación
disease	el	enfermedad
dismissal	el	despido
distributor	la	distribuidora;
	el	distribuidor
diving	el	submarinismo
diving equipment	el	equipo de inmersión
dizzy		mareada/o
to do		hacer

What are you doing?
¿Qué hace?
I didn't do it.
No lo hice.

doctor	la	doctora;
	el	doctor;
	la/el	médica/o

a documentary	un	documental
dog	la/el	perra/o
dole	el	paro
dolls	las	muñecas
donkey	el	burro
door	la	puerta
dope	la	droga
double	el	doble
a double bed	una	cama de matrimonio
a double room	una	habitación doble
a dozen	una	docena
drama	el	drama
dramatic		dramática/o
draughts	las	damas
to draw		dibujar; pintar
to dream		soñar
dress	el	vestido
a drink	una	copa
to drink		beber; tomar
to drive		conducir
driver's licence	el	carnet; permiso de conducir
drug	la	medicina
drug addiction	la	toxicomanía
drug dealer	el	traficante de drogas camello (slang)
drugs	las	drogas
drums	la	batería
to be drunk		emborracharse
to dry (clothes)		secar
duck	el	pato
dummy (baby's)	un	chupete

E

each		cada
eagle	la	águila
ear	la	oreja

English		Spanish
early		temprano
It's early.		Es temprano.
to earn		ganar
earrings	los	pendientes
ears	las	orejas
Earth	la	Tierra
earth	la	tierra
earthquake	un	terremoto
east		este
Easter		Pascua; Semana Santa
easy		fácil
to eat		comer
economy	la	economía
ecstasy (drug)	el	éxtasis
editor	la/el	editora/editor
education	el	educación
eight		ocho
eighteen		dieciocho
eighth		octava/o
eighty		ochenta
elections	las	elecciones
electorate	el	electorado
electricity	la	electricidad
elevator	el	ascensor
eleven		once
embarassed		avergonzada/o
embarassment	la	vergüenza
embassy	la	embajada ...
emergency exit	la	salida de emergencia
employee	la/el	emleada/o
employer	la/el	jefa/e
empty		vacía/o
end	el	fin
to end		acabar; terminar
endangered species		
los **especies en**	peligro de extinción
engagement	el	compromiso

engine	el	motor
engineer	la/el	ingeniera/o
engineering	la	ingeniería
England		Inglaterra
English		inglés
to enjoy (oneself)		divertirse
enough		bastante; suficiente
Enough!		Basta!
to enter		entrar
entertaining		entretenido
envelope	el	sobre
environment	el	medio ambiente
epileptic		epiléptica/o
Epiphany	el	día de los reyes magos
epoch	la	época
equal opportunity	la	igualdad de oportunidades
equality	la	igualdad
equipment	el	equipo
erection	la	erección
erotic literature	la	literatura erótica
etching	la	aguafuerte
european	una/un	europea/o
euthanasia	la	eutanasia
evening	la	noche
every day		cada día
example	el	exemplo
For example, ...		
Por exemplo, ...		
excellent		excelente; fantástica/o
exchange (money)	el	cambio
to exchange; give gifts		regalar
exchange rate	el	tipo de cambio
excluded		no incluido
Excuse me.		Perdón.
to exhibit		exponer

English		Spanish
exhibition	la	exposición
exit	la	salida
expensive		cara/o
exploitation	la	explotación
express		expreso
express mail	el	correo urgente
eye	el	ojo

F

face	la	cara
factory	la	fábrica
factory worker	una/un	obrera/o
fall (autumn)	el	otoño
family	la	familia
famous		conocida/o; famosa/o
fan (hand held)	el	abanico
fan (machine)	el	ventilador
fans (of a team)	la	afición
Fantastic! (swear word)		¡De puta madre!
far		lejos
farm	la	granja
farmer	la	agricultora; el agricultor; la/el granjera/o
fast		rápida/o
fat		gorda/o
father	el	padre; papá
father-in-law	el	suegro
fault (in manufacture)	un	desperfecto
fault (someone's)	la	culpa
faulty		defectuosa/o
fear	el	miedo
February		febrero
to feel		sentir
feelings	los	sentimientos
fence	la	cerca
fencing	la	esgrima
festival	el	festival

English		Spanish
fever	la	fiebre
few		pocos
fiancée/fiancé	la/el	novia/o
fiction	la	ficción
field	el	campo
fifteen		quince
fifth		quinta/o
fifty		cincuenta
fight	la	lucha
to fight		luchar contra; combatir
figures	las	cifras
to fill		llenar
a film (negatives)	la	película
film (cinema)	el	cine
film (for camera)	un	carrete
film speed	la	sensibilidad
film noir	el	cine negro
films	el	cine
filtered		con filtro
to find		encontrar
a fine	una	multa
finger	el	dedo
fir	el	abeto
fire (controlled)	el	fuego
fire (uncontrolled)	un	incendio
firewood	la	leña
first		primera/o (1r)
first-aid kit	el	maletín de primeros auxilios
fish (alive)	el	pez
fish (as food)	el	pescado
fish shop	la	pescadería
five		cinco
flag	la	bandera
flash	la	bombilla; flash
flat (land, etc)		plana/o
flea	la	pulga
flashlight	una	linterna
flight	el	vuelo

domestic flight	un	vuelo doméstico
floor	el	suelo
floor (storey)	el	piso
flour	la	harina
flower	un	flor
flower seller	la/el	vendedora; vendedor de flores
fly	una	mosca
It's foggy.		Hay niebla.
to follow		seguir
food	la	comida
foot	el	pie
football	el	fútbol
footpath	el	camino
foreign		extranjera/o
forest	el	bosque
forever		[para] siempre
to forget		olvidar
I forget.		
Me olvido.		
Forget about it!; Don't worry!		
¡No te preocupes!; ¡No hay de qué!		
to forgive		perdonar
fortnight	la	quincena
fortune teller	una	adivinadora
	un	adivinador
forty		cuarenta
four		cuatro
fourteen		catorce
fourth		cuarta/o
fox	el	zorro
foyer	el	vestíbulo
free (not bound)		libre
free (of charge)		gratis
to freeze		helar; congelar
Friday		viernes
friend	una/un	amiga/o;
	una/un	colega
It's frosty.		Está helando.

frozen foods	los	productos congelados
fruit picking	la	recolección de fruta
to fuck		follar; echar un polvo; joder
full		llena/o
fun	un	diversión
for fun		en broma
to have fun		divertirse
to make fun of		burlarse de
funeral	el	funeral
future	el	futuro

G

gallop	el	galope
game (games)	el	juego
game (sport)	la	partida
a game show	un	concurso
garage (mechanic's)	el	taller
garbage	la	basura
gardening	la	jardinería
gardens	los	jardines
gas cartridge	el	cartucho de gas
gate	la	puerta
gay		gay
gear stick	el	cambio de marchas
general		generale
genet	una	gineta
Get lost!		¡Hasta nunca!
gift	el	regalo
gig	un	bolo
girl	la	chica
girlfriend	la	novia
to give		dar
Could you give me ...?		
¿Podría darme ...?		

H

glacier	el	glaciar
glandular fever	la	fiebre glandular
glass	el	vidrio
gloves	los	guantes
to go		ir; partir

Let's go.
Vamos; Vámonos.
We'd like to go to ...
Queremos ir a ...
Go straight ahead.
Vaya derecho.
to go out with
salir con

goal	el	gol
goalkeeper		portera/o
goat	la	cabra
God		Dios
of gold		de oro
Good afternoon.		Buenas tardes.
(until about 8pm)		
Good evening/night.		Buenas noches.
Good health; Cheers!		¡Salud!
good hotel	un	buen hotel
Good luck!		¡buena suerte!
Good morning.		Buenos días.
Goodbye.		¡Adiós!
goose	el	ganso
gorilla	la	gorila
gorse	la	aulaga
goth		siniestra/o
Gothic art	el	arte gótico
government	el	gobierno
gram	un	gramo
grandchild	una/un	nieta/o
grandfather	el	abuelo
grandmother	la	abuela
grapes	las	uvas
graphic art	el	arte gráfico
grass	la	hierba
grave	la	tumba

great		fantástica/o
Great!		¡Por supuesto!
green		verde
greengrocer	la	verdulería; frutería
grey		gris
to guess		adivinar
guide(person)	la/el	guía
guide (audio)	la	guía audio
guidebook	la	guía
guide dog	el	perro lazarillo
guided trek	un	excursión; guiada
guinea pig	el	conejillo de indias
guitar	la	guitarra
gums	las	encías
gym	el	gimnasio
gymnastics	la	gimnasia rítmica

H

hair	el	pelo
hairbrush	el	cepillo (para el cabello; pelo)
half		media/o
half a litre	un	medio litro
to hallucinate		alucinar
ham	el	jamón
hammer	el	martillo
hammock	la	hamaca
hand	la	mano
handbag	el	bolso
handicrafts	la	artesanía
handlebars	los	manillar
handmade		hecho a mano
handsome		hermoso
happy		feliz
Happy birthday!		¡Feliz cumpleaños!
Happy saint's day!		¡Feliz santo!

**D
I
C
T
I
O
N
A
R
Y**

harbour	el	puerto
hard		dura/o
hare	el	liebre
harness	el	arnés
harrassment	el	acoso
hash	el	hachís; chocolate (slang)
to have		tener; haber
		see page 31

Do you have ...?

¿Tiene usted ...?

I have ...

Tengo ...

hayfever	la	alergia al polen
he		él
head	la	cabeza
a headache	un	dolor de cabeza
health	la	salud
to hear		oír
hearing aid	el	audífono
heart	el	corazón
heat	el	calor
heater	una	estufa
heather	el	brezo
heavy		pesada/o
Hello.		¡Hola!
Hello! (answering a call)		¿Diga?
helmet	el	casco
Help!		¡Ayudo!
to help		ayudar

Can you help me?

¿Puede ayudarme?

hen	la	galina
hepatitis	el	hepatitis
herbs	las	hierbas
herbalist	la	herborista
here		aquí
heroin	la	heroína; jaco; caballo (slang)

heroin addict	una/un	heroinómana/o; yonki (slang)
high		alta/o
high school	el	instituto
to hike		ir de excursión
hiking	el	excursionismo; senderismo
hiking boots	las	botas de montaña
hiking routes	los	caminos rurales
hill	la	colina
Hindu		hindú
to hire		alquiler
holidays (vacation)	los	vacaciones

Where can I hire a bicycle?

¿Dónde puedo alquilar un bicicleta?

to hitchhike		hacer dedo; hacer auto stop
HIV positive		seropositiva/o
holiday	un	día festivo
Holy Week	la	Semana santa
homelessness		los sin hogar
homeopathy	la	homeopatía
homosexual	la/el	homosexual
honey	el	miel
honeymoon	la	luna de miel
horns	los	cuernos
horrible		horrible
horse	el	caballo
horse riding	la	equitación
hospital	el	hospital
hot		caliente

It's hot.

Hace calor; Hará calor.

to be hot		tener calor
hot water	la	agua caliente
house	la	casa
housework	el	trabajo de casa

how	cómo
How do I get to ...?	
¿Cómo puedo llegar a ...?	
How do you say ...?	
¿Cómo se dice ...?	
hug	un abrazo
human rights	los derechos humanos
a hundred	cien; ciento
to be hungry	tener hambre
husband	el esposo; marido

I

I	yo
ibex	una cabra montés
ice	el hielo
ice axe	un piolet
icecream	un helado
identification card	el carnet de identidad
identification	el identificación
idiot	una/un idiota
if	si
ill	enferma/o
immigration	la inmigración
important	importante
It's important.	Es importante.
It's not important.	No importa.
in a hurry	prisa
in front of	enfrente de; delante de
included	incluido
income tax	el impuesto sobre la renta
incomprehensible	incomprensible
indicator	el intermitente
indigestion	la indigestión
industry	la industria
inequality	la desigualdad

an infection	una infección
an inflammation	una inflamación
influenza	la gripe
inhaler	el inhalador
to inject	inyectarse; chutarse
injection	una inyección
injury	una herida
inside	adentro
instructor	la/el profesor
insurance	el seguro
intense	intensos
interesting	interesante
intermission	el descanso; media parte
international	internacional
interview	una entrevista
Ireland	Irlanda
iris	el lirio
island	la isla
itch	un comezón; picazón
itinerary	el itinerario
IUD	un DIU

J

jack (for car)	un gato
jacket	una chaqueta chupa
jail	el cárcel
January	enero
jar	una jarra
jaw	la mandíbula
jealous	celosos
jeans	los tejanos; vaqueros
jeep	un yip
jewellery	la joyería
Jewish	judía/o
job	el trabajo
job advertisement	un anuncio de trabajo

job centre	el	INEM
job description	un	descripción del trabajo
jockey	un	jockey
joke	una	broma
to joke		bromear
journalist	un	periodista
journey	el	viaje
judge	una/un	juez
judo	el	judo
juice	el	jugo
July		julio
to jump		saltar
jumper (sweater)	el	jersey; pullover; suéter
June		junio
justice	el	justicia

K

kestrel	el	cernícalo
key	la	llave
keyboard	el	teclado
kick	un	chut
kick off	el	saque inicial
kidney	un	riñón
to kill		matar
kilogram	un	quilo
kilometre	un	kilómetro
kind		amable
kindergarten	la	escuela de párvulos
king	el	rey
kiss	un	beso
to kiss		besar
Kiss me.		Bésame.
kitchen	la	cocina
kite (bird)	el	milano
kitten	la/el	gatita/o
knapsack	la	mochila

knee	la	rodilla
knife	un	cuchillo
knight	el	caballo
to know (someone)		conocer
to know (something)		saber
I don't know.		
No lo sé.		

L

lace	el	encaje
lake	el	lago
lamb	el	cordero
land	la	tierra
languages	las	idiomas; lenguas
large		grande
last	la/el	última/o
last month	el	mes pasado
last night		anoche
last week	la	semana pasada
last year	el	año pasado
late		tarde
It's late.		
laugh		reírse
launderette	la	lavandería
lavendar	la	lavanda
law	la	ley
	el	derecho
lawyer	una/un	abogada/o
laxatives	la	xantes
laziness	la	pereza
lazy		perezosa/o
leaded(petrol; gas)	la	gasolina con plomo
leader	un	jefe
league	la	liga
to learn		aprender
leather	el	cuero

leather wine bottle	las botas de vino	little (small)		pequeña/o; poca/o
leathergoods	los artículos de cuero	a little (amount)	un poquito	
ledge	el saliente	a little bit	un poco; un poquito	
to be left (behind/ over)	quedar	to live (life)		vivir
left (not right)	izquierdo	to live (somewhere)		vivir; ocupar
left luggage	la consigna	Long live ...!		¡Arriba ...!
left-wing	de izquierda; izquierdista	local		de cercanías
		local council	los municipales	
left-winger (inf)	un progre	local; city bus	el autobús	
leg	la pierna	location	el terreno para rodaje de exteriores	
leg (in race)	una etapa			
legalisation	la legalización			
legislation	la legislación	lock	la cerradura	
lens	el objetivo	to lock		cerrar
Lent	la Cuaresma	long		larga/o
Leo	leo	long distance		de largo recorrido
lesbian	una lesbiana			
less	menos	long-distance bus; coach		autocar; autobús
letter	una carta			
liar	una/un mentirosa/o	to look		mirar
library	la biblioteca	to look after		cuidar
lice	los piojos	to look for		buscar
to lie	mentir	looking after children		como canguro; en cuidar niñas/os
life	la vida			
lift (elevator)	el ascensor			
light (n)	la luz	lookout point	un mirador	
light (adj)	leve; ligera/o	loose change	las monedas sueltas	
light (blonde)	rubia/o	to lose		perder
light (clear)	claro	loser	la/el perdedora/ perdedor	
light bulb	la bombilla			
light meter	el fotómetro	loss	la pérdida	
lighter	el encendedor; mechero	a lot		mucho
		lottery ticket seller	el vendedor de lotería	
to like	gustar(le); apreciar			
		loud		ruidosa/o
line	la línea	to love		amar; querer
lips	los labios	lover	la/el amante	
lipstick	el lápiz de labios	low		baja/o
to listen	escuchar	low/high blood pressure	la presión baja/ alta	

loyal		leales
luck	la	suerte
lucky		afortunada/o
ludo	el	parchís
luggage	el	equipaje
luggage lockers	la	consigna automática
lump	un	bulto
lunch	el	almuerzo;
	la	comida
lunchtime	el	hora de comer
luxury	el	lujo
lynx	un	lince

M

machine	una	máquina
mad		loca/o
made (of)		estar hecho de
magazine	una	revista
magician		maga/o
mail	el	correo
mailbox	el	buzón
main road	la	carretera
main square	el	Plaza Mayor
majority	la	mayoría
to make		hacer; fabricar
make-up	el	maquillaje
male	un	masculino
man	un	hombre
manager	la/el	jefa/e de sección; manager; gerente
	la	directora
	el	director
manual worker	la/el	obrera/o; trabajadora/ trabajador
many		muchas/os
Many happy returns!		¡Que cumplas muchos más!

map	un	mapa
Can you show me on the map?		
¿Puede mostrar en el mapa?		
March		marzo
mare	la	yegua
margarine	la	margarina
marijuana	la	marihuana maría (slang)
marital status	el	estado civil
market	el	mercado
marriage	el	matrimonio
to marry		casarse
marvellous		maravillosa/o
mass	la	misa
massage	el	masaje
mat	la	esterilla
match	el	partido
matches	los	fósforos; cerillas
[It doesn't] matter.		No importa.
[What's the] matter?		¿Qué pasa?
mattress	el	colchón
May		mayo
mayor	la/el	alcalde
mechanic	una	mecánica
	uno	mecánico
medal	una	medalla
medicine	la	medicina;
	el	medicamento
meditation	la	meditación
to meet		encontrar
member	el	miembro
menstruation	la	menstruación; regla
menthol (cigarettes)	los	(cigarillos) mentolados
menu	un	menú;
	la	carta
message	un	mensaje
metal	el	metal
meteor	el	meteorito
metre	el	metro

midnight	la medianoche	mother-in-law	la suegra
migraine	una migraña	motorboat	una motora
military service	el servicio militar	motorcycle	una motocicleta; moto
milk	la leche		
millimetre	un milímetro	motorway (tollway)	un autopista
million	un millón	mountain	la montaña
mind	la mente	mountain bike	una mountain bike; bicicleta de montaña
mineral water	la agua mineral		
a minute	un minuto		
Just a minute.	Espera un segundo.	mountain hut	un refugio de montaña
in [five] minutes	dentro de [cinco] minutos	mountain path	el sendero
		mountain range	la cordillera
mirror	el espejo	mountaineering	el alpinismo
miscarriage	un aborto natural	mouse	el ratón
to miss (feel absen	extrañar	mouth	la boca
mistake	un error	movie	el cine
to mix	mezclar	mud	el lodo
mobile breath testing unit	el control de alcoholemia	Mum	Mamá
		muscle	el músculo
mobile phone	el teléfono móbil	museum	el museo
modem	un modem	music	la música
Modernism	el modernismo	musician	una/un música/o
moisturising cream	la crema hidratante	Muslim	una musulmana
			un musulmán
monastery	el monasterio	mute	muda/o
Monday	lunes		
money	el dinero	**N**	
mongoose	la mangosta	name	el nombre
monk	el monje	nappy	un pañal
monkey	el mono	nappy rash cream	la crema para la irritación de los pañales
month	el mes		
this month	este mes		
monument	el monumento	national park	el parque nacional
moon	la luna		
more	más	nationality	la nacionalidad
morning (6am - 1pm)	de la mañana	nature	la naturaleza
this morning	esta mañana; madrugada	naturopath	la naturópata
		nausea	la náusea
mosque	la mezquita	near	cerca
mother	la madre; mamá		

nearby hotel	un	hotel cercano	nose	la nariz
nebula		nebulosa	notebook	un cuaderno
necessary		necesaria/o	nothing	nada
necklace	un	collar	It's nothing.	
to need		necesitar	No es nada.	
needle (sewing)	una	aguja	not yet	todavía no
needle (syringe)	la	jeringa	noughts & crosses	tres en raya
neither		tampoco	novel	la novela
net	el	red	November	noviembre
never		nunca	now	ahora
new		nueva/o	nuclear energy	la energía nuclear
news	las	noticias	nuclear testing	las pruebas
newsagency	el	quiosco		nucleares
newspaper	un	periódico	nun	una monja
newspaper in	un	periódico en	nurse	una/un enfermera/o
English		inglés		
newspapers	los	periódicos		
New Year's Day	el	año nuevo		
New Year's Eve	la	Nochevieja		
New Zealand	la	Nueva Zelanda	**O**	
next		próximo	oak	el roble
next month	el	mes que viene	obvious	obvia/o
next to		al lado de	ocean	el océano
next week	la	semana que	October	octubre
		viene	offence	una ofensa
next year	el	año que viene	office	la oficina
nice		simpática/o;	office work	el trabajo de
		agradable		oficina
nickname	un	apodo	office worker	una/un oficinista;
night	la	noche		empleada/o
nine		nueve	offside	fuera de juego
nineteen		diecinueve	often	a menudo
ninety		noventa	oil (cooking)	el aceite
ninth		novena/o	oil (crude)	el petróleo
noise	el	ruido	OK	regular;
noisy		ruidosa		De acuerdo.
non-direct		semidirecto	old	vieja/o
non-fiction	el	ensayo	old city	la ciudad antigua
none		nada		el barrio viejo
noon	la	mediodía		el casco antiguo
north	la	norte	olive oil	el aceite de oliva
			olives	la aceitunas

Olympic Games	los	juegos olímpicos
omelette	la	tortilla
on		en; sobre
on time		a tiempo
once; one time	una	vez
one		uno; una; un
one million	un	millón
one-way (ticket)	un	(billete) sencillo
only		sola/o; solamente
open		abierta/o
to open		abrir
opening	el	inauguración
opera	la	ópera
opera house	el	teatro de la ópera
operation	una	operación
operator	una/un	operadora
opinion	un	opinión
opposite		frente a
optician	una/un	óptica
or		o
oral		oral
orange	una	naranja
orchestra	la	orquesta
orchid	una	orquídea
order	el	orden
to order		ordenar
ordinary		corriente; normal
organise		organizar
orgasm	el	orgasmo
original	el	original
other		otra/o
otter	la	nutria
outgoing		abiertos
outside	el	exterior; fuera
over		sobre
overcoat	un	sobretodo
overdose	un	sobredosis
to owe		deber

owl	un	búho
owner	la/el	dueña/o
ox	el	buey
oxygen	el	oxígeno
ozone layer	la	capa de ozono

P

pacifier	un	chupete
package	un	paquete
packet (cigarettes)	un	paquete; una cajetilla
padlock	el	candado
page	una	página
a pain	un	dolor
painful		dolorosa/o
pain in the neck (bore)	una/un	plasta
painkillers	los	analgésicos
to paint		pintar
painter	una/un	pintora/pintor
painting (the art)	la	pintura
paintings	los	cuadros
pair [of gloves]	un	par [de guantes]
pair (a couple)	una	pareja
palace	el	palacio
pan	una	cazuela
panty liners	la	salva slip
pap smear	una	citología
paper	el	papel
paraplegic	una/un	parapléjica/o
parcel	un	paquete
parents	los	padres
a park	un	parque
to park		estacionar
parliament	el	parlamento
parrot	el	loro

part	una parte
party	la fiesta
party politics	los partidos políticos
pass	un pase
passenger	un pasajero
passive	pasiva/o
passport	el pasaporte
passport number	el número de pasaporte
past	el pasado
path	el sendero
patient (adj)	paciente
to pay	pagar
payment	un pago
peace	la paz
peak	el cumbre
pedestrian	una/un peatón
pelota	la pelota vasca
pelota player	el pelotari
pen (ballpoint)	el bolígrafo
pencil	un lápiz
penicillin	la penicilina
penis	el pene
penknife	la navaja
pensioner	una/un pensionista
people	la gente
pepper	la pimienta
percent	por ciento
performance	la actuación
performance art	la interpretación
performing artist	el artista callejero
period pain	el dolor menstrual
permanent	permanente
permanent collection	un exposición permanente
permission; permit	el permiso
person	una persona
personality	la personalidad
to perspire	sudar

petition	una petición
petrol	la gasolin; bencina
pharmacy	la farmacia
phone book	una guía telefónica
phone box	la cabina telefónica
phonecard	la tarjeta de teléfono
photo	una fotografía; foto
Can (May) I take a photo?	
¿Puedo sacar una foto?	
photographer	una/un fotógrafa/o
photography	la fotografía
pick; pickaxe	una piqueta
to pick up	ligar
pie	un pastel
piece	el pedazo; trozo
pig	el cerdo
pill	una pastilla
the Pill	la píldora
pillow	la almohada
pillowcase	una funda de almohada
pinball	el millón
pine	el pino
pink	rosa
pipe	una pipa
place	el lugar; sitio
place of birth	el lugar de nacimiento
plain	la llanura
plane	el avión
planet	la planeta
plant	una planta
to plant	sembrar
plastic	el plástico
plate	un plato
plateau	la meseta
platform	el andén
play	la obra; pieza
to play	jugar

(sport/games)	
to play (music)	tocar
player (sports)	una jugadora
	un jugador
player	una/un música/o
playing cards	los naipes
to play cards	jugar a cartas
plug (bath)	un tapón
plug (electricity)	un enchufe
pocket	el bolsillo
poetry	la poesía
point (tip)	el punto
point (games)	un tanto
to point	apuntar
poker	el póquer
police	la policía
politics	la política
political speech	el mitin
politicians	los políticos
pollen	el polen
polls	los sondeos
pollution	la contaminación
pool (swimming)	la piscina
pool (game)	el billar americano
poor	pobre
popcorn	las palomitas (de maíz)
Pope	el Papa
popular magazines	las revistas del corazón
port	el puerto
portrait sketcher	la/el retratista; caricaturista
possible	posible
It's (not) possible.	(No) es posible.
postcard	la postal
post code	el código postal
postage	el franqueo
poster	un póster
post office	el Correos

pot (ceramic)	la olla
pot (dope)	el costo
pottery	la alfarería; cerámica
poverty	la pobreza
power	el poder
prayer	un oración
prayer book	un devocionario
to prefer	preferir
pregnant	embarazada
prehistoric art	el arte prehistórico
pre-menstrual tension	la tensión premenstrual
to prepare	preparar
present (gift)	un regalo
present (time)	el presente
presentation	la presentación
presenter	una presentadora
	un presentador
president	la/el presidenta/e
pressure	la presión
pretty	bonita/o
prevent	prevenir
price	el precio
pride	el orgullo
priest	un sacerdote
prime minister	la primera ministra
	el primer ministro
a print (artwork)	un grabado
prison	el cárcel; prisión
prisoner	una/un prisionera/o
private	privada/o
private hospital	la clínica
privatisation	la privatización
to produce	producir
producer	una productora
	un productor
profession	una profesión
profit	el beneficio
profitability	la rentabilidad

programme	la	programa
projector	el	proyector
promise	una	promesa
proposal	una	propuesta
to protect		proteger
protected forest	el	bosque pretegida
protected species	los	especies pretegidos
protest	una	protesta
to protest		protestar
public toilet	los	servicios; aseos públicos
to pull		jalar
pump	la	bomba
puncture	un	pinchazo
to punish		castigar
puppy	una/un	cachorra/o
pure		pura/o
purple		púrpura; lila
to push		empujar
to put		poner

qualifications	los	cualificaciones
quality	la	calidad
quarrel	una	pelea; riña
quarter	un	cuarto
queen	la	reina
question	una	pregunta
to question		preguntar
question (topic)	el	asunto;
	la	cuestion
queue	una	cola
quick		rápida/o
quiet (adj)		tranquila/o
quiet	el	silencioso
	la	tranquilidad
to quit		dejar

R		
rabbit	el	conejo
race (breed)	la	raza
race (sport)	la	carrera
racing bike	la	bicicleta de carreras
racism	el	racismo
racquet	una	raqueta
radiator	el	radiador
railroad	el	ferrocarril
railway station	la	estación
rain	la	lluvia
It's raining.		Llueve.
rally	una	concentración
rape	la	violación
rare		rara/o
a rash	la	irritación
rat	una	rata
rate of pay	el	salario
raw		cruda/o
razor	la	afeitadora
razor blades	las	cuchillas de afeitar
to read		leer
ready		lista/o

Are you ready?
¿Estás lista/o?
I'm ready.
Estoy lista/o.

to realise		darse cuenta de
realism (movies)	el	cine realista
Realism	el	realismo
reason	el	razón;
	el	motivo
receipt	el	recibo
to receive		recibir
recent		reciente
recently		recientemente
to recognise		reconocer
to recommend		recomendar
record	un	disco

record shop	la	tienda de discos	
recording	un	grabación	
recyclable		reciclable	
recycling	el	reciclar	
recycling bin	el	contenedor de reciclaje	
red		roja/o	
referee	el	árbitro	
reference	las	referencias	
reflection (mirror)	el	reflejo	
reflection (thinking)	el	reflexión	
reflexology	la	reflexología	
refrigerator	una	nevera	
refugee	una/un	refugiada/o	
refund	un	reembolso	
to refund		reembolsar	
to refuse		negar(se)	
regional		regional	
registered mail	el	correo certificado	
to regret		lamentar	
relationship	la	relación	
to relax		relajar	
religion	el	religión	
religious procession	la	procesión religiosa	
to remember		recordar	
remote		remota/o	
remote control	el	mando a distancia	
rent	el	alquiler	
to rent		alquilar	
to repeat		repetir	

Could you repeat that please?
¿Puede repetirlo, por favor?

republic	una	república	
reservation	una	reservación	
to reserve		reservar	
resignation	la	dimisión	
respect	el	respecto	
rest (relaxation)	el	descanso	

rest (what's left)	el	resto	
to rest		descansar	
restaurant	un	restaurante	
resumé	el	currículum	
retired		jubilada/o	
to return		volver; regresar	
return (ticket)	un	(billete) de ida y vuelta	
review	la	crítica	
rhythm	el	ritmo	
ribs	las	costillas	
rich (wealthy)		rica/o	
to ride (a horse)		montar (a caballo)	
right (correct)		correcta/o; exacta/o	
right (not left)		derecho	
to be right		tener razón	
You're right.		tienes razón	
civil rights		derechos civiles	
right now		en este momento	
right-wing		derechista	
ring (on finger)	el	anillo	
ring (of phone)	la	llamada	
I'll give you a ring.		Te llamaré.	
ring (sound)	el	sonido	
ring-road	el	cinturón	
	la	carretera de circunvalación	
rip-off	un	estafa	
risk	un	riesgo	
river	el	río	
road (main)	la	carretera	
road map	la	mapa de carreteras	
roadie	un	transportista	
to rob		robar	
rock	la	roca	
rock climbing	el	escalar	
[wall of] rock; crag	un	peñón	

rock group	un grupo de rock		to say	decir
rolling	de liar		to scale/climb	trepar
romance	el amor		scarves	los pañuelos; bufandas
room (in hotel)	una habitación			
room (in any building)	un cuarto		school	la escuela
			science	las ciencias
room number	el número de la habitación		science-fiction	la ciencia ficción
			sci-fi movies	el cine de ciencia ficción
rope	la cuerda			
rosemary	el romero		scientist	una/un científica/o
round	redonda/o		scissors	las tijeras
[at the] roundabout	[en la] rotonda		to score	marcar
rowing	el remo		scoreboard	el marcador
rubbish	la basura		Scotland	la Escocia
rug	una alfombra; un tapete		screen	la pantalla
			script	el guión
ruins	las ruinas		scriptwriter	una/un guionista
rules	las reglas		scrum	el melé
to run	correr		sculptor	una/un escultora/escultor
			sculpture	la escultura

sad	triste		sea	el mar
saddle	el sillín		seasick	mareada/o
safe (adj)	segura/o		seaside	la costa
safe (n)	una caja fuerte		seat	un asiento
safe sex	el sexo seguro		seatbelt	el cinturón de seguridad
saint	santa/o			
(when followed by a saint's name)	san		second (n)	un segundo
			second	segunda/o
saint's day	el santo		secretary	una/un secretaria/o
salary	el salario		to see	ver
[on] sale	estar en venta		We'll see!	Ya veremos!
sales department	el departamento de ventas		I see. [understand]	Ya entiendo.
			See you later.	Hasta luego.
salt	el sal		See you tomorrow.	Hasta mañana.
same	la/el misma/o		self-employed	una trabajadora; autónoma
sand	la arena			
sanitary napkins	las compresas			un trabajador; autónomo
Saturday	sábado			
to save	salvar		selfish	egoísta
			self-service	el autoservicio

320

to sell	vender
to send	enviar
send-off	un expulsión
sensible	juiciosa/o
sentence (grammatical)	una frase
sentence (judiciary)	una sentencia
to separate	separar
September	setiembre/ septiembre
series	una serie
serious	seria/o
service (assistence)	el servicio
service (religious)	el oficio
seven	siete
seventeen	diecisiete
seventh	séptima/o
seventy	setenta
several	varias/os
to sew	coser
sex	el sexo
sexism	el machismo
shade; shadow	la sombra
shampoo	el champú
shape	la forma
to share (with)	repartir (entre); dividir (entre)
to share a dorm	compartir un dormitorio
to shave	afeitarse
shaving foam	la espuma de afeitar
she	ella
sheep	una oveja
sheet (bed)	la sábana
sheet (of paper)	una hoja
shell	una concha
shelves	las estanterías
ship	un barco
to ship	enviar; transportar

	por vía marítima
shirt	una camisa
shoe shop	la zapatería
shoes	los zapatos
to shoot	disparar
shop	una tienda
to go shopping	ir de compras
short (length)	corta/o
short (height)	baja/o
short films	los cortos
short stories	los cuentos
shortage	una escasez
shorts	los pantalones cortos
shoulders	los hombros
to shout	gritar
a show	un espectáculo
to show	mostrar
Can you show me on the map? ¿Me puede mostrar en el mapa?	
shower	la ducha
shrine	la capilla (in a church); altar
to shut	cerrar
shuttle	la lanzadera espacial
shy	tímida/o
sick	enferma/o
a sickness	un enfermedad
side	el lado
a sign	un señal
to sign	firmar
signature	la firma
silk	la seda
of silver	de plata
similar	similar
simple	secilla/o
sin	un pecado
since (May)	desde (mayo)
to sing	cantar
singer	una/un cantante

singer-songwriter	una	cantautora	soap	el	jabón
	un	cantautor	soap opera	una	telenovela
single (person)		soltera/o		una	culebrón
single (unique)		sola/o; única/o			(generally used for Latin American soaps)
single room	una	habitación individual	soccer	el	fútbol
sister	una	hermana	social-democratic	la	socialdemócrata
to sit		sentarse	social sciences	las	ciencias sociales
six		seis	social security	la	seguridad social
sixteen		dieciséis	social welfare	el	estado del bienestar
sixth		sexta/o			
sixty		sesenta	socialist	una/un	socialista
size (of anything)	el	tamaño	socks	los	calcetines
size (clothes)	la	talla	solid		sólida/o
size (shoes)	el	número	some		algún; algunas/os
ski slope	la	pista			
ski-boots	las	botas	somebody		alguien
ski-lift	el	tele-arrastre	something		algo
ski-pass	el	forfait	sometimes		de vez en cuando
ski-suit	el	traje de esquí			
skiing	el	esquí	son	el	hijo
to ski		esquiar	song	la	canción
skin	la	piel	soon		pronto
skirt	una	falda	sore throat	un	dolor de garganta
skis	los	esquíes			
sky	el	cielo	I'm sorry.		Lo siento.
to sleep		dormir	sound	el	sonido
sleeping bag	un	saco de dormir	south		sur
sleeping car	el	coche cama	South America	la	América del Sur/ Sudamérica
sleeping pills	las	pastillas para dormir			
			souvenir	un	recuerdo
sleepy	el	sueño	souvenir shop	la	tienda de recuerdos
slide (film)	la	diapositiva			
slow; slowly		despacio	space	el	espacio
small		pequeña/o	space exploration	la	exploración espacial
a smell	un	olor			
to smell		oler	Spanish		español
to smile		sonreír	sparrowhawk	un	gavilán
to smoke		fumar	to speak		hablar
snake	el	serpiente	special		especial
snow	el	nieve	specialist	una/un	especialista

speed	la	velocidad
speed limit	la	límite de velocidad
spicy		picante
spider	una	araña
spine	la	columna (vertebral)
sport	los	deportes
sportsperson	una/un	deportista
a sprain	una	torcedura
spring (season)	la	primavera
spring (coil)	el	muelle
square (shape)	un	cuadro; cuadrado
square (town)	la	plaza
stables	la	cuadra
stadium	el	estadio
stage	el	escenario
stainless steel	el	acero inoxidable
stairway	la	escalera
stallion	el	semental
stamps	los	sellos
standard (usual)		normal
standard of living	el	nivel de vida
stars	las	estrellas
to start		comenzar
station	la	estación
stationers	la	papelería
statue	el	estatua
to stay (remain)		quedarse
to stay (somewhere)		alojarse; hospedarse
an STD (sexually transmitted disease)	una	enfermedad de transmisión sexual
to steal		robar
steam	el	vapor
steep		escarpada/o
step	un	paso
stepbrother	el	hemanastro

stepfather	el	padrastro
stepmother	la	madrastra
stepsister	la	hermanastra
stockings; pantyhose	las	medias
stomach	el	estómago
stomachache	un	dolor de estómago
stone	una	piedra
stoned		ciega/o
stop	una	parada
to stop		parar
Stop!		¡Parada!
stork	la	cigüeña
storm	una	tormenta
story	una	cuenta
stove	la	estufa; cocina
straight		recta/o; derecha/o; extraña/o
strange		
stranger	una/un	extranjera/o
stream	un	arroyo
street	la	calle
	el	paseo
street demonstration	una	manifestación
street-seller	una	vendedora callejera
	un	vendedor callejero
strength	la	fuerza
a strike (stop work)	la	huelga
on strike		en huelga
string	la	cuerda
stroll; walk	el	pasear
strong		fuerte
stubborn		testaruda/o
student	un	estudiante
studio	un	estudio
stupid		estúpida/o

style	el	estilo	synthetic		fibra/o
subtitles	los	subtítulos	syringe	la	jeringa; (chuta)
suburb	el	barrio			
suburbs of ...	las	fueras de ...			
subway station	la	parada de metro	**T**		
			table	la	mesa
success	el	éxito	table football	el	futbolín
to suffer		sufrir	table tennis	el	ping pong
sugar	el	azúcar	tackle	el	placaje
suitcase	la	maleta	tail	el	rabo
summer	el	verano	to take (away)		llevar
sun	el	sol	to take (food; the train)		tomar
sunblock	la	crema solar	to take photographs		hacer fotos
sunburn	una	quemadura de sol	to talk		hablar
			tall		alta/o
Sunday		domingo	tampons	los	tampones
sunflower oil	el	aceite de girasol	tasty		sabrosa/o
			tax	los	impuestos
sunglasses	las	gafas de sol	taxi stand	la	parada de taxis
sunny		Hace sol; Hará sol	teacher	una	profesora
				un	profesor
sunrise	el	amanecer	teaching	la	enseñanza
sunset	la	puesta del sol;	team	el	equipo
	el	atardecer	tear (crying)	una	lágrima
			technique	la	técnica
sunstroke	una	insolación	teeth	los	dientes
supermarket	el	supermercado	telegram	un	telegrama
supporters	las	hinchas	telephone	el	teléfono
Sure.		Claro.	to telephone		llamar (por teléfono)
surface mail		por vía terrestre			
surfboard	la	tabla de surf	telephone office	la	centralita telefónica
surname	el	apellido			
a surprise	una	sorpresa	telescope	el	telescopio
to survive		sobrevivir	television	la	televisión
sweet		dulce	temperature (fever)	el	fiebre
to swim		nadar	temperature (weather)	la	temperatura
swimming	la	natación			
swimming pool	la	piscina	temple	un	templo
swimsuit	el	bañador	ten		diez
sword	la	espada	tennis	el	tenis
sympathetic		comprensiva/o	tennis court	la	pista de tenis
synagogue	la	sinagoga			

tent	una tienda (de campaña)
tent pegs	las piquetas
tenth	décima/o
term of office (political)	un mandato
terrible	de pena/de puta pena
test	una prueba
to thank	dar gracias
Thank you.	Gracias.
theatre	el teatro
theme park	un parque de atracciones
they	ellas/ellos
thick	gruesa/o
thief	un ladrón
thin	delgada/o
to think	pensar
third	un tercio
third (adj)	tercera/o
thirsty	el sed
I'm thirsty.	
Tengo sed.	
thirteen	trece
thirty	treinta
thought	un pensamiento
thousand	mil
three	tres
three of a kind	un trío
three-quarters	tres cuartos
thrillers (movie)	el cine de suspense
throat	la garganta
thrush (bird)	el zorzal; tordo
thrush (illness)	la afta
Thursday	jueves
thyme	el tomillo
ticket	un billete
ticket (theatre)	la entrada
ticket collector	la/el revisora/ revisor

ticket machine	la venta automática de billetes
ticket office	la aquilla
ticket scalping	la reventa
tide	la marea
tight	apretada/o
time	el tiempo
What time is it?	
¿Qué horas son?	
timetable	el horario
tin (can)	la lata
tin opener	las abrelatas
tip (gratuity)	una propina
tired	cansada/o
tissues	los pañuelos de papel
toad	el sapo
toast	la tostada
tobacco	el tabaco
tobacco kiosk	el quiosco de tabaco
today	hoy
together	juntas/os
toilet paper	el papel higiénico
toilets	los servicios
toll-free motorway	la autovía
tomorrow	mañana
tomorrow afternoon; evening	
mañana por la tarde; noche	
tomorrow morning	
mañana por la mañana	
tonight	esta noche
too (as well)	también
too expensive	demasiado cara/o
too much; many	demasiado/s
tooth (front)	el diente
tooth (back)	la muela
toothache	me duele una muela
toothbrush	el cepillo de dientes

toothpaste	la	pasta dentífrica
torch (flashlight)	una	linterna
tortoise	una	tortuga
to touch		tocar
tour	una	excursión;
	un	viaje
tourist	una	turista
tourist	el	guiri (slang)
tourist information office		
la oficina de turismo		
tournament	el	torneo
towards		hacia
towel	una	toalla
tower	la	torre
town (large, city)	un	ciudad
town (small, village)	un	pueblo
toxic waste	los	residuos tóxicos
track (car-racing)	el	autódromo
track (footprints)	el	rastro
track (sports)	la	pista
track (path)	el	sendero
trade union	los	sindicatos
traffic	el	tráfico
traffic lights	los	semáforos
trail; route	el	camino;
		sendero
train	el	tren
train station	la	estación de tren
tram	el	tranvía
transit lounge	el	tránsito
to translate		traducir
to travel		viajar
travel agency	la	agencia de viajes
travel sickness	el	mareo
travel (books)	los	libros de viajes
traveller	una/uno	viajera/o
traveller's cheques	los	cheques de viaje
tree	un	árbol
trek	un	excursión

trendy (person)		moderna/o
trip	un	viaje
trousers	los	pantalones
truck	un	camión
It's true.		Es verdad.
trust	la	confianza
to trust		confiar
truth	la	verdad
to try		intentar; probar
to try [to do something]		intentar [de hacer algo]
T-shirt	una	camiseta
Tuesday		martes
tune	una	melodía
Turn left ...		Doble a la izquierda ...
Turn right ...		Doble a la derecha ...
TV	la	tele
TV set	el	televisor
twelve		doce
twenty		veinte
twice		dos veces
twin beds		dos camas
twins	los	gemelos
two		dos
two pairs		doble pareja
two tickets		dos billetes
to type		escribir a máquina
typical		típica/o
tyres	los	neumáticos

U

ultrasound	un	ultrasonido
umbrella	el	paraguas
underpants (men)	los	calzoncillos
underpants (women)	las	bragas
to understand		entender; comprender

326

unemployed	en el paro
unemployment	el desempleo; paro
unions	los sindicatos
universe	el universo
university	la universidad
unleaded	sin plomo
unsafe	insegura/o
until (June)	hasta (junio)
unusual	extraña/o
up	arriba
uphill	la cuesta arriba
urgent	urgente
USA	Los Estados Unidos
useful	útil
usher	una acomodadora
	un acomodador

V

vacant	vacante; libre
vacation	los vacaciones
vaccination	una vacunación
valley	el valle
valuable	preciosa/o
value (price)	el precio
van	una caravana; furgoneta
vegetable	un legumbre
vegetarian	una/un vegetariana/o
vegetation	la vegatación
vein	la vena
venereal disease	una enfermedad venérea
venue	un local
very	muy
video tape	la cinta de vídeo
view	una vista

view of the sea; mountain
las vistas al mar; a la montaña

village	un pueblo; pueblecito
vine	un vid
vineyard	un viñedo
virus	un virus
visa	un visado
to visit	visitar
vitamins	las vitaminas
voice	el voz
volume	el volumen
to vote	votar
vulture	el buitre

W

Wait!	Esperal
waiter	la/el camarera/o
waiting room	la sala de espera
Wales	el País de Gales
to walk	caminar
wall (inside)	la pared
wall (outside)	el muro
want	querer; desear
war	la guerra
wardrobe	el vestuario
warm	caliente
to warn	advertir
to wash (something)	lavar
to wash (oneself)	lavarse
washing machine	una lavadora
watch	el reloj
to watch	mirar
water	el agua
mineral water	el agua mineral
water bottle	la cantimplora
waterfall	una cascada
waterskiing	el esquí acuático
waterskis	los esquís para el agua
wave	la ola
way	el camino

Please tell me the way to ...
¿Por favor, como llego a ...
Which way?
¿Por dónde?; ¿En qué dirección?

Way Out		Salida
we		nosotras/ nosotros
weak		débil
wealthy		rica/o
to wear		llevar
weather	el	tiempo
wedding	la	boda
wedding anniversary	el	aniversario de bodas
wedding cake	la	tarta nupcial
wedding present	el	regalo de bodas
Wednesday		miércoles
week	la	semana
this week		esta semana
weekend	la	fin de semana
to weigh		pesar
weight	el	peso
welcome		benvenida
welfare	el	bienestar social
well		bien
west		oeste
wet		mojada/o
what		qué

What is he saying?
¿Qué está diciendo?
What time is it?
¿Qué horas son?

wheel	la	rueda
wheelchair	la	silla de ruedas
when		cuándo
When does it leave?		¿Cuándo sale?
where		dónde

Where is the bank?
¿Dónde está el banco?

white		blanca/o
who		quién

Who is it?
¿Quién es?
Who are they?
¿Quiénes son?

whole		todo
why		porqué

Why is the museum closed?
¿Por qué está cerrado el museo?

wide		ancha/o
wife	la	esposa, mujer
wild animal	un	animal salvaje
to win		ganar
wind	el	viento
window	la	ventana
window (car; ticket office)	la	ventanilla
window (shop)	la	vetrina

to [go] window-shopping
mirar los escaparates

windscreen; windshield	el	parabrisas
wine	el	vino
winery	la	bodega
wing	la	ala
winner	la/el	ganadora/ ganador
winter	el	invierno
wire	el	alambre
wise		sabia/o
with		con
within		dentro de
within an hour/ month		dentro de una hora/ un mes
without		sin
without filter		sin filtro
wolf	el	lobo
woman	una	mujer
wonderful		maravillosa/o
wood	la	madera

woodpecker	el	pico
wool	la	lana
word	una	palabra
work	el	trabajo
to work		trabajar
workout	el	entreno
work permit	el	permiso de trabajo
workshop	un	taller
world	el	mundo
worms	los	lombrices
worried		preocupada/o
worship	la	adoración
worth	el	valor
wound	una	herida
to write		escribir
writer	una/un	escritora/escritor
wrong		falsa/o

I'm wrong. (my fault)
Tengo la culpa
I'm wrong. (not right)
No tengo razón.

Y

year	el	año
this year	este	año
yellow		amarilla/o
yesterday		ayer

yesterday afternoon; evening
ayer por la tarde; noche
yesterday morning
ayer por la mañana; madrugada

yet		todavía
you (pol)		usted
(inf)		tú
(pl, pol)		ustedes
(pl, inf)		vosotras/os
young		joven
youth (collective)	la	juventud

youth hostel	un	albergue juvenil; de juventud

Z

zebra	la	cebra
zero	el	cero
zodiac	el	zodíaco

SPANISH – ENGLISH

In this dictionary we have included the definite (**la** or **el**, corresponding to 'the' in English) or indefinite article (**una** or **un**, corresponding to 'a' or 'one' in English) with each noun. We have chosen either the definite or indefinite article according to the way the word is most likely to be used. However, note that in most cases the articles are interchangeable. Thus **un abanico**, 'a fan' may also be **el abanico**, 'the fan'. **La abuela**, 'the grandmother', may also be **una abuela**, 'a grandmother'. Just remember, **el** becomes **un**, while **la** becomes **una**.

Note that the letter 'll' is listed within the 'l' listing. This is because contemporary Spanish no longer has the 'll' listed as a separate letter. If you are using an older dictionary as well, you'll probably find it still listed separately.

The letters 'ch' are considered one letter in Spanish, and therefore come between the letter 'C' and 'D'. When looking for anything with 'ch' in it, remember that it will be listed after the alphabetical listings containing 'c'. For example, **enchufe** (plug) will be after **encontrar** (to meet), *not* between **encendedor** (electricity) and **encima de** (above).

The letter 'ñ' is always listed after the letter 'n'. Thus you will find **año** (year) *after* all words beginning with 'an'.

A

	abajo	below
un	abanico	fan
las	abejas	bees
el	abeto	fir
	abierta/o	open
una/un	abogada/o	lawyer
	a bordo	aboard
el	aborto	abortion
un	aborto natural	miscarriage
un	abrazo	cuddle
las	abrelatas	can opener
el	abrigo	coat
	abril	April
	abrir	to open

la	abuela	grandmother
el	abuelo	grandfather
	aburrida/o	boring
	acabar	to end
	acampar	to camp
	¿Está permitido acampar aquí?	
	Can we camp here?	
el	acantilado	cliff
un	accidente	accident
el	aceite	oil
el	aceite de girasol	sunflower oil
el	aceite de oliva	olive oil
la	aceitunas	olives
el	acero inoxidable	stainless steel

331

una	acomodadora	usher
un	acomodador	
el	acoso	harrassment
una/un	activista	activist
una	actriz	actor
un	actor	
una	actuación	performance
	adentro	inside
una/un	adicta/o	addict
	¡Adiós!	Goodbye!
una/un	adivina/o	fortune teller
	adivinar	to guess
la	adoración	worship
la	aduana	customs
una/o	adulta/o	adult
una	aerograma	aerogram
la	afeitadora	razor
	afeitarse	to shave
el	afición	fan
una/o	aficionada/o	amateur; enthusiast
	afortunada/o	lucky
la	afta	thrush (illness)
la	agencia de viajes	travel agency
la	agenda	diary
	agosto	August
	agradable	nice
	agresivos	aggressive
una	agricultora	farmer
un	agricultor	
la	agricultura	agriculture
el	agua	water
la	agua caliente	hot water
el	agua fría	cold water
una	aguafuerte	etching
la	agua mineral	mineral water
el	águila	eagle
una	aguja	needle (sewing)
	ahogar	to drown
	ahora	now

el	aire	air
un	aís	country
el	ajedrez	chess
	al lado de	next to
la/el	alcalde	mayor
un	alcornoque	cork oak
una	alergia	an allergy
la	alergia al polen	hayfever
la	alfarería	pottery
una	alfombra	rug
	algo	something
el	algodón	cotton
	alguien	somebody
	algunas/os	some
la	almohada	pillow
el	almuerzo	lunch
	alojarse	to stay (somewhere)
el	alpinismo	mountaineering
	alquilar	to rent; hire
	¿Dónde puedo alquilar un bicicleta?	
	Where can I hire a bicycle?	
el	alquiler	the rent
	alta/o	high
la	altura	altitude
	alucinar	to hallucinate
	amable	kind
el	amanecer	sunrise
la/el	amante	lover
una	amapola	poppy
	amar	to love
	amarilla/o	yellow
	a menudo	often
la	América del Sur	South America
	amiga/o	friend
una	ampolla	blister
los	analgésicos	painkillers
un	análisis de sangre	blood test
una/un	anarquista	anarchist
	andar en bicicleta	to cycle
la	anemia	anaemia

el	anillo	ring (on finger)
un	animal salvaje	wild animal
el	aniversario de bodas	wedding anniversary
	anoche	last night
	anteayer	day before yesterday
la	antena	antenna
la	antena parabólica	satellite dish
	antes	before
los	anticonceptivos	contraceptives
	antigua/o	ancient
los	antigüedades	antiques
las	antologías	anthologies
	anual	annual
un	anuncio de trabajo	job advertisement
el	año	year
el	año nuevo	New Year's Day
el	año pasado	last year
el	año que viene	next year
un	aparato de transparencias	overhead projector
el	apellido	surname
el	apéndice	appendix
un	apodo	nickname
	apreciar	to like
	aprender	to learn
una	apuesta	a bet
	aquí	here
la	aquilla	ticket office
una	araña	spider
el	árbitro	referee
la	ardilla	squirrel
la	arena	sand
el	armario	cupboard
el	arnés	harness
	arriba	above
	¡Arriba ...!	Long live …!

un	arroyo	stream
el	arte cibernético	cyber art
el	arte gótico	Gothic art
el	arte prehistórico	prehistoric art
el	arte renacentista	Renaissance art
el	arte y ensayo	art films
la	artesanía	handicrafts
los	artículos de cuero	leathergoods
un	artista callejera/o	busker; performing artist
la	ASA; sensibilidad	ASA; film speed
el	ascensor	lift (elevator)
un	asiento	seat
el	asunto	question (topic)
el	atardecer	sunset
	a tiempo	on time
el	atletismo	athletics
el	audífono	hearing aid
	autocar	long-distance bus; coach
las	autonómicas	regional
una	autónoma	self-employed
un	autónomo	
un	autopista	motorway (with tolls)
el	autoservicio	self-service
el	autovía	toll-free motorway
	avenida	avenue
	avergonzada/o	embarrassed
el	avión	plane
	ayer	yesterday
	ayer por la mañana; madrugada	yesterday morning
	ayer por la tarde; noche	yesterday afternoon; evening

la	ayuda	aid (help)
	ayudar	to help
	¡Ayudo!	Help!
el	azúcar	sugar
	azul	blue

B

el	babero	bib
	bailar	to dance
el	bailar	dancing
	baja/o	low; short (height)
un	balde	bucket
el	balonmano	handball
la	bandera	flag
el	bañador	swimsuit
el	baño	bathroom
una	baraja	deck (of cards)
el	barco	boat
el	barrio	suburb
el	barrio viejo	old city
	Basta!	Enough!
	bastante	enough
la	basura	garbage
el	bate	bat
la	batería	battery; drums
lel	bautizo	baptism
un	bebé	baby
	beber	to drink
	bendecir	to bless
el	beneficio	profit
	besar	to kiss
	Bésame.	Kiss me.
un	beso	kiss
el	biberón	feeding bottle
la	Biblia	the Bible
la	biblioteca	library
un	bici	bike

la	bicicleta aeroestática	exercise bicycle
la	bicicleta de carreras	racing bike
una	bicicleta de montaña	mountain bike
un	bicho	bug
	bien	well
	bien escrita/o	well-written
el	bienestar social	welfare
el	billar español/ americano	billiards/ pool
un	billete	ticket
un	billete de ida y vuelta	return ticket
un	billete sencillo	one-way ticket
los	billetes (de banco)	banknotes
las	biografías	biography
la	bios	lips
	blanca/o	white
	blanco y negro	B&W (film)
la	boca	mouth
la	boda	wedding
el	bolígrafo	pen (ball point)
un	bolo	gig
la	bolsa	carrier bag
el	bolsillo	pocket
el	bolso	handbag
la	bomba	pump
la	bombilla	flashlight; light bulb; torch
	bondadosos	caring
	bonito	beautiful
	bordar	to embroider
el	bosque	forest
el	bosque pretegida	protected forest
las	botas	boots
las	botas	ski-boots
las	botas de montaña	hiking boots

C

las	botas de vino	leather wine bottle
la	botella	bottle
los	botones	buttons
el	boxeo	boxing
las	bragas	underpants (women)
	brava/o	brave
el	brezo	heather
una	broma	joke
	bromear	to joke
el	bronquitis	bronchitis
la	brújula	compass
una	budista	Buddhist
	buena/o	good
	¡Buena suerte!	Good luck!
	Buenas noches.	Good evening; night.
	Buenas tardes.	Good afternoon.
	Buenos días.	Good morning.
	¡Buen provecho!	Bon apetit!
	¡Buen viaje!	Bon voyage!
el	buey	ox
el	búho	owl
el	buitre	vulture
un	bulto	lump
	burlarse de	to make fun of
el	burro	donkey
	buscar	to look for
el	buzón	mail box

C

una/un	camella/o	drug dealer (slang)
el	canario	canary
el	caballo	horse; heroin (slang)

la	cabeza	head
la	cabina telefónica	phone box
el	cable	cable TV
la	cabra	goat
una	cabra montés	ibex
	cabronaza/o	bastard
un	cacto	cactus
una/un	cachorro/a	puppy
	cada	each
	cada día	every day
la	caja	box
la	caja	cashier
una	caja fuerte	safe (n)
la	caja registradora	cash register
el	cajero automático	automatic teller
una	cajetilla	packet
los	calcetines	socks
el	calendario	calendar
la	calidad	quality
	caliente	hot
la	calle	street
el	calor	heat
los	calzoncillos	underpants (men)
la	cama	bed
una	cama de matrimonio	double bed
la	cámara	room camera
la/el	camarera/o	waiter
	cambiar	to change
el	cambio	exchange; change (coins)
el	cambio de marchas	gear stick
	caminar	to walk
el	camino	trail; route
los	caminos rurales	hiking routes
el	camión de catering	catering truck

C

una	camisa	shirt	el	cartucho de gas	gas cartridge
una	camiseta	T-shirt	la	casa	house
los	campeonatos	championships		casarse	to marry
el	camping	campsite	una	cascada	waterfall
el	campo	countryside; field	el	casco	helmet
el	canal	canal; channel	el	casco antiguo	old city
la	canasta	basket	el	casete	cassette
	cancelar	to cancel		casi	almost
la	canción	song		castigar	to punish
la	cancha	court	el	castillo	castle
el	candado	padlock	un	catarro	cold
	cansada/o	tired		catorce	fourteen
	cantar	to sing	el	cava (champán)	champagne
una	cantautora	singer-song writer	una	cazuela	pan
				celebrar	to celebrate (an event)
un	cantautor			celosos	jealous
la	cantimplora	water bottle	la	cena	dinner
la	capa	cape	el	cenicero	ashtray
la	capa de ozono	ozone layer	la	centralita telefónica	telephone office
	ser capaz de	to be able to do (can)	el	centro de la ciudad	city centre
la	capilla	shrine; altar	el	cepillo de dientes	toothbrush
el	capote	cloak			
	cara	expensive	el	cepillo (para el cabello; pelo)	hairbrush
la	cara	face			
una	caravana	van		cerca	near
el	cárcel	jail	la	cerca	fence
un	cardenal	bruise		de cercanías	local
el	carnet	driver's licence	el	cerdo	pig
el	carnet de identidad	identification card	el	cernícalo	kestrel
			el	cero	zero
la	carrera	race (sport)		cerrado	closed
un	carrete	film (camera)	la	cerradura	lock (n)
la	carretera	main road		cerrar	to close; lock
un	carro	trolley	la	cesta	basket
una	carta	letter; menu		ch	see separate list after 'C'
la	carta astral	chart (astro-logical)			
las	cartas	cards		ciega/o	blind; stoned (slang)
el	cartón	carton			

el	cielo	sky
	cien; ciento	hundred
la	ciencia ficción	science fiction
las	ciencias	science
las	ciencias sociales	social sciences
una/un	científica/o	scientist
el	ciervo	deer
una	cifra aproximada	ballpark figure
las	cifras	figures
los	cigarrillos	cigarettes
un	cigarro	a cigarette
la	cigüeña	stork
	cinco	five
	cincuenta	fifty
el	cine	film (cinema)
el	cine negro	film-noir
el	cine realista	realism
la	cinta de vídeo	video tape
el	cinturón	ring-road
el	cinturón de seguridad	seatbelt
el	circo	circus
una	cita	date; appointment
	citarse	to date
una	citología	pap smear
la	ciudad	city
la	ciudad antigua	old city
la	ciudadanía	citizenship
	claro	light
	Claro.	Sure.
la	clínica	private hospital
el	cobrador	conductor (bus)
una/un	cocainómana/o	cocaine addict
la	cocina	kitchen; stove
	cocinar	to cook
el	coche	car
el	coche cama	sleeping car
el	código postal	post code

	cojonuda/o	brilliant
una	cola	queue
el	colchón	mattress
la	colina	hill
un	collar	necklace
la	columna (vertebral)	spine
	combatir	to fight
la	comedia	comedy
la	comedia negra	black comedy
	comenzar	to start
	comer	to eat
el	comerciante	business person
un	comezón	itch
la	comida	food
la	comida de bebé potitos	baby food
	cómo	how
	¿Cómo puedo llegar a ...?	How do I get to ...?
	¿Cómo se dice ...?	How do you say ...?
	cómoda/o	comfortable
el	compact	CD
una/un	compañera/o	companion
	compartir (un dormitorio)	to share (a dorm)
	comprender	to understand
	comprensiva/o	sympathetic
las	compresas	sanitary napkins
el	compromiso	engagement (appointment; to marry)
	con aire acondicionado	air-conditioned
una	concentración	rally
un	concierto	a concert
un	concurso	a game show

una	concha	shell
un	condón	condom
	conducir	to drive
el	conductor	driver
el	conejillo de indias	guinea pig
el	conejo	rabbit
una	confesión	confession
	con filtro	filtered
	confirmar	to confirm
	congelar	to freeze
	conocer	to know (someone)
	conocida/o	famous
el	consejo	advice
	conservador	conservative
la/el	conservadora/ conservador	curator
la	consigna	left luggage
	estar constipada/o	to have a cold
la	construcción	construction work
la	contaminación	pollution
	contar	to count
el	contenedor de reciclaje	recycling bin
el	contestador automático	answering machine
el	contrarreloj	race against the clock
el	contrato	contract
el	control de alcoholemia	mobile breath testing unit
una	copa	drink; cup
el	corazón	heart
el	cordero	lamb
la	cordillera	mountain range
el	corredor de apuestas	bookmaker
el	correo	mail

el	correo certificado	registered mail
el	Correos	post office
el	correo urgente	express mail
	correr	to run
la	corrida	bullfight
	corriente	ordinary
	corrupta/o	corrupt
	corta/o	short
	cortar	to cut
los	cortos	short films
el	corzo	deer
	coser	to sew
la	costa	seaside; coast
	costar	to cost
	Cuesta bastante.	It costs a lot.
	¿Cuánto cuesta?	How much is it?
las	costillas	ribs
el	costo	pot (dope)
	costruir	to build
la	crema hidratante	moisturising cream
la	crema solar	sunblock
la	crítica	review
	cruda/o	raw
el	cruz	cross (religious)
un	cuaderno	notebook
la	cuadra	stables
un	cuadrado; cuadro	square (shape)
los	cuadros	paintings
	¿Cuánto?	How much; many?
	¿Cuánto cuesta?	How much is it?
	cuarenta	forty
la	Cuaresma	Lent
	cuarta/o	fourth

un	cuarto	room
un	cuarto	quarter
	cuatro	four
un	cubo	bucket
una	cucaracha	cockroach
las	cuchillas de afeitar	razor blades
un	cuchillo	knife
la	cuenta	bill
una	cuenta	story
los	cuentos	short stories
la	cuerda	rope
los	cuernos	horns
el	cuero	leather
el	cuerpo	body
	cuesta arriba	uphill
las	cuevas	caves
	¡Cuidado!	Careful!
una	culebrón	soap opera (Latin American)
el	culo	bum; ass
	cuidar	to look after
	cuidar de	to care (someone)
la	culpa	fault; blame; guilt
el	cumbre	peak
los	cumpleaños	birthday
	¡Que cumplas muchos más!	Many happy returns!
uno	cupón	coupon
el	currículum	resumé

CH

	chachi	great
una	chaqueta chupa	jacket
la	charcutería	delicatessen
los	cheques de viaje	travellers' cheques

la	chica	girl
el	chicle	chewing gum
el	chico	boy
el	chupete	dummy; pacifier
la	chuta (slang)	syringe
un	chut	kick

D

los	dados	dice; die
	dar	to give
	darse cuenta (de)	to realise
un	dato	piece of information
	De acuerdo.	OK
	deber	to owe
	débil	weak
	de cercanías	local
	décima/o	tenth
	decidir	to decide
	decir	to say
	¿Cómo se dice ...?	How do you say ...?
un	decorado	prop
el	dedo	finger
	defectuosa/o	faulty
	de izquierda; izquierdista	left-wing
	delante de	in front of
	delantero	forward
	de largo recorrido	long distance
	de liar	rolling
	delirante	delirious
	demasiado cara/o	too expensive
	demasiado/s	too much; many
una	demora	a delay
	dentro de (seis) días	in (six) days
	dentro de una hora/un mes	an hour/month

el	departamento de ventas	sales department
	de pena; de puta pena	terrible
la	dependencia	addiction; dependence
los	deportes	sport
una/un	deportista	sportsperson
	De puta madre	Fantastic! (swearword)
	derechista	right-wing
	derecho	right (not left)
el	derecho	law
el	desayuno	breakfast
	descansar	to rest
el	descanso	intermission
	descompuesta/o	broken (out of order)
un	descripción del trabajo	job description
	descubrir	to discover
un	descuento	discount
	desde (mayo)	since (May)
	desear	to want
el	desempleo; paro	unemployment
una/un	desgraciada/o	creep (colloquial)
el	desierto	desert
la	desigualdad	inequality
el	desodorante	deodorant
	despacio	slow; slowly
un	despertador	alarm clock
el	despido	dismissal
	después	after
	después de	after
el	destapador	bottle opener
	destemplada/o	shivery
el	destino	destination; destiny
	destruir	to destroy
una	desventaja	disadvantage
	detrás de	behind

	de vez en cuando	sometimes
un	devocionario	prayer book
el	día	day
el	día de los reyes magos	Epiphany
un	día festivo	holiday
la	diapositiva	slide
	diariamente	daily
	dibujar	to draw
los	dibujos animados	animation; comics
el	diccionario	dictionary
	diciembre	December
los	dientes	teeth
	diez	ten
	¿Diga?	Hello! (answering a call)
la	dimisión	resignation
el	dinero	money
la	dirección	address
	directo	direct
la/el	directora/director	director
un	disco	record
	discutir	to argue
el	diseño	design
	disparar	to shoot
un	DIU	IUD
un	diversión	fun
	divertirse	to have fun
	dividir (entre)	to share (with)
	Doble a la derecha ...	Turn right ...
	Doble a la izquierda ...	Turn left ...
el	doble	double
	doce	twelve
una	docena	dozen
el	dolor	pain
un	dolor de cabeza	headache
un	dolor de estómago	stomachache

un	dolor de garganta	sore throat	
el	dolor menstrual	period pain	
	dolorosa/o	painful	
	domingo	Sunday	
	dormir	to sleep	
	dónde	where	

¿Dónde está ...?
Where is ...?

¿Dónde puedo alquilar una bicicleta?
Where can I hire a bicycle?

	dos	two
	dos veces	twice
la	drogadicción	addiction
las	drogas	drugs
la	ducha	shower
	duele una muela	toothache
la/el	dueña/o	owner

E

la	economía	business; economy
la	edad	age
el	edificio	building
	él	he
	ella	she
	ellas/ellos	they
	embarcarse	to board (ship)
la	embajada ...	embassy
	embarazada	pregnant
el	embrague	clutch
la/el	emleada/o	employee
	empujar	to push
	en	on
	en broma	for fun; joking
el	encaje	lace
	encantadores	charming
	encargada/o de luces	lighting operator
el	encendedor	lighter
las	encías	gums

	encima de	above
	encontrar	to meet
un	enchufe	plug (electricity)
	en el paro	unemployed
	enero	January
	enferma/o	sick
el	enfermedad	disease
una/un	enfermera/o	nurse
	enfrente de	in front of
	enojada/o	angry
el	ensayo	non-fiction
la	enseñanza	teaching
	entender	understand
	[Ya] entiendo.	I see. (understand)
la	entrada	ticket (theatre)
	entrar	to enter
	entre	between
la	entrenadora	coach; trainer
el	entrenador	
el	entreno	workout
	entretenido	entertaining
una	entrevista	interview
	enviar	to send
	epiléptica/o	epilectic
el	equipaje	luggage
el	equipo	team; equipment
el	equipo de inmersión	diving equipment
la	equitación	horseriding
el	escalar	rock climbing
	escalera	straight
	escarpada/o	steep
una	escasez	shortage
el	escenario	stage
la	Escocia	Scotland
	escoger	to choose
	escribir	to write
	escribir a máquina	to type

una	escritora	writer
un	escritor	
el	escrutinio	counting of votes
	escuchar	to listen
la	escuela	school
la	escuela de párvulos	kindergarten
una	escultora	sculptor
un	escultor	
la	esgrima	fencing
el	espacio	space
la	espada	sword
la	espalda	back
	español	Spanish
los	especies en peligro de extinción	endangered species
los	especies protegidos	protected species
un	espectáculo	show
el	espejo	mirror
	Esperal	Wait!
la	esposa; mujer	wife
el	esposo; marido	husband
la	espuma de afeitar	shaving foam
el	esquí	skiing
el	esquí acuático	waterskiing
	esquiar	to ski
la	esquina (exterior)	corner
	esta mañana; madrugada	this morning
	esta noche	tonight
	esta semana	this week
	esta tarde	this afternoon
	Está helando.	It's frosty.
	Está nublado	It's cloudy.
la	estación	station
	estacionar	to park
el	estadio	stadium
el	estado civil	marital status

el	estado del bienestar	social welfare
Los	Estados Unidos	USA
una	estafa	rip-off
las	estanterías	shelves
	este	east
	este año	this year
	este mes	this month
la	esterilla	mat
el	estilo	style
el	estómago	stomach
las	estrellas	stars
el	estreñimiento	constipation
	estropeado/a	broken
la	estufa	stove; heater
una	etapa	leg (in race)
	europea/o	european
la	eutanasia	euthanasia
un	excursión	trek
una	excursión	tour group
un	excursión guiada	guided trek
el	excursionismo	hiking
un	exemplo	example
el	exito	success
la	exploración espacial	space exploration
la	explotación	exploitation
	exponer	to exhibit
una	exposición	exhibition
un	exposición permanente	permanent collection
	expreso	express
un	expulsión	send-off
el	éxtasis	ecstasy (drug)
el	exterior; fuera	outside
	extranjera/o	foreign
una	extranjera	stranger
un	extranjero	
	extraña/o	unusual
	extrañar	to miss (feel the absence of)

F

la	fábrica	factory
	fabricar	to make
	fácil	easy
una	falda	skirt
una	falta	fault; foul
	febrero	February
la	fecha	date
la	fecha de nacimiento	date of birth
	¡Felicidades!	Congratulations!
	feliz	happy
	¡Feliz cumpleaños!	Happy birthday!
	¡Feliz santo!	Happy saint's day!
el	ferrocarril	railway
	festejar	to celebrate
	fibra/o	synthetic
la	ficción	fiction
las	fichas	pieces
la	fiebre	fever
la	fiebre glandular	glandular fever
la	fiesta	party
el	fin	end
la	fin de semana	weekend
la	firma	signature
un	flor	flower
	follar	to fuck
	[en el] fondo	[at the] bottom
el	forfait	ski-pass
la	forma	shape
los	fósforos; cerillas	matches
el	fotómetro	light meter
el	franqueo	postage
los	frenos	brakes
	frente a	opposite
	fría/o	cold (adj)
la	frontera	border
el	frontón	wall
la	frutería	greengrocer

el	fuego	fire (controlled)
la	fuera	outside
	fuera de juego	offside
las	fueras de ...	suburbs of ...
	fuerte	strong
la	fuerza	strength
	fumar	to smoke
una	funda de almohada	pillowcase
una	furgoneta	van
el	fútbol sala	indoor soccer
el	futbolín	table soccer

G

las	gafas de sol	sunglasses
la	gallina	hen
el	gallito	cockerel
el	gamo	deer
la	ganadora	winner
el	ganador	
	ganar	to earn
el	ganso	goose
la	garganta	throat
la/el	gata/o	cat
un	gato	jack (for car)
la/el	gatita/o	kitten
un	gavilán	sparrowhawk
el	gel de baño	shower gel
los	gemelos	twins
la	gente	people
una	gineta	genet
el	glaciar	glacier
el	gobierno	government
	gorda/o	fat
un	grabado	print
un	grabación	recording
	grande	big
los	grandes almacenes	department stores

la	granja	farm
la/el	granjera/o	farmer
la	gripe	influenza
	gris	grey
	gritar	to shout
una	grulla	crane (bird)
el	grupo sanguíneo	blood group
los	guantes	gloves
la	guardarropía	cloakroom
la	guardería	childminding service
	guay (slang)	cool
la	guía	guidebook; guide(person)
el	guión	script
una/un	guionista	scriptwriter
el	guiri (slang)	tourist
	gustar(le)	to like (it)

H

	haber	to have see page 31
	habilidosa/o	crafty
la	habitación	room (in hotel)
una	habitación doble	double room
una	habitación individual	single room
	hablar	to talk
	Hace calor; Hará calor.	It's hot.
	Hace frío; Hará frío.	It's cold
	Hace sol; Hará sol.	It's sunny
	hace un rato	[a while] ago
	hace [media hora]	[half hour] ago
	hace [tres días]	[three days] ago
	hacer	to do

	hacer dedo; hacer auto stop	to hitchhike
	hacer fotos	to take photographs
	hacer	to make
el	hachís	hash
la	hamaca	hammock
la	hambre	hungry
la	harina	flour
	Hasta luego.	See you later.
	¡Hasta nuncal	Get lost!
	hasta (junio)	until (June)
	Hay niebla.	It's foggy.
	hecho a mano	handmade
	¡Hecho!	Agreed!
un	helado	icecream
	helar	to freeze
	hemanastro	stepbrother
una	herida	wound
la	hermana	sister
la	hermanastra	stepsister
el	hermano	brother
	hermoso	handsome
la	heroína	heroin
una/un	heroinómana/o	heroin addict
el	hielo	ice
la	hija	daughter
el	hijo	son
los	hijos/niños	children
el	hilo dental	dental floss
las	hinchas	supporters
una	hoja	sheet (of paper)
	¡Hola!	Hello.
un	hombre	man
los	hombros	shoulders
el	hora de comer	lunchtime
la	hormiga	ant
	hortera	dag; bozo
	hospedarse	to stay (somewhere)

un	hotel barato	cheap hotel
un	hotel cercano	nearby hotel
un	hotel limpio	clean hotel
	hoy	today
la	huelga	strike (work)
	en huelga	on strike
el	hueso	bone
los	huevos	eggs
los	huevos de chocolate	chocolate eggs

I

las	idiomas	languages
una	iglesia	church
la	igualdad	equality
la	igualdad de oportunidades	equal opportunity
	iguales	deuce
	No importa.	It doesn't matter.
el	impuesto sobre la renta	income tax
los	impuestos	tax
el	inauguración	opening
un	incendio	fire (uncontrolled)
	no incluido	excluded
el	INEM	job centre
	infantil	child's
	informativo	current affairs
la/el	ingeniera/o	engineer
la	ingeniería	engineering
	ingeniosa/o	crafty
	Inglaterra	England
el	inhalador	inhaler
una	injuria	an insult
una	insolación	sunstroke
el	instituto	high school
	intentar [de hacer algo]	to try [to do something]
	intentar; probar	to try

el	intermitente	indicator (car)
la	interpretación	interpretation; performance art
el	invierno	winter
una	inyección	injection
	inyectarse	to inject oneself
	ir de compras	to go shopping
	ir de excursión	to hike
	ir; partir	to go
	Irlanda	Ireland
la	irritación	a rash
la	isla	island
	de izquierda; izquierdista	left-wing
	izquierdo	left (not right)

J

un	jabalí	boar
el	jabón	soap
	jalar	to pull
el	jamón	ham
la	jardinería	gardening
el	jardíne	garden
una	jarra	jar
la/el	jefa/e	employer
la/el	jefa/e de sección	manager
la	jeringa	syringe
	joder	to fuck
la	joyería	jewellery
	jubilada/o	retired
	judía/o	Jewish
el	judo	judo
el	juego	game
los	juegos de ordenador	computer games
los	juegos olímpicos	Olympic Games
	jueves	Thursday
una/un	juez	judge
una	jugadora	player (sports)
un	jugador	

L

	jugar	to play (sport; games)
	jugar a cartas	to play cards
el	jugo	juice
	juiciosa/o	sensible
	julio	July
	junio	June
el	juzgado	court (legal)
	¡Jesús!	Bless you! (sneezing)

L

el	lado	side
el	lago	lake
	lamentar	to regret
la	lana	wool
la	lanzadera espacial	shuttle
un	lápiz	pencil
el	lápiz de labios	lipstick
	larga/o	long
	de largo recorrido	long-distance
la	lata	can (tin; aluminium)
el	latón	brass
la	lavandería	launderette
la	lazona	regional
	leales	loyal
la	leche	milk
	leer	to read
	lejos	far
la	leña	firewood
los	lentes de contacto	contact lenses
las	letras	humanities
el	levantamiento de pesas	weightlifting
	leve	light
	libre	free (not bound)
la	librería	bookshop
los	libros	books

los	libros de viajes	travel books
el	liebre	hare
el	lienzo	canvas
	ligar	to chat up
	ligera/o	light
	lila	lilac; purple
la	límite de velocidad	speed limit
	limpia/o	clean
un	lince	lynx
la	línea	line
una	linterna	torch (flashlight)
el	lirio	iris
	lista/o	ready
	¿Estás lista/o?	Are you ready?
	Estoy lista/o.	I'm ready.
la	llamada	ring (of phone)
la	llanura	plain
la	llave	key
	llegadas	arrivals
	llegar	to come; arrive
	¿Cómo puedo llegar a ...?	How do I get to ...?
	llena/o	full
	llenar	to fill
	llevar	to take (away); carry
	Llueve.	It's raining.
la	lluvia	rain
el	lobo	wolf
	loca/o	crazy
un	local	venue
el	lodo	mud
los	lombrices	worms
el	loro	parrot
los	sin hogar	homeless
los	luces	lights
la	lucha	fight

el luchar contra — to fight
el lugar — place
el lugar de nacimiento — place of birth
el lujo — luxury
la luminosa — light
la luna — moon
la luna de miel — honeymoon
lunes — Monday

Readers looking for a word beginning with 'll' should look in the previous listing. In contemporary Spanish, the 'll' is no longer listed as a separate letter.

M

el machismo — sexism
la madera — wood
madrastra — stepmother
la madre; mamá — mother
la madrugada — dawn
maga/o — magician
mala/o — bad
la maleta — suitcase
el maletín de primeros auxilios — first-aid kit
un mandato — term of office
la mandíbula — jaw
el mando a distancia — remote control
los manillar — handlebars
la mano — hand
la manta — blanket
la mantequilla — butter
mañana — tomorrow
de la mañana — morning (6am–1pm)
mañana por la mañana — tomorrow morning

mañana por la tarde; noche — tomorrow afternoon; evening
la mangosta — mongoose
la mapa de carreteras — road map
¿Me puede mostrar en el mapa? — Can you show me on the map?
una máquina — machine
la máquina de tabaco — cigarette machine
el mar — sea
maravilloso — marvellous
el marcador — scoreboard
marcar — to score
la marea — tide
mareada/o — dizzy; seasick
el mareo — travel sickness
la mariposa — butterfly
por vía marítima — by sea; sea mail
marrón — brown
martes — Tuesday
el martillo — hammer
marzo — March
más — more
el masaje — massage
la masajista — massage therapist
matar — to kill
la matrícula — car registration
el matrimonio — marriage
mayo — May
la mayoría — majority
el mechero — lighter
la media parte — halftime
media/o — half
la medianoche — midnight
las medias — stockings; pantyhose
la medicina; medicamento — medicine

la/el médico	doctor	el mitin	political speech
un medio galope	canter	el mochila	backpack
medio litro	half a litre	la mona de pascua	chocolate figures
la mediodía	noon	las monedas	coins
la/el mejor	best	las monedas sueltas	loose change
el melé	scrum	una monja	nun
la/el mendiga/o	beggar	un monje	monk
menos	less	la/el mona/o	monkey
un mensaje	message	la montaña	mountain
la mente	mind	montar a caballo	to ride a horse
mentir	to lie	una mordedura	bite (dog)
una mentirosa	liar	la mosca	fly
un mentiroso		mostrar	to show
los (cigarillos) mentolados	menthol (cigarettes)	¿Me puede mostrar en el mapa? Can you show me on the map?	
el mercado	market	el motivo del viaje	reason for travel
el mes	month	muchas/os	many
el mes pasado	last month	muda/o	mute
el mes que viene	next month	el muelle	spring (coil)
la mesa	table	muerta/o	dead
la mesa de ping pong	table tennis table	la muerte	death
la meseta	plateau	una multa	a fine
el metro	metre	los municipales	local council
mezclar	to mix	las muñecas	dolls
la mezquita	mosque	las murallas	city walls
el miedo	fear	el músculo	muscle
la miel	honey	el museo	museum; art gallery
el miembro	member		
miércoles	Wednesday	una musulmana	Muslim
mil	thousand	un musulmán	
el milano	kite (bird)		
un millón	one million	**N**	
el millón	pinball		
minusválida/o	disabled	nada	none
mirar los escaparates	window-shopping	No es nada. It's nothing.	
un mirador	lookout point	nadar	to swim
mirar	to look	una naranja	orange
la misa	mass	la nariz	nose
la/el misma/o	same	la natación	swimming
		la naturaleza	nature

la	navaja	nature
la	Navidad	penknife
	nebulosa	Christmas Day
	necesitar	nebula
	negar	to need
	negarse	to deny
	negra/o	to refuse
los	neumáticos	black
una	nevera	tyres
una/un	nieta/o	refrigerator
el	nieve	grandchild
un	nivel	snow
el	nivel de vida	a level; standard
		standard of
la	noche	living
la	Nochebuena	evening; night
la	Nochevieja	Christmas Eve
el	nombre	New Year's Eve
el	nombre de pila	name
la	norte	christian name
	nosotras/os	north
las	noticias	we
la	novela negra	news
		crime; detective
las	novelas	novels
	novena/o	novels
	noventa	ninth
la	novia	ninety
el	novio	girlfriend
el	nube	boyfriend
	nueva/o	cloud
	nueve	new
el	número de	nine
	andén	platform number
el	número de la	
	habitación	room number
el	número de	
	pasaporte	passport number
	nunca	never
la	nutria	otter

O

	o	or
el	objetivo	lens
una	obra de arte	artwork
una	obrera/o	factory worker
	obvia/o	obvious
	octava/o	eighth
	octubre	October
	ocupar	to live (some-where)
	ochenta	eighty
	ocho	eight
	oeste	west
la	oficina central	head office
una/un	oficinista;	office worker
	empleada/o	
el	oficio	service (religious)
	oír	to hear
el	ojo	eye
	¡Ojo!	Careful!
la	ola	wave
	oler	to smell
la	olla	pot (ceramic)
un	olor	a smell
	olvidar	to forget
	Me olvido.	I forget.
	once	eleven
la	ópera	opera; opera house
una	oración	prayer
el	orden	order
	ordenar	to order
la	oreja	ear
el	orgullo	pride
el	oro	gold
el	orso	bear
	oscuro	dark
	otoño	autumn
	otra/o	other
una	oveja	sheep

P

el	(película) en color	colour (film)
	padrastro	stepfather
el	padre; papá	father
los	padres	parents
	pagar	to pay
una	página	page
un	pago	payment
el	País de Gales	Wales
el	pájaro	bird
la	pala	table tennis bat
las	palomitas (de maíz)	popcorn
el	pan	bread
la	panadería	bakery
la	pantalla	screen
los	pantalones	trousers
los	pantalones cortos	shorts
un	pañal	nappy
los	pañales	disposable nappies
los	pañuelos de papel	tissues
los	pañuelos; bufandas	scarves
el	Papa	Pope
	papá	dad
el	papel	paper
el	papel de fumar	cigarette papers
el	papel higiénico	toilet paper
la	papelería	stationers
un	par [de guantes]	pair [of gloves]
el	parabrisas	windscreen; windshield
una	parada	a stop
el	paraguas	umbrella
una/un	parapléjica/o	paraplegic

el	parchís	ludo
la	pareja	pair (a couple)
los	parientes	relations
el	paro	dole
un	parque de atracciones	theme park
la	partida	game (sport)
la	partida de nacimiento	birth certificate
el	partido	match
los	partidos políticos	political parties
	partir	to depart; leave
	partir de	to depart to
	pasado	past
	pasado mañana	day after tomorrow
un	pasajero	passenger
un	pase	pass
el	pasear	a stroll
un	paso	step
la	pasta dentífrica	toothpaste
un	pastel	pie
el	pastel de cumpleaños	birthday cake
la	pastelería	cake shop
una	pastilla	pill
las	pastillas para dormir	sleeping pills
el	pato	duck
la/el	payasa/o	clown
la	paz	peace
una/un	peatón	pedestrian
un	pecado	sin
el	pecho	chest; breast
un	pedazo	piece
	pedir	to ask (for something); borrow
un	peine	comb
una	pelea	a quarrel
una	película	a film (camera)

	Spanish	English
el	pelo	hair
la	pelota de juego	game ball
la	pelota de partido	match ball
la	pelota de ping pong	ping pong ball
la	pelota vasca	pelota
el	pelotari	pelota player
los	pendientes	earrings
el	pene	penis
el	peñón	[wall of] rock; crag
	pequeña/o	small
la	perdedora	loser
el	perdedor	loser
	perder	to lose
	perdonar	to forgive
la	pereza	laziness
	perezosa/o	lazy
un	periódico	newspaper
un	periódico en inglés	newspaper in English
una/un	periodista	journalist
el	permiso de conducir	driver's licence
el	permiso de trabajo	work permit
	pero	but
la/el	perra/o	dog
el	perro lazarillo	guide dog
	pesada/o	heavy
las	pesas	weights
el	pescado	fish (as food)
el	pez	fish
	picante	spicy
un	picazón	itch
un	pico	beak;
el	pie	foot
la	piedra	stone
la	piel	skin
la	pierna	leg

	Spanish	English
	pija/o	flash; nouveau-riche type
la	pila	battery
la	píldora	the Pill
la	pimienta	pepper
un	pinchazo	puncture
el	pino	pine
	pintar	to paint
una	pintora	painter
un	pintor	
la	pintura	painting (art of)
los	piojos	lice
el	piolet	ice axe
una	pipa	pipe
una	piqueta	pick; pickaxe
las	piquetas	tent pegs
la	piscina	swimming pool
el	piso	floor (storey)
la	pista	race track; tennis court; ski slope
el	placaje	tackle
	plana/o	flat (land, etc)
una	planta	plant
una/un	plasta	pain in the neck; a bore
el	plástico	plastic
la	plata	silver
un	plato	plate
la	playa	beach
el	Plaza Mayor	main square
la	plaza	square (in town)
la	plaza de toros	bullring
	pobre	poor
la	pobreza	poverty
un	poco; poquito	a little bit
	pocos	few
el	poder	power
	poder	to be able to do; can

¿Podría darme ...?
Could you give me ...?

¿Puede ayudarme?
Can you help me?
¿Puedo sacar una foto?
Can (May) I take a photo?

el	pollo	chicken
	poner	to put
un	poquito	a little (amount)
	por	for
	por ciento	percent
	Por exemplo, ...	For example, ...
	porque	because
los	portales	arcades
	por vía terrestre;	surface; sea
	marítima	mail
una	postal	a postcard
los	postales	postcards
el	precio	price
una	pregunta	a question
	preguntar	to ask (question)
	preocupada/o	worried
	preocuparse por	to care (about something)
	¡No te preocupes!	Forget about it!; Don't worry.
	preparar	to prepare
los	preservativos	condoms
la	presión arterial	blood pressure
la	presión baja/ alta	low/high blood pressure
	prevenir	to prevent
la	primavera	spring (season)
el	primer	first
la	primera ministra	prime minister
el	primer ministro	
	primera/o (1r)	first
	prisa	in a hurry
los	prismáticos	binoculars
	privada/o	private
	probar	to try

la	procesión religiosa	religious procession
los	productos congelados	frozen foods
los	productos lácteos	dairy products
	profunda/o	deep
un	progre	lefty
una	promesa	promise
	pronto	soon
una	propuesta	proposal
la	prórroga	extra time
	proteger	to protect
	próximo	next
el	proyector	projector
un	prueba de embarazo	pregnancy test kit
las	pruebas nucleares	nuclear testing
un	pueblo; pueblecito	a village
el	puente	bridge
la	puerta	gate
el	puerto	harbour; port
la	puesta del sol	sunset
la	pulga	flea
el	punto	point (tip)

Q

	¿Qué?	What?
	¿Qué hace?	
	What are you doing?	
	¿Qué pasa?	
	What's the matter?	
	quedar	to be left (behind) over)
	quedarse	to stay (remain)
una	quemadura	a burn
una	quemadura de sol	sunburn
	querer	to want; love

Queremos ir a ...
We'd like to go to ...

el	queso	cheese
un	quilo	kilogram
	quince	fifteen
la	quincena	fortnight
	quinta/o	fifth
el	quiosco	newsagency
el	quiosco de tabaco	tobacco kiosk
	quitar	to take away

R

el	rabo	tail
una	rata	rat
el	ratón	mouse
el	ratonero	buzzard
la	raza	race (breed)
el	razón	reason
	realizar	to carry out
una	rebaja	discount
	recibir	to receive
el	recibo	receipt
	reciente	recent
	recientemente	recently
la	recogida de equipajes	baggage claim
	reconocer	to recognise
	recordar	to remember
	de largo recorrido	long-distance
un	recuerdo	souvenir
el	red	net
	redonda/o	round
	reembolsar	to refund
un	reembolso	refund
el	reflejo	reflection (mirror)
el	reflexión	reflection (thinking)
una/un	refugiada/o	refugee

un	refugio de montaña	mountain hut
	regalar	to exchange; give gifts
un	regalo	present (gift)
el	regalo de bodas	wedding present
la	regla	menstruation
las	reglas	rules
	regresar	to return
	Regular	OK
la	reina	queen
	reírse	laugh
la	relación	relationship
	relajar	to relax
el	reloj	watch; clock
el	remo	rowing
la	rentabilidad	profitability
	repartir	to deal
	repartir (entre)	to share (with)
un	resfriado	a cold
la	residencia de estudiantes	college
los	residuos tóxicos	toxic waste
	respirar	to breathe
una	respuesta	answer
el	retablo	altarpiece
un	retén	checkpoint (police)
la/el	retratista	portrait sketcher
la	reventa	ticket scalping
	revisar	to check
la/el	revisora/revisor	ticket collector
una	revista	magazine
las	revistas del corazón	popular magazines
el	rey	king
	rica/o	rich (wealthy)
un	riesgo	risk
el	rincón	corner (interior)

el	río	river
una	riña	a quarrel
el	riñón	kidney
el	ritmo	rhythm
	robar	to rob; steal
el	roble	oak
la	rodilla	knee
	roja/o	red
el	romero	rosemary
la	ropa	clothing
	rosa	pink
el	roscón de pascua	easter cake
	rota/o	broken (out of order)
	[en la] rotonda	[at the] round-about
el	rubio	light
la	rueda	wheel
el	ruido	noise
	ruidosa/o	loud

S

	[para] siempre	forever
	sábado	Saturday
la	sábana	sheet
	saber	to know (something)
un	saco de dormir	sleeping bag
el	sal	salt
la	sala	salon
la	sala de espera	waiting room
la	sala de fiestas	ballroom
	Salida	Way Out
la	salida	exit
la	salida de emergencia	emergency exit
las	salidas	departures
el	saliente	ledge
	salir con	to go out with

	salir de	to depart (leave)
	saltar	to jump
la	salud	health
	¡Salud!	Bless you! (sneezing)
la	salva slip	panty liners
	salvar	to save
	san	saint (when followed by a saint's name)
	sangrar	to bleed
el	sangre	blood
	santa/o	saint
el	sapo	toad
	secar	to dry (clothes)
	secilla/o	simple
	sed	thirsty
la	seda	silk
	seguir	to follow
	segura/o	safe
el	seguro	insurance
	seis	six
los	sellos	stamps
	[en el] semáforo	[at the] traffic lights
la	Semana santa	Holy Week
la	semana	week
la	semana pasada	last week
la	semana que viene	next week
	sembrar	to plant
el	semental	stallion
el	senderismo	hiking
el	sendero	trail; mountain path
los	senos	breasts
la	sensibilidad; ASA	film speed; ASA
	sensible	sensitive
	sentarse	to sit
	sentir	to feel
	séptima/o	seventh

S

	ser;	to be
	(estar see page 32)	
	seria/o	serious
	seropositiva/o	HIV positive
el	serpiente	snake
el	servicio de	babysitter
	canguros	
los	servicios	toilets
	sesenta	sixty
	setenta	seventy
	setiembre/	September
	septiembre	
el	sexo seguro	safe sex
	sexta/o	sixth
un	señal	a sign
la	SIDA	AIDS
	siempre	always
	Lo siento.	I'm sorry.
	siete	seven
la	silla	chair
la	silla de ruedas	wheelchair
el	sillín	saddle
	simpática/o	nice; friendly
	sin filtro	without filter
	sin plomo	unleaded
los	sindicatos	trade unions
el	síndrome de	cold turkey
	abstinencia (mono)	
el	sitio	place
	sobornar	to bribe
un	soborno	a bribe
	sobre	above; on
el	sobre	envelope
un	sobredosis	overdose
un	sobretodo	overcoat
el	sol	sun
	sola/o	alone
	sola/o;	only
	solamente	
	sola/o	single (unique)
	soltera/o	single (person)

la	sombra	shade
los	sondeos	polls
el	sonido	sound
	sonreir	to smile
	sorda/o	deaf
	soñar	to dream
	subir	to climb
el	submarinismo	diving
	sucia/o	dirty
el	sucursal	branch office
la	Sudamérica	South America
	sudar	to perspire
la	suegra	mother-in-law
el	suegro	father-in-law
el	suelo	ground; floor
el	sueño	sleepy
la	suerte	luck
	sufrir	suffer
el	sujetador	bra
	¡Por supuesto!	Great!
	sur	south

T

la	tabla de surf	surfboard
el	tablero de	chess board
	ajedrez	
el	talco	baby powder
la	talla	size (clothes)
el	taller	garage
el	tamaño	size (of anything)
	también	also
	tampoco	neither
	tan grande como	as big as
un	tanto	point (games)
un	tapete	rug
	tarde	late
	[de la] tarde	[in the] afternoon
		(3pm - 8pm)
una	tarjeta de crédito	credit card

la	tarjeta de embarque	boarding pass
la	tarjeta de teléfono	phonecard
una	tarjeta postal	postcard
la	tarta nupcial	wedding cake
la	tasa del aeropuerto	airport tax
el	teclado	keyboard
los	tejanos	jeans
el	tejón	badger
la	tele	TV
el	tele-arrastre	ski-lift
el	teleférico	cable car
una	telenovela	soap opera
el	telescopio	telescope
el	televisor	TV set
un	templo	temple
	temprano	early
	tener razón	to be right
	tener	to have
	see page 32	
	¿Tiene usted ...?	Do you have ...?
	tercera/o	third (adj)
un	tercio	a third
	terminar	to end
el	ternero	calf
un	terremoto	earthquake
el	terreno para rodaje de exteriores	location
	por vía terrestre	surface mail
	testaruda/o	stubborn
el	tiempo	weather
una	tienda (de campaña)	tent
la	tienda de alimentación; almacén	general store; shop
una	tienda de	craft shop

	artesanía	
la	tienda de discos	record shop
la	tienda de fotografía	camera shop
la	tienda de recuerdos	souvenir shop
la	Tierra	Earth
la	tierra	earth
las	tijeras	scissors
el	tipo de cambio	exchange rate
el	tiro	hit
el	título	degree
una	toalla	towel
el	tobillo	ankle
	todavía no	not yet
	todo	all
	tomar	to take (food; the train)
el	tomillo	thyme
una	torcedura	sprain
el	tordo	thrush (bird)
el	torneo	tournament
el	toro	bull
el	toro bravo	fighting bull
los	toros	bullfighting
el	torre	castle
una	tortuga	tortoise
un	tos	a cough
la	toxicomanía	drug addiction
una/un	trabajador	manual worker
una	trabajadora; autónoma	self-employed
un	trabajador; autónomo	
el	trabajo	job
el	trabajo de oficina	office work
	traer	to bring
el	traficante de drogas (camell	drug dealer
el	traje de esquí	ski-suit

una/un	**tramposa/o**	a cheat
el	**tranvía**	tram
	trece	thirteen
	treinta	thirty
el	**tren**	train
	trepar	to scale; climb
	tres	three
	tres cuartos	three-quarters
	tres en raya	noughts & crosses
el	**tribunal**	court (legal)
un	**trío**	three of a kind
	triste	sad
un	**trozo**	piece
	tú	you (inf)
la	**tumba**	grave

U

el	**último**	last
un	**ultrasonido**	ultrasound
	única/o	single (unique)
	una/o	one
	usted	you (pol)
	ustedes	you (pl, pol)
las	**uvas**	grapes

V

	va	he/she/it goes
la	**vaca**	cow
	vacía/o	empty
el	**vagón restaurante**	dining car
	valer	to cost
	¿Cuánto vale ir a ...?	How much is it to go to ...?
el	**valle**	valley
	Vámonos.	Let's go.
el	**vapor**	steam
los	**vaqueros**	jeans
	varias/os	several
	veinte	twenty

la	**vela**	candle
la	**vena**	vein
la/el	**vencedora/ vencedor**	winner
un	**vendaje**	bandage
una	**vendedora callejera**	street-seller
	vender	to sell
	venir	to come
la	**venta automática de billetes**	ticket machine
	[estar en] venta	[to be on] sale
una	**ventaja**	advantage
la	**ventana**	window
la	**ventanilla**	window (car; ticket office)
el	**ventilador**	fan
	ver	to see
	¡Ya veremos!	We'll see!
el	**verano**	summer
	verde	green
la	**verdulería**	greengrocer
el	**vestíbulo**	foyer
el	**vestido**	dress
el	**vestuario**	wardrobe
los	**vestuarios**	changing rooms
la	**vetrina**	window (shop)
una	**vez**	once
	viajar	to travel
el	**viaje**	journey
la	**vida**	life
el	**vidrio**	glass
	vieja/o	old
el	**viento**	wind
	viernes	Friday
un	**viñedo**	vineyard
la	**violación**	rape
un	**visado**	visa
la	**vista**	view
	vivir	to live (life & somewhere)

el	volumen	volume
	volver	to return
	vosotras/os	you (pl, inf)
el	voz	voice
el	vuelo	flight
el	vuelo doméstico	domestic flight

X

| la | xantes | laxatives |

Y

	y	and
	ya	already
la	yegua	mare
un	yip	jeep
	yo	I
una/un	yonki	junkie

Z

la	zapatería	shoe shop
los	zapatos	shoes
el	zorro	fox
el	zorzal; tordo	thrush (bird)

INDEX

CROSSWORD ANSWERS

GETTING AROUND (page 64)

Across:
1. barco
3. Peligro
4. lejos
5. avión

Down:
1. billete
2. regional

GOING OUT (page 86)

Across:
2. leer
4. bésame
5. (la) comida
6. manos

Down:
1. soltero
3. esta noche
4. bailar

INTERESTS (page 110)

Across:
3. aburrido
5. (bienestar) social
6. (los) sin (hogar)

Down:
1. surrealismo
2. ficción
4. bonito

HEALTH (page 194)

Across:
1. naturópata
5. dedo
7. farmacia

Down:
2. tos
3. píldora
4. sangre
6. débil

BASQUE (page 240)

Across:
2. udaltzaingoa
4. (ni) naiz
6. gazta
7. larogei

Down:
1. egunkaria
3. Donostia
5. xaboia

CATALAN (page 264)

Across:
4. vídua
5. metge
6. esmorzar

Down:
1. infermera
2. quiosc
3. dutxa

GALICIAN (page 288)

Across:
4. postre
5. enderezo
6. (vós) internos

Down:
1. estudante
2. venres
3. xuño

LONELY PLANET PHRASEBOOKS

Complete your travel experience with a Lonely Planet phrasebook. Developed for the independent traveller, the phrasebooks enable you to communicate confidently in any practical situation – and get to know the local people and their culture.

Skipping lengthy details on where to get your drycleaning ironed, information in the phrasebooks covers bargaining, customs and protocol, how to address people and introduce yourself, explanations of local ways of telling the time, dealing with bureaucracy and bargaining, plus plenty of ways to share your interests and learn from locals.

Arabic (Egyptian)
Arabic (Moroccan)
Australian
*Introduction to Australian English,
Aboriginal and Torres Strait languages.*
Baltic States
*Covers Estonian, Latvian and
Lithuanian.*
Bengali
Brazilian
Burmese
Cantonese
Central Europe
*Covers Czech, French, German,
Hungarian, Italian and Slovak.*
Eastern Europe
*Covers Bulgarian, Czech, Hungarian,
Polish, Romanian and Slovak.*
Ethiopian (Amharic)
Fijian
French
German
Greek
Hindi/Urdu
Indonesian
Italian
Japanese
Korean
Lao
Latin American (Spanish)
Malay
Mandarin
Mediterranean Europe
*Covers Albanian, Greek, Italian,
Macedonian, Maltese, Serbian &
Croatian and Slovene.*

Mongolian
Nepali
Papua New Guinea (Pidgin)
Pilipino
Quechua
Russian
Scandinavian Europe
*Covers Danish, Finnish, Icelandic,
Norwegian and Swedish.*
South-East Asia
*Covers Burmese, Indonesian, Khmer,
Lao, Malay, Tagalog (Pilipino), Thai and
Vietnamese.*
Spanish
Sri Lanka
Swahili
Thai
Thai Hill Tribes
Tibetan
Turkish
Ukrainian
USA
*Introduction to US English,
Vernacular Talk, Native American
languages and Hawaiian.*
Vietnamese
Western Europe
*Useful words and phrases in Basque,
Catalan, Dutch, French, German,
Irish, Portuguese and Spanish
(Castilian).*

PLANET TALK

Lonely Planet's FREE quarterly newsletter

Every issue is packed with up-to-date travel news
and advice including:

* a letter from Lonely Planet co-founders Tony and
  Maureen Wheeler
* go behind the scenes on the road with a Lonely
  Planet author
* feature article on an important and topical travel
  issue
* a selection of recent letters from travellers
* details on forthcoming Lonely planet promotions
* complete list of Lonely Planet products

To join our mailing list contact any Lonely Planet office.

LONELY PLANET PUBLICATIONS

AUSTRALIA
PO Box 617, Hawthorn 3122, Victoria
tel: (03) 9819 1877 fax: (03) 9819 6459
e-mail: talk2us@lonelyplanet.com.au

USA
Embarcadero West,
155 Filbert St, Suite 251,
Oakland, CA 94607
tel: (510) 893 8555
TOLL FREE: 800 275-8555
fax: (510) 893 8563
e-mail: info@lonelyplanet.com

UK
10 Barley Mow Passage, Chiswick,
London W4 4PH
tel: (0181) 742 3161 fax: (0181) 742 2772
e-mail: 100413.3551@compuserve.com

FRANCE:
71 bis rue du Cardinal Lemoine, 75005
Paris
tel: 1 44 32 06 20 fax: 1 46 34 72 55
e-mail: 100560.415@compuserve.com

World Wide Web: http://www.lonelyplanet.com